Permissible Progeny?

PERMISSIBLE PROGENY?

The Morality of Procreation and Parenting

Edited by Sarah Hannan,

Samantha Brennan,

and

Richard Vernon

OXFORD
UNIVERSITY PRESS

OXFORD
UNIVERSITY PRESS

Oxford University Press is a department of the University of Oxford.
It furthers the University's objective of excellence in research, scholarship,
and education by publishing worldwide.

Oxford   New York
Auckland   Cape Town   Dar es Salaam   Hong Kong   Karachi
Kuala Lumpur   Madrid   Melbourne   Mexico City   Nairobi
New Delhi   Shanghai   Taipei   Toronto

With offices in
Argentina   Austria   Brazil   Chile   Czech Republic   France   Greece
Guatemala   Hungary   Italy   Japan   Poland   Portugal   Singapore
South Korea   Switzerland   Thailand   Turkey   Ukraine   Vietnam

Oxford is a registered trade mark of Oxford University Press
in the UK and certain other countries.

Published in the United States of America by
Oxford University Press
198 Madison Avenue, New York, NY 10016

Library of Congress Cataloging-in-Publication Data
Permissible progeny? : the morality of procreation and parenting / [edited by]
Sarah Hannan, Samantha Brennan, [and] Richard Vernon.
    p.   cm.
 Includes bibliographical references and index.
  ISBN 978-0-19-937811-1 (hardcover : alk. paper) —
ISBN 978-0-19-937812-8 (pbk. : alk. paper) 1. Human reproduction—Moral
and ethical aspects. 2. Parenting—Moral and ethical aspects. 3. Child rearing—
Moral and ethical aspects. I. Hannan, Sarah, joint editor.
  HQ766.15.P47 2015
  176—dc23
                    2014047891

9 8 7 6 5 4 3 2 1

Printed in the United States of America on acid-free paper

CONTENTS

ACKNOWLEDGMENTS

This book arises from a conference held at Western University, Canada in June 2013. We gratefully acknowledge financial assistance from the Social Sciences and Humanities Research Council Connections Grant Program, as well as the Deans of Social Science and of Arts and Humanities, the Rotman Institute of Philosophy, and the Department of Women's Studies and Feminist Research, all at Western University, Canada.

CONTRIBUTORS

David Benatar is Professor and Head of Philosophy at the University of Cape Town, South Africa. He is the author of *Better Never to Have Been: The Harm of Coming into Existence* (Oxford, 2006) and of *The Second Sexism: Discrimination Against Men and Boys* (Wiley-Blackwell, 2012).

Andrew Botterell is an Associate Professor at the University of Western Ontario, where he is jointly appointed to the Department of Philosophy and the Faculty of Law. In addition to his work on the ethics of reproduction, he also teaches and researches in philosophy of law and metaphysics. He is a former Supreme Court of Canada clerk, and currently serves as the Associate Editor of the *Canadian Journal of Law & Jurisprudence*.

Elizabeth Brake is an Associate Professor of Philosophy at Arizona State University. She was educated at the universities of Oxford (B.A.) and St. Andrews (MLitt, Ph.D.) and previously taught at the University of Calgary, Canada. Her work is primarily in feminist ethics and political philosophy. Her book, *Minimizing Marriage* (Oxford University Press, 2012), won an Honorable Mention for the 2014 APA Book Prize. She has written on parental rights and obligations as well as liberal theory, and is currently working on a project on disaster ethics. She has held a Murphy Institute Fellowship at Tulane and a Canadian SSHRC Grant.

Samantha Brennan is a philosopher who works in the area of moral and political philosophy, with a special interest in feminist ethics. In addition, Samantha is cross-appointed to the Department of Woman's Studies and Feminist Research. She is also eligible to supervise doctoral dissertations in political science. Her work falls into three main areas: contemporary moral theory, feminist ethics and political philosophy, and theory of justice for families and children. Brennan served as Chair of the Department of Philosophy at Western University, 2002–2007 and 2008–2011.

Matthew Clayton is Associate Professor of Political Theory at the University of Warwick. He is the author of *Justice and Legitimacy in Upbringing* (Oxford University Press, 2006) and has co-edited *The Ideal of Equality* (Palgrave Macmillan, 2000) and *Social Justice* (Blackwell, 2004).

Jurgen De Wispelaere is an occupational therapist turned political philosopher. He currently works at the McGill Institute for Health and Social Policy, following a stint as a postdoctoral fellow with the Montreal Health Equity Research Consortium (MHERC), McGill University. Before that he taught at University College Dublin, Trinity College Dublin, and the Universitat Autònoma de Barcelona. His publications span a wide variety of topics in ethics and politics, including unconditional basic income, disability, organ procurement, and family-making policy. With Daniel Weinstock he has written several papers on the state's role in procreation and parenting, especially focused on adoption. With Gideon Calder and Anca Gheaus he is currently editing the *Routledge Handbook on the Philosophy of Childhood and Children*.

Anca Gheaus is a researcher at Umeå University, where she works on a project on "Close Personal Relationships, Children and the Family," and is a De Velling Willis Fellow in the Philosophy Department at the University of Sheffield. She has published articles on children and the family in the *Journal of Political Philosophy*, the *Journal of Social Philosophy*, *Social Theory and Practice*, the *Critical Review of International Social and Political Philosophy*, *Ethical Perspectives*, *Ethics and Social Welfare*, *Raison Publique*, and *Hypatia*. She authored book chapters on these topics in several recent collections and co-edits a special issue of the *Journal for Applied Philosophy* on the nature and value of childhood.

Sarah Hannan is an Assistant Professor in Political Studies and an Associate Director of the Centre for Professional and Applied Ethics at the University of Manitoba. She earned her D.Phil. from Oxford University and was a postdoctoral fellow at Stanford University's Center for Ethics in Society. Sarah works primarily in contemporary moral and political philosophy. She is currently focusing on the morality of procreation and parenting. Some of her other research interests include: autonomy, bioethics, and philosophy of education.

Meena Krishnamurthy is Assistant Professor in the Department of Philosophy and an Associate Director of the Centre for Professional and Applied Ethics at the University of Manitoba. Before this, she was a Research Postdoctoral Fellow at Novel Tech Ethics, Dalhousie University. She completed her Ph.D. in Philosophy at Cornell University. She works mainly in political philosophy. Her current research focuses on the notions of exploitation, coercion, and oppression. She has published papers in the *Canadian Journal of Philosophy*, *Social Theory and Practice*, and *Public Health Ethics*.

Steven Lecce teaches political theory in the Department of Political Studies at the University of Manitoba, where he is also Associate Dean, Faculty of Arts. His research is primarily concerned with contemporary theories of social and distributive justice, and the ethical bases of the liberal-democratic state. He is the author of *Against Perfectionism: Defending Liberal Neutrality* (Toronto: University of Toronto Press, 2008), and numerous articles about political philosophy. Recently, he was a Visiting Scholar at Oxford University's Centre for the Study of Social Justice.

Corey MacIver is a D.Phil. student in the Department of Politics and International Relations at the University of Oxford. His research focuses on environmental theory. He is writing a dissertation on which methodologies green political philosophers should adopt in light of real-world environmental politics.

Colin Macleod is Associate Professor of Philosophy and Law at the University of Victoria. His research focuses on issues in contemporary moral, political, and legal theory with a special focus on distributive justice and equality; children, families, and justice; and democratic ethics. He is the author of *Liberalism, Justice, and Markets* (OUP 1998); co-editor with David Archard of *The Moral and Political Status of Children* (OUP 2002); and co-editor with Alexander Bagattini of *The Nature of Children's Well-Being: Theory and Practice* (Springer 2014).

Erik Magnusson is a D.Phil. student in the Department of Politics and International Relations at the University of Oxford. His research focuses on contemporary moral and political theory and its application to procreation and parenthood. He is currently working on a dissertation project entitled "Procreative Justice."

Jason Marsh is Assistant Professor of Philosophy at St. Olaf College in Minnesota. He works on theoretical ethics, applied ethics, and the philosophy of religion and has published in such journals as *The Monist*, *Bioethics*, and *Philosophy and Phenomenological Research*. One of his long-term goals is to provide a systematic justification of procreation and to think harder about human happiness and our obligations to future generations.

Carolyn McLeod is Professor of Philosophy and an affiliate member of Women's Studies and Feminist Research at Western University, Canada.

Her main research areas are reproductive ethics, moral psychology, and feminist philosophy. McLeod is co-editor (with Françoise Baylis) of *Family-Making: Contemporary Ethical Challenges* (Oxford University Press, 2014) and author of *Self-Trust and Reproductive Autonomy* (MIT Press, 2002). In addition to her academic research, she has contributed to public policy about reproductive health care and adoption services in Canada.

Richard Vernon is Distinguished University Professor in the Political Science Department at Western University (Canada), where he teaches political philosophy. His publications are in the history of political thought and contemporary political theory, on topics including toleration, global justice, and historical redress.

Daniel Weinstock teaches in the Faculty of Law at McGill University, where he is also the Director of the Institute for Health and Social Policy. His research interests have to do with the interface between normative moral and political philosophy, and issues of public policy. Over the years, he has written numerous scholarly articles on issues like multiculturalism and religious diversity; public policy issues that relate to childhood, families, and education; and the governance of cities. A regular participant in public policy debates in Canada, he presently sits on a provincial commission tasked with making recommendations on increasing justice and equity in the Quebec school system.

Permissible Progeny?

Introduction: On the Morality of Procreation and Parenting

SARAH HANNAN

Choosing whether to become a parent and how to go about raising a child are two of the most important decisions humans can make.[1] The impacts of these choices are weighty and far-reaching. Assuming responsibility for a child changes the character of parents' daily lives, and usually results in irrevocable lifelong shifts in parents' priorities and motivations. Deciding whether and how to parent also has profound impacts on children, as well as on the adults they will grow up to be. Finally, parenting choices affect third parties who are not directly involved in the parent-child relationship. These third parties include human and non-human animals that exist at present, and those who will come to exist in the future.

It is important to note that not everyone chooses to become a parent (this is more true of procreative parents than adoptive parents). There are pressing practical and philosophical issues surrounding safe and affordable access to birth control and abortion. Women can also become pregnant as a result of involuntary sex. These topics are not taken up in this volume. But even setting aside cases of unwanted and unavoidable pregnancy, it seems that a significant proportion of people who conceive do not chose to do so in any robust sense.

Children are often the causal result of a choice to have sex, and not the intention to create a new human life. Moreover, even those who do set out to become parents often do so without giving much thought to why they want to be parents, how to go about becoming a parent, and how to raise a child. There is some sense then in which the talk of parental *choices* with which I began does not match up with many people's experiences of parenthood.

The fact that people often become parents without meaning to, or without giving serious thought to the matter, is one of the main motivations for this volume. Each of the chapters in this book urges us to take seriously questions surrounding both procreation and parenthood. This collection aims to illustrate that there are pressing moral, political, and public policy choices to be made with respect to the bearing and rearing of children. It offers some unique perspectives on what is at stake in these choices, and how to think about their implications. The collection also introduces new arguments for how choices about the bearing and rearing of children should be made. Several of the chapters take up issues that have received little to no attention in the literature, while others develop and deepen the discourse by offering novel takes on subjects that are already provoking debate.

Of course, we make many choices on a daily basis without giving much thought to them. For instance, this is how we generally decide what to wear and what route to take to work. Choices about procreation and parenthood are just as common, but we ought to take these decisions more seriously because the impacts of these decisions are usually much more significant. In the following four sections I will lay out: (1) important problems of bearing and rearing children that we are generally inattentive to, (2) why these problems are the proper targets of moral and political assessment, (3) how philosophy can help us to solve these problems, and (4) the contributions to solving these problems made by each chapter of the volume.

Some of the problems raised in this introduction will not be explored further in the collection. The hope is that drawing attention to these problems will allow the reader to appreciate the complicated web of issues and questions surrounding the bearing and rearing of children. The aim of this volume is to advance the debate on these issues and stimulate further work in the field. Each chapter contributes something important to the literature, but even taken together these chapters do not provide an exhaustive treatment of the many issues surrounding procreation and parenthood.

THE UNDERAPPRECIATED MORAL PROBLEMS OF BEARING AND REARING CHILDREN

In this section, I introduce a number of questions related to the morality of bearing and rearing children that we tend to neglect in our daily lives and in our philosophical theories. Since my aim in this section is to confront our everyday thinking about these problems, I frame them colloquially and unsystematically here, though I provide a more systematic framework for thinking about them in the section titled, "How Can Philosophy Help?"

To begin with, many individuals do not seriously consider *whether to become parents.*[2] The dominant societal narrative expects people to enter monogamous heterosexual marriages and to have children. While this narrative is slowly changing, many still experience its pressures. People who do not want to parent, or who want to parent in unconventional ways, often face judgment, ostracism, and even legal barriers.

Perhaps even more worrying, however, is that there are those who do not stop to consider whether having a child is the right thing for them, or for the many others that will be affected. The pervasiveness of the expectation that one will become a parent is so entrenched that it can often go unnoticed even while having an impact on our choices. Having a child is just what you do, unless you cannot, which is regarded as regrettable. As a result, people are not socially required to justify becoming parents. As Christine Overall points out, those who do not have children are regarded an owing an explanation, while "no one says to a newly pregnant woman or the proud father of a newborn, 'Why did you choose to have that child? What are your reasons?'"[3] This volume suggests that we should be asking ourselves and one another for such explanations—though perhaps more delicately, and ideally before we become parents. Is having a child good for everyone? In virtue of what is parenting valuable?[4] Could there ever be a duty to raise a child?

A related issue that is not given sufficient attention is *how many children to have.*[5] The societal norms associated with parenthood do not just press in favor of having children, but of having several. As soon as someone has a child, questions quickly follow about when she will have the next. There are widely held and negative views about the hazards of having only one child: the child will be selfish, she will be lonely when she gets older, and so forth. Having just one child is thought to be bad for the child, but also for the parents, and for society at large. But is this true? This is worth asking when, as we will see, the costs associated with having multiple children can be quite high.

In addition to the expectation to become a parent several times over, there are also strong norms concerning *how to become a parent.*[6] The social pressure is not merely to become a parent—it is to become a parent to a biologically related child via procreation. Issues of procreation and parenthood can be separated because it is possible to do either one in isolation. You can bring a child into existence through your genetic contribution without parenting him or her, and you can parent a child that you are not genetically related to. Although the two can be separated, the expectation that you will parent your own biological child is so strong that many people do not stop to consider other options.

Interestingly, the perceived importance of having children the "old-fashioned way" has led to a plethora of reproductive options. Now it is possible for some people to have biologically related children using historically unconventional methods. With the availability of gamete donation, surrogacy, and new reproductive technologies (such as in vitro fertilization and preimplantation genetic diagnosis) there are now several ways to genetically reproduce.

Adoption has historically been regarded as a second-best option, which is only to be explored when one cannot have children "the natural way." The increased availability of new reproductive technologies means that some people who experience difficulty procreating have additional options before turning to adoption. This is often heralded as a highly beneficial advance because it allows more people to realize their procreative goals, and thereby to bring immense meaning to their lives. This is no doubt true to some extent, but it is worth pointing out that there are often extreme emotional and financial costs associated with such procedures as well.

Moreover, the availability of reproductive technologies often demotes adoption from a second-best to a fifth- or sixth-best option. But why should this be the case? What is the significance of having a biologically related child?[7] Is there something special about this way of becoming a parent? If so, is it important enough to outweigh the needs of children waiting to be adopted, or the environmental costs of creating more people, for example? Just because we have reproductive technologies, and can develop more, should we? Are there instances where we are obliged to use technologies, such as preimplantation genetic diagnosis? Might we have duties to make our children as genetically well off as we can?[8] These are just some of the questions about the means by which people become parents that we give insufficient moral and political attention, and which some of the chapters collected here encourage us to examine in greater detail.

A related group of questions surrounds *which child to have or raise.* Whether we are talking about procreation or adoption, there are choices about which specific children should be brought into existence or taken under our care. With respect to procreation, there are some options surrounding the gametes used, embryos selected, or fetuses aborted. For example, prospective parents can use preimplantation genetic selection (where it is legal and available) to decide which embryos to implant, thereby choosing which embryos will get a chance to develop into children. This technique allows parents to select against fetuses who possess particular traits—for instance, those who suffer from genetic disorders like Huntington's disease and Sickle cell disease. It can also be used to select for particular traits, as when parents select for genetically deaf children. Parents can also choose which child to bring into existence by aborting particular fetuses, whether in singleton or multiple pregnancies. There are many moral and political questions we should ask surrounding these practices. For example, should people be able to intentionally select embryos that will result in deaf children, or embryos with other traits conventionally considered to significantly disadvantage children? In a racist or sexist society, could arguments levelled against the selection of embryos that will result in deaf children also be used to condemn selecting female embryos, or using gametes from an oppressed racial minority? With respect to adoption, there is an even greater array of questions surrounding which child prospective parents should choose to raise. Should parents adopt a child who is a member of the same racial group? A child born in the same country? The child who is most in need within their own community? The child who is most in need internationally? A child who shows skills, propensities, or interests that they share? In short, after deciding whether and how to have a child, there are still choices to be made about which particular child one will create or adopt.

Another set of questions left largely unexplored concerns *when to have children*. Which conditions ought to obtain before parents create or adopt a child? Is there an age at which one is too young to procreate or become a parent? Children are reaching sexual maturity at increasingly younger ages, meaning that they can reproduce earlier in their lives than was possible in the past.[9] Should anyone intervene in the lives of children to prevent them from conceiving, carrying fetuses to term, or parenting their biological children? How young is it permissible for adoptive parents to be? Is it unfair that people can procreate and be considered the default parents of a child before they can adopt a child?

Despite the fact that people are able to procreate at younger ages, the average parental age is on the rise in Western societies. People are waiting longer to have children, which is likely due to a host of factors including increased education, career demands, more effective birth control, and rising life expectancies. Moreover, some individuals—women in particular—are able to use reproductive technologies to produce genetic offspring later than would be possible without such interventions. How old is too old for the creation of a child? Much attention has been paid to the increased risks associated with advanced maternal age for both the child and the mother.

More recent discoveries, however, suggest that advanced paternal age is responsible for greater risks to the fetus and resulting child than was previously believed.[10] Men can continue to produce children well into their lives, but should they? At what age should people cease adopting children? Are there reasons to make differential cutoffs depending on whether you adopt or create a child?

The question of when to have children need not be interpreted as a question of age. Perhaps age is simply a proxy for other more relevant preconditions that people ought to meet before becoming parents (whether by procreation or adoption). After all, age often correlates with factors like a stable home life and economic security. We might reasonably think that you should only create or assume responsibility for a life when you have the means to support that child through their nonage. What sort of personal traits and external resources do we think people ought to possess before procreating or parenting a child?

To say that people should not procreate or parent before they have the means to successfully raise a child is to exclude some people from procreation and parenthood altogether. This is because some people will never have sufficient levels of whatever internal and external resources we deem necessary. Some of these deficits can, and arguably should, be compensated for by outside intervention and social restructuring.[11] However, even when appropriate measures are instituted, there will be individuals who will lack the traits and resources included on any reasonable list of parental requirements. Therefore, questions about when people ought to procreate or parent can sometimes shift into questions about *who should procreate or parent*, since the appropriate answer to when some people should undertake these activities will be "never."

Consideration of who should procreate or parent demands a systematic account of which traits and resources these activities require. Such an account may include certain internal motivational states associated with people's own answers to whether they think they should parent, but it need not. One could be very well-motivated—that is, have appropriate, genuine, and strong feelings about wanting to procreate or parent—without being well-suited to bear or rear children. Should people raise children when they possess excellent parenting skills, but lack the motivation to parent? May people who are aware that they have a low life expectancy parent children? What degree of financial resources and domestic stability must prospective parents possess?

The foregoing are questions about who should parent, but there are also many questions about who should procreate. Should people with certain genetic problems procreate? What about people with rare but beneficial genetic gifts? Should the list of genetic gifts and problems that bear on procreation vary from one society to another?

Individuals may want to bring these considerations about who should parent to bear on their own decisions about *who to procreate or parent with*. There are plenty of people who are excellent romantic partners, but may not make good parents. With respect to procreation, and gamete donation in particular, there is evidence that some people are extremely interested in what the donor looks like.[12] Is this the most important feature to consider in deciding whose genetic material to use in creating a life?

Cases where one partner wishes to create or raise a child and the other does not also occur with some regularity. When such disagreements occur it is important to consider whether bringing a new person into existence, or assuming care of an existing vulnerable person, are things that we ought to convince or pressure others into doing. All of this is to say that it is important to ask: should I create or raise a child with this particular person?

At this stage we can also call attention to questions about *how many parents a child should have*.[13] Why is there an assumption that we should parent with one other person rather than several? In the first instance, we might think that this is the case because of the linkage in our society between procreation and parenting. Most people parent their biological children, and most children have two biological parents. It is worth noting, however, that it is currently possible for children to have three genetic parents.[14] In the future, it is likely that cloning will allow for children that are the genetic result of just one person (and their genetic linage) rather than two. So even genetics does not neatly lend itself to the idea that two is the natural number of parents children ought to have.

What is more, there is already a recognized divide between procreation and parenthood. Many genetic parents are not involved in the lives of their children for the following sorts of reasons: they have died; they were anonymous donors; they agreed, whether formally or informally, that they would not have any involvement with the resulting child (as when procreators give up children for adoption); they became estranged from the child, as often happens when the relationship with the child's other genetic parents breaks down.

Leaving genetics aside, we might think that the structure of romantic personal relationships recommends two as the appropriate number of parents. It may seem obvious that children should be reared by a romantic couple, whether they are genetically related to the child or not. However, this is not a very stable or obvious foundation either, as many romantic relationships break down, and not all are conducted in pairs to begin with.

There are many people who parent children they are not genetically related to, and who co-parent children with people whom they are not romantically involved with. Take, for example, the common case of a family where the biological parents have separated and remarried, with both step-parents involved in the parenting of their partner's biological children. Here, more than two individuals parent the children, and the children recognize all parties involved as parents.

If we recognize that the structure of procreative and romantic relationships does not necessarily single out two parents as the obvious number, questions arise about the appropriate number of parents a child may have. First we may wonder: what number of co-parents best serves the interests of parental caregivers? For example, parents' lives go better when they are allowed to parent and pursue a number of non-parental interests. Having a larger number of co-parents may free up more time for the pursuit of non-parental projects. At the same time, larger parental groups may detract from the goods we derive from parenthood, by diminishing the intimacy of the parent-child relationship, and making it more difficult for parental groups to agree on rearing policies. Similar considerations arise when we consider what number of parents best serves children's interests. Children may benefit from exposure to different parental perspectives. They may also enjoy "safety in numbers," since children with a greater number of parents are often more protected if one of their parents is, for example, unfit, away a lot, incapacitated, or dies. However, the presence of too many parents may impair children's ability to become close to their caregivers, and thus benefit from the presence of multiple parents.

The final group of questions to be raised here, which are often neglected despite their importance, are questions concerning *how to parent*.[15] Once an individual has procreated and assumed care of the resulting child, or come to parent a child via non-procreative means, a host of issues regarding how to appropriately raise that child comes to the fore. What makes for good parenting, and how should parents understand and conduct their relationships with their children? Should all children be parented in the same manner? There are obviously many ways of raising children that are unacceptable; on the other hand, it seems that one can parent well in a number of morally appropriate ways. Different modes of parenting may suit particular parents and particular children. We should consider why some modes are acceptable and others are not, as well as how much leeway parents have in deviating from optimal strategies. It is clearly unacceptable to abuse one's child, but does spanking constitute abuse, or is it an acceptable form of punishment? If the amount of time that parents should ideally spend with their children would make certain careers incompatible with excellent parenting, are prospective parents obliged to forgo those careers? Economically disadvantaged parents are often unable to spend optimal amounts of time with their children because they have to work extra hours to make ends meet. Does this mean that more privileged parents should spend less time with their children than they otherwise would, in order to avoid unfairly advantaging their children relative to disadvantaged children?[16] These are a small sample of the many questions one should ask about how to parent.

In this section I have called our attention to questions concerning the following issues: whether to have children, how many children to have, how to have children, which particular children to have, when to have children, who should have children, with whom to have children, how many individuals to co-parent with, and how to parent. This list does not exhaust the questions one should consider regarding procreation and parenthood. Moreover, I have only touched on a small number of sub-questions that belong to these sets. The purpose of this section is not to raise all of the relevant questions related to procreation and parenthood. Instead, I have aimed to illustrate that there are a number of such interesting questions, corresponding to difficult problems that individuals face and that we as a society should care about.

THE APPROPRIATENESS OF MORAL AND POLITICAL ASSESSMENT

The last section raised questions that people neglect in their everyday lives. Moral and political philosophers have also historically failed to devote much attention to these questions in their scholarly work. What explains this inattention?

In some cases the neglect is the result of believing that procreative and parenting choices are not proper subjects of moral or political assessment. Some people believe that choices in particular domains are private. They point to persons' practices in matters of religion, or to their sexual proclivities, and argue that these choices are not appropriately singled out for moral or political scrutiny.

But whatever one thinks of this suggestion as applied to religious or sexual choices, it is surely only plausible where these choices do not adversely affect nonconsenting others. For instance, individuals' religious practices are not plausibly regarded as immune from moral assessment when they involve the exercise of violence against apostates. Similarly, one's sexual decisions are clearly subject to moral censure when they involve harassment or assault. Since children cannot consent to being brought into the world or parented, decisions about procreation and parenthood necessarily involve nonconsenting others. So the thought that these decisions are private is implausible. The presence of nonconsenting third parties who are also affected by individuals' procreative and parenting decisions strengthens the conclusion that these decisions are properly subject to moral assessment.

In other cases, people may fail to attend to moral questions of procreation and parenting from the belief that choices in these areas are "natural" and thereby justified. This position cannot be correct. We can plausibly regard everything occurring in nature as natural, so the position would suggest that there is no space available for moral evaluation. Murder is something that occurs naturally, both in the sense that it occurs in the natural world, and in the sense that people have certain natural drives, observable in many other species, to kill one another under certain conditions. But we do not regard murder as immune from moral or political assessment by virtue of being "natural".

In the foregoing paragraphs, I compared procreative and parenting decisions to religious violence, rape, and murder. My point is not that these actions are morally analogous. Instead, the comparison illustrates that we need to say more about what distinguishes procreative and parenting choices from those morally unacceptable decisions. Claims to privacy and naturalness are insufficient for explaining the distinction.

Of course, many people have given some thought to the moral and political status of decisions to procreate and parent, and some of these people think that the justification of these decisions is obvious. This is false. Myriad interests are involved in decisions about procreation and parenting, and these interests often come into complicated conflicts with one another. Sorting out such conflicts is unlikely to be simple or straightforward.

For example, many people think it is obvious that we are justified in procreating as we see fit. The question of whether it is permissible to procreate is commonly regarded as one of the most easily answered moral questions concerning procreation and parenting. However, decisions to procreate affect core interests of many parties in ways that make it unlikely that unlimited procreation is permissible. In an overpopulated world, our decision to procreate takes away scarce resources from others. It may also deprive prospective adoptees of an opportunity to be raised by parents. And by imposing high population burdens, unrestricted procreative decisions harm the interests of future persons and non-human animals. In light of these effects, it is far from obvious that we are at moral liberty to procreate. Determining whether it is permissible to procreate requires considerable thought. Many other questions about procreative and parenting choices are liable to be even more complicated, in light of the interests and entitlements they engage.

Finally, one might think that even if these questions surrounding the bearing and rearing of children are normatively complicated and important enough to deserve sustained moral attention, we should not focus on them because doing so can lead to terrible practical outcomes. History offers us many policy nightmares that have stemmed from moral views about certain people's suitability as procreators and parents. For example, eugenics programs, forced sterilization, forced abortion, and the mass removal of children from their parents all rightly evoke concern that the state has overstepped its bounds. Looking forward we ought to be concerned about the racism, classism, ableism, and sexism that have informed, and been reinforced by, political policies with respect to procreation and parenthood. However, it seems that this is a reason to engage in careful philosophical discussion of procreation and parenting policies, rather than a reason to avoid it. Contentious philosophical inquiry into procreation and parenting policy could help us to avoid the imposition of unjust future harms in these areas.

Moreover, there is reason to expect that such an inquiry might reveal some modes of procreation and parenting regulation to be acceptable. Tax incentives to reduce procreation, for instance, are not evidently objectionable in the way that forced abortion policies are. Moreover, even if certain procreative or parental choices are wrongful, that does not necessarily mean we should implement political policies prohibiting them. Sometimes our moral assessments of actions may not have any bearing on what we should do in politics. Certain moral values may not be appropriately considered when making policy decisions. And even where values are relevant, concerns about feasibility, the clumsiness of state regulation, or the effects of regulation on third parties, may mean that a morally inappropriate practice should remain politically unregulated. For these reasons, the objection from past political abuses is unpersuasive.

HOW CAN PHILOSOPHY HELP?

Earlier, I raised the following questions about bearing and rearing children: whether to have a child, how many children to have, how to have a child, which particular child to carry to term or rear, when to have a child, who should have a child, with whom should we create or raise a child, how many people should we co-parent with, and how to parent.

I then provided reasons for thinking that such procreative and parenting choices are appropriate subjects of moral and political assessment. But how can philosophers begin to make headway on the complicated web of questions listed above?

The works in this collection illustrate many of the ways that philosophy can contribute to our understanding of the morality of procreation and parenting. In this third section, I briefly outline two general strategies that philosophers often use to make progress on difficult moral and political questions. The first strategy is to draw conceptual distinctions that allow us to divide the problems into their constituent parts so that we can see them more clearly and thereby better discern the appropriate answers. The second strategy is to identify interests that are relevant to a given set of problems. I will outline these strategies and discuss one way in which each strategy can be profitably applied to the case of bearing and rearing children.

Dividing and Classifying Problems

I begin with the strategy of dividing the problems raised earlier. These problems all pertain to parenting and procreation, and we often experience them rising up simultaneously in our lives. In the first section, I presented these problems in a way that is faithful to this experience. However, when we subject these problems to philosophical scrutiny, we see that they are importantly different from one another, and should often be analyzed separately. Recognizing this clears the ground for a more plausible treatment of each problem.

In what follows, I outline what I take to be one profitable way of utilizing this strategy to further our understanding of the morality of procreation and parenthood. Of course, different philosophers may want to divide the conceptual space in different ways, but hopefully this example has some substantive appeal, in addition to helping to illustrate the general strategy.

I choose to classify the problems associated with bearing and rearing children as problems about the moral rights of parents, but the distinction could easily be fleshed out other ways—for instance, by focusing on the moral responsibilities of parents instead of on their moral rights. Note that while my focus is on moral rights, a similar classification could be used to disambiguate the political rights of parents and procreators. Note also that while my division is cast in terms of the rights of parents and procreators, the entitlements of children play a central role in determining the scope and content of these rights. A different classification could foreground the rights of children, allowing the entitlements of parents and procreators to play a secondary role.

I distinguish between the following categories of parental rights, each of which can be further elaborated or specified into associated sub-rights: (1) the right to procreate, (2) the right to parent, (3) the right to parent specific children, and (4) the rights of parents.[17]

The Right to Procreate

As the name suggests, the right to procreate is a right to bring new people into existence. Obvious candidates for moral procreative rights include the right to try to conceive fetuses with consenting partners and the right to decide whether to bring existing fetuses to term when one has contributed to creating them. These rights are contingent and dependent on the circumstances in which people find themselves. There is no fundamental right to bring children into existence; as will be discussed later, no right to procreate can be blind to the consequences that it will have for the children created or for nonconsenting third parties. This, of course, still leaves open the question of whether the world in which we presently live is one in which it is permissible to procreate, and of what factors determine the extent of our procreative rights. Even if we decide that some people have rights to procreate, further questions arise, such as whether these rights place limits on the number of offspring that can be created, and whether third parties have duties to assist would-be procreators in reproducing.

The Right to Parent

The right to parent is the entitlement to vie for and, in some cases, occupy the role of parent. Where there are children, someone must possess rights to parent them. This is because young children are incapable of providing for even their own basic interests. Insofar as they are brought into the world involuntarily and in a helpless state, children have a right to be cared for. Correspondingly, some people must be under a duty to do this caring—that is, to be parents. The difficulty is that many individuals want to assume these duties, and some of them will be unfit. Therefore, we need a way of settling who is entitled to fulfill the necessary parenting duties.

Sometimes there will be fewer children in need of parents than there are persons who possess the right to parent. When this happens, the right to parent does not necessarily entitle its holder to occupy the role of parent. Instead, it gives her some claim to vie for the role—to be considered for that role based on her qualifications as a parent, to have a fair chance at occupying the role, or something similar.

Even in cases where the right to parent does entitle holders to be parents, acknowledging this right does not tell us anything about the form of authority that parents wield over their children. Rights to parent only indicate that, insofar as someone has to care for children, and this caring will require holding authority over them, the individual with the right to parent is entitled to exercise such authority (or to vie for such an entitlement to parent). The question of what counts as legitimate parental authority concerns a distinct category of rights discussed later—namely, the rights of parents.

The right to parent is also distinct from the right to procreate as described earlier. This is evidenced by the fact that one can imagine there being procreative rights to conceive and carry fetuses to term, without the existence of an accompanying right to parent the resulting children. We might grant procreative rights out of respect for bodily integrity but maintain that individuals are not entitled to raise the children they create once these children are born. For instance, biological parents might be obliged to redistribute their children to individuals who are better suited to rear them. Conversely, it is possible to possess a right to parent without also possessing a right to procreate. In a world like our own, with children in need of adoptive parents, it might be that parents at risk of passing on a severe genetic disease to their children are entitled to a chance to adopt a child, but not entitled to procreate.

The Right to Parent Particular Children

Another set of parental rights concerns the parenting of particular children. Establishing that someone has a right to parent leaves open which specific children they have a claim to parent, and how they come to have claims to parent these children rather than others. It could be possible for one to possess the right to procreate and the right to parent, but not the right to parent the biological children she creates. In such a circumstance individuals might produce children, be required to redistribute these children, and then be entrusted with other non-biologically related children to parent. Alternatively, adults could be permitted to parent some of their genetic children—say, one—but then be obliged to give up subsequent children they create to those who also have rights to parent but who are unable to conceive their own biological children. Some children could remain with their biological parents, but it would not follow that such parents possessed rights to parent all the children they created.

Trying to determine whether people have rights to parent their genetic offspring opens up interesting questions. Issues to be considered include whether raising biologically related children contributes uniquely to parental flourishing, and whether it is better for children to be raised by their genetic parents.

Whether anyone holds rights to parent particular children, and how they come to hold them, also has implications for adoption schemes. For example, we may wonder if parents who adopt one child have a greater claim to raise that child's genetic siblings than other would-be parents do. Another important issue concerns the moral status of trans-racial adoption: should adoptive parents' claims to raise children of their own race be stronger than their claims to raise children of another race? In settling both of these issues, we would need to establish whether parents', children's, or third parties' interests are advanced by such arrangements.

The Rights of Parents

The final set of parental rights is the rights of parents. As I argued earlier, young children must rely on adults to provide for their needs. Those with rights to parent children play a primary role in seeing to it that children's needs are met. In order to help satisfy children's fundamental interests, parents will need to hold rights over their children. This allows parents to prevent children from taking actions that harm their interests, and, in certain instances, to induce children to take actions that will further their interests. The rights that parents hold over their children are the rights of parents. They are the rights that give substance to the role of parent.[18] The rights of parents set the terms of legitimate parental authority; the right to parent, by contrast, gives parents claims to hold this authority over children.[19]

The rights of parents give the individuals entrusted with them the ability to shape many aspects of young children's lives. These rights change as children age. For example, when children are young, their parents will have rights to force them to eat vegetables and go to school. But as children grow older, such forms of control become illegitimate. Parents of older children may still have entitlements to exert parental control, but the extent of this control lessens as children become more capable of managing their own lives.

There is considerable debate about the scope and content of the rights of parents. Contested topics include whether parents have rights to determine matters such as what school children attend, and for how long; how children worship; and what medical treatment children receive. If the rights of parents do not extend to cover these areas, then we need to determine which other individuals or groups can exercise authority over children, and in what domains. This is also a controversial issue.

Identifying Interests

In addition to distinguishing between different sorts of rights, another way of making philosophical progress on the difficult problems related to parenting and procreation is to identify the interests that bear on these problems. The first step in implementing this strategy is to identify the affected parties. Then we must determine what interests they have in the problem being resolved one way rather than another. Sometimes everyone's interests will point in the same direction, and the right course of action will be clear. At other times, a single individual may have conflicting interests, or disparate parties' interests may conflict with one another. In these cases, we must make a determination about whose interests take precedence, and how to weigh competing interests against one another.

There is not space to fully engage this strategy, but I will discuss the parties whose interests are most relevant to the procreation and parenting questions raised earlier, and briefly indicate the content of some of these interests. Broadly speaking, there are four sets of interests at stake in the morality of parenting and procreation: the interests of children, of parents, of affected third parties, and of the state. I leave it up to the reader to think about how these parties' interests should be weighed against one another.

The Interests of Children

Although there are complicating issues, like the non-identity problem, the interests of both existing and would-be children seem relevant to settling many of the moral questions surrounding procreation and parenting.[20] For instance, when we try to determine whether it is appropriate to procreate, how many children to have, or how we may permissibly exercise our parental authority, we must consider how children fare when we adopt one answer rather than another.

Consider the question of whether it is appropriate to procreate. The potential child's interest in leading a good life seems central to the determination of the permissibility of creating a new life.[21] Is the child likely to be loved?[22] Are there enough natural and economic resources to provide for a good life for the child? Will she have options to exercise her freedom and lead a life of her choosing?[23] Will she have genetic traits that are compatible with her living a good life? Unless the answers to all of these questions are "yes," the potential child's interests will speak strongly against the permissibility of procreation. Taking an extreme case: if there has just been a nuclear holocaust, it seems inappropriate to bring children into the world. Even in more mundane cases, there are often real questions as to whether children's interests in leading a good life are likely enough to be satisfied as to render procreation permissible. If a child is likely to suffer from a genetic condition that would leave them with a short and extremely painful life, many people think the child's interests speak against the permissibility of her creation.

Now consider the questions of whether to adopt rather than procreate, and of which children should be given priority in adoption. Here, the interests of actual children—those waiting to be adopted—bear importantly. Consider, for example, a would-be parent deliberating between adopting and procreating (without the resources to do both). When the developmental costs of not being adopted are high, and there are fewer adoptive parents than there are adoptees, the would-be parent should regard the interests of potential adoptees as weighing heavily against the permissibility of procreation. As those costs decrease, or as the supply of adoptive parents exceeds the number of adoptees, the interests of adoptees no longer speak as strongly against the would-be parent's procreation.

The Interests of Parents

A second set of interests belongs to parents and would-be parents. There is a strong assumption that raising a child contributes to the well-being of many adults. Some philosophers even suggest that parenting a child uniquely contributes to our flourishing, such that we cannot enjoy particular significant goods in the absence of the parent-child relationship.[24] When we ask ourselves how rights to parent are distributed, it seems important to take into account would-be parents' interests in raising a child. If we set the bar for adequate parenting too high, for instance, by insisting that parents maximally meet children's interests, then many adults will be morally excluded from parenting. This would be a significant loss for those that would benefit immensely from the parenting project. Some people should be regarded as unfit parents, but the potential loss that accompanies such a designation should not be overlooked.

While many agree that there is a strong interest in parenting, there is more controversy regarding whether there is a special interest in rearing a biologically related child.[25] For those who accept that there is an interest in parenting a biological child, this interest will bear on the moral permissibility of procreation. It can seem as though this interest speaks clearly in favor of a right to procreate. However, there is something strange about the claim that a person's interest in occupying the role of parent can ground a right to procreate. Apparently analogous role cases illustrate that we do not normally think it is permissible to put individuals in a helpless state—even temporarily—so that we might help them out of it. For instance, it is clear that one should not injure others in order to create a need for doctors, and thus satisfy her interest in occupying that role. Even if this worry can be overcome so that the interest in parenting a biological child can ground some qualified procreative right, it seems that the same interest will also impose limits on the right to procreate. This is because some people's attempts to fulfill their procreative interests may interfere with other people's ability to do the same. For example, if some people create many children, and our population becomes too large to sustain, then would-be procreators will have to forgo creating children of their own, so as to avoid the harms associated with overpopulation.

There are also important questions concerning how parental interests should bear on the rights of parents, the rights which determine what one may permissibly do to and with their child. There is a debate about whether to assign any weight to the interests of parents, and if so how much, when determining the appropriate scope and content of the rights of parents. Consider the issue of whether parents may require children to attend religious services or be baptized.[26] A parent's interest in perpetuating her culture may support the permissibility of her forcing her child to attend church. On the other hand, it is not clear how much weight this interest should be given relative to the child's interests. The difficulty of weighing these interests against each other may sometimes be a product of the content of the interests. But, more generally, the difficulty results from the fact that it is hard to know how much the terms of parental authority should be responsive to any parental interests at all.

The Interests of Affected Third Parties

A third set of interests belongs to third parties positively or negatively affected by other people's procreation and parenting choices. When we make decisions about whether to create children, assume care of them, and how to raise them, these decisions affect others. Take, for example, the norms that we pass on to our children. The ways that we teach and encourage our children to behave will likely play a role in how they interact with other people, as children and as future adults. Consequently, it is important to consider which bearing and rearing decisions are liable to harm and which are liable to benefit third parties.

Some of the chapters in this collection note that the earth contains a finite amount of natural resources and that humans require these resources to live. In procreating, we bring into existence another consumer of resources and thus unilaterally alter the resource entitlement of existing people by adding another mouth to feed, another body to house, and so on. A related perspective is how our bearing and rearing decisions affect the interests of non-human animals. I think that this is an important and underdeveloped aspect of the morality of procreation and parenting, which deserves considerably more attention. It is obvious that when we add another human being to the earth we not only reduce the share of resources left for other humans, but also for non-human animals. One of the many interesting questions that pit the interests of humans against those of non-human animals asks: whether and on what grounds may we prioritize our own species survival over that of other species? Another asks: given the costs to non-human animals, should we raise children as vegans, meat eaters, or something in between?

In considering the interests of third parties, an additional set of interests to keep in mind is that of *future* humans[27] and non-human animals. Attending exclusively to the interests of existing third parties could have disastrous consequences for subsequent generations. Important questions to consider here concern whether we can sensibly think about the interests of nonexistent creatures, whether their interests are likely to match those of existing creatures, and how to weigh these interests against those of existing generations. One pressing debate surrounds the extent to which we should discount the interests of future humans when deciding on policies that will affect current and future generations.

The Interests of the State

A fourth set of interests, which one may or may not want to isolate from the other three categories, are the interests of states.[28] On one popular reading, the state merely arbitrates, represents, and promotes the interests of parents, children, and third parties. This view holds that it would be a mistake to think of the state as having interests that do not bottom out in some amalgamation of its citizens' interests. Even if you take this view, however, the state plays an important role in securing long-term political stability and security, something that is necessary for citizens to pursue most of their interests. In other words, even if what we might colloquially refer to as "state interests" are ultimately best understood as citizen interests, the state is still uniquely suited to protect and promote certain interests of its citizens, as well as to secure the background conditions for the realization of all their interests more generally.

In its capacity as the protector and promoter of its citizens' interests, the state has an interest in bringing about the conditions necessary for the perpetuation of just institutions. It is in virtue of this goal that states plausibly have a derivative interest in procreation and parenting. For example, states could be said to have an interest in ensuring that enough citizens are born to keep vital services, such as social security, operational. Another topic, which has received more attention, centers on the interests the state has in rearing children. The state has interests in its children growing up to be responsible and contributing members of the polity. At present, the primary mechanism that the state has for satisfying this interest is its schools. Debates surround whether the state can force parents to send their children to state-run schools and, if so, for how long; what schools may permissibly teach; and so forth. Here there is a potential tension between the interests that parents have in rearing their children in particular ways (say, to be anarchists) and the interests that the state has in rearing them differently (say, to be liberal democrats).

This section has called our attention to two strategies that philosophers commonly bring to bear on moral problems. The first strategy was that of drawing conceptual distinctions between different sorts of rights or moral entitlements. The ultimate goal of disambiguating these different sets is to carefully consider what justifies each subgroup, how these justifications might differ, and how they relate to one another. The four-part distinction of parental rights drawn here was as follows: the right to procreate, the right to parent, the right to parent particular children, and the rights of parents. Acknowledging these different sets of rights allows us to make progress on difficult problems, by narrowing in on which aspects of alleged parental authority are at stake in these problems. We can correctly say that people hold certain parental rights but not all of them, and that they hold the rights that they do for different reasons, which may bear on how they can permissibly exercise these rights.

The second and related strategy explored here was that of identifying the interests that are relevant to the morality of procreation and parenthood. Another four-fold distinction was drawn, this time between the interests of children, the interests of parents, the interests of third parties, and the interests of the state. Separating out who has a stake in the resolution of bearing and rearing problems, of the sorts raised in earlier sections of this chapter, allows us to consider which interests should take precedence in a particular case, and how conflicting interests should be weighed against one another. I have not offered any thoughts on the priority or weighting of these four groups of interests; my goal has been to leave the reader better positioned to make such judgments for herself.

I hope that the preceding section also suggests how the two strategies might be helpfully employed together, in order to make progress on the moral problems surrounding procreation and parenthood. Having identified different subsets of rights, and the different relevant interests, we can ask which interests might ground each set of rights. This will help us to determine who holds these rights, and to establish their scope, content, and strength.

These two strategies are by no means exhaustive of what philosophy has to offer us in this context. Some of the chapters that follow utilize these approaches, while others exhibit different methodologies. Taken as a whole, the chapters assembled here deepen our understanding of the moral problems surrounding procreation and parenthood, by advancing philosophical discussion of existing debates and laying the foundation for new ones.

CHAPTER CONTRIBUTIONS

The bulk of the chapters in this collection are about procreation, though they approach the topic from different perspectives and with different questions in mind. It is appropriate for procreation to take center stage here, since the philosophical discourse on parenthood has tended to neglect this topic. There is a small but burgeoning literature on the rights of parents and children, and the responsibilities of government and other third parties in the rearing of children. By contrast, relatively little attention has been paid to whether we should bring new people into existence at all. Six of the chapters in this collection take procreation as their main subject.

The collection also discusses other issues in the morality of parenting. There is a chapter about the rationality of becoming a parent (whether by procreation or adoption). Two chapters focus explicitly on adoption, and two consider how we should rear children once they are in our care. The chapters will be briefly introduced here in the order they appear in the collection.

The book opens with a chapter from David Benatar, which offers an argument for anti-natalism, the position that is wrong to bring someone into existence. Benatar has historically offered what he calls a "philanthropic" argument for anti-natalism: bringing a human being into existence is harmful, so we should refrain from procreating out of concern for the welfare of the would-be person. Here he presents new "misanthropic" arguments for anti-natalism, which defend the anti-natalist conclusion by appealing to the terrible harms humans inflict on one another, on nonhuman animals, and on the environment. From these facts he argues that we have a (presumptive) duty to desist from bringing into existence new members of our species, since they are likely to cause incredible pain, suffering, and death. Benatar offers this as a moral argument that gives each of us reason to desist from creating new human lives, and stresses that it does not tell us to cull existing members of our species, or prevent others from procreating. He goes on to make the case that—despite initial appearances—misanthropic and philanthropic anti-natalist arguments are consistent with one another. Benatar's chapter also includes an appendix, which makes an aesthetic case for anti-natalism.

Benatar uses the term "evil" in his chapter to describe the sorts of suffering that humans inflict. The next chapter in the book also explores the connections between evil and procreative morality. Jason Marsh argues that many philosophers' views about procreation are in tension with their views about the problem of evil. He contends that there is an asymmetry in thinking that the presence of evil provides evidence against the existence of a benevolent God, while simultaneously thinking that humans can permissibly create children who will experience this same evil. Marsh asserts that arguments are needed to show that the evil that threatens theism does not also threaten human procreation. The chapter considers some candidate arguments but finds them lacking. Marsh suggests that those who think procreation is justified need to develop a systematic defence of the practice, which he, along with many other authors in this volume, thinks is conspicuously missing. His distinctive contribution is to bring perspectives from the philosophy of religion to bear on the morality of procreation and vice versa; highlighting the tensions between these fields, but also stressing that examining the relationship between them could prove profitable.

While the first two chapters question whether procreation can be justified, Anca Gheaus's contribution leads us in a different and interesting direction by taking up the question of whether there could ever be a *duty* to procreate. Gheaus argues that there is a collective responsibility to have enough children to ensure that future people will not be significantly harmed by depopulation. More controversially, she takes the position that states can incentivize and even coerce individuals into having children if there is not enough voluntary procreation, so as to avoid the material and psychological suffering that would accompany being amongst the last generations of humans. Gheaus allows that the world we currently inhabit is not one in which these circumstances obtain. Given current overpopulation, Gheaus is doubtful that there is a right to unrestricted procreation. Nevertheless, she argues that considering whether there is a duty to procreate is profitable because it bears on the important question of who should pay for children. Gheaus contends that since there is a collective responsibility to have children, fairness demands that those who do not procreate share some of the morally mandatory costs with those who fulfill their duty by bringing new children into existence.

The next chapter, by Corey MacIver, challenges the idea that children are positive externalities in the way Gheaus suggests. MacIver's chapter is more interested in the problems associated with overpopulation than with underpopulation. He begins by pointing out that humans must use scarce natural resources in order to live. MacIver goes on to argue that procreation is a form of consumption, since it involves bringing into existence a being with needs for these scarce resources, thereby diminishing the amount left over for others. He maintains that this consumptive act should be treated as morally on par with our other environmental impacts, arguing that procreative decisions should be incorporated into ecological footprint analysis. MacIver argues that procreative acts can be subject to moral scrutiny and even intervention. This conclusion runs afoul of the popular opinion that choosing to create a child is a private and prepolitical act. An individual's decision to procreate can have massive impacts on others; this chapter narrows in on the environmental impacts and illustrates that allowing unlimited procreative autonomy is not consistent with protecting existing people's legitimate claims to the natural world.

Elizabeth Brake's chapter also takes seriously the environmental harms associated with procreation. Brake points out that, for most procreators, creating a child will be their single largest effect on the environment, since it brings about another lifetime's worth of pollution and resource depletion. Brake also draws our attention to the fact that the decision to procreate rather than adopt imposes significant burdens on children in need of families. Given the significant moral costs associated with procreation, Brake asks how we could justify this act. Her answer is that procreation can sometimes be justified, in light of the value of genetic ties between parents and children. Producing a genetically related child does not guarantee that he or she will be exactly like you, but Brake contends that there is a likelihood of physical and behavioral family resemblances. She believes the value of these resemblances can provide a justification for procreation. Rather than foucsing on procreative impacts, environmental and otherwise, to call into question the morality of creating children, Brake stresses the great impact procreation can have on the future as a possibly justifying feature. She argues that procreation allows us a powerful means of world creation, as it gives us an opportunity to pass on desirable genetic traits that can enrich the future. Brake makes it clear, however, that her argument provides only *pro tanto* justification for procreation, which can be outweighed by other considerations. World creation may not justify creating new people in all circumstances, but Brake thinks that it is the most plausible justification for procreation available.

Thus far all of the chapters have been about procreation, with several of them considering whether particular interests in, or features of, procreation might render procreation morally permissible. The next chapter in the collection considers the political and legal treatment of procreation, focusing on how government should treat procreative motives. For instance, if Brake is right that the desire to pass on certain genetic traits is a morally superior motive, should the state treat it as such when regulating procreation? Steven Lecce and Erik Magnusson approach this question from a liberal neutralist perspective. There is reasonable disagreement about which procreative motives are morally acceptable, which stems from deeper divergence on what constitutes a good life. Given this, Lecce and Magnusson contend that a neutral state must tolerate the morally suspect motives of some prospective parents, so long as these parents do not infringe on the justice-based entitlements of others. Correspondingly, they hold that the state should not permit violations of justice even when they result from morally acceptable motives. Lecce and Magnusson do allow for one circumstance in which procreative motives can inform family law or public policy, namely when the presence of these motives is a reliable indication of the procreative act's likely consequences for the resultant children or third parties. They consider stronger and weaker versions of their view by examining what it could say about savior siblings and sex-selective abortion. In the end, Lecce and Magnusson endorse a position on *how* we should think about procreative motives in the political domain, and invite us to think about which policies ought to be pursued in particular cases given the framework they have laid out.

The next chapter, by Meena Krishnamurthy, marks a shift in two respects. First, Krishnamurthy's chapter considers whether becoming a parent can ever be *rational* rather than whether it should be morally or politically permitted. Second, Krishnamurthy's contribution also moves away from a specific concern with procreation, asking whether becoming a parent via procreation or adoption can ever be rational. She takes on L.A. Paul's claim that we cannot make a rational decision about whether or not to raise a child, because rearing a child is a transformative experience, whose expected value we cannot determine in advance. Contrary to Paul, Krishnamurthy argues that we can rationally choose to be parents. She points out that we might place value on having children for moral reasons such as perpetuating an ethnic or cultural group. Moreover, she argues that we can place value on going through transformative experiences themselves, like having a child, without knowing how they will turn out. Krishnamurthy also contends that Paul is incorrect to claim that we cannot know what it is like to parent, and thus judge its value for us, without already being a parent. This is because we can have experiences of a related type, like spending time with a friend's child, which provide evidence of what it would be like to raise your own child. Finally the chapter stresses that we need not have concrete knowledge of what it will be like for us to have children in order to assess the value for us and make a rational decision about whether to in fact have children. What is needed for a rational choice is an estimate of the value having children would hold for us, which is something we can have if Krishnamurthy's arguments succeed.

Many people, whether accurately or not, place a high value on raising children and pursue that goal accordingly. As earlier sections of this introduction pointed out, there is more than one way of becoming a parent. The next two chapters deal with adoption. Adopting a child can be tremendously rewarding for the parents and children involved, but it is not without significant costs. While one could argue that this is true of parenting more generally, individuals wishing to adopt are subjected to requirements, such as home studies and background checks, to which the parents of biologically related children are not normally subjected. Andrew Botterell and Carolyn McLeod's chapter asks whether this unequal treatment can be morally justified. Specifically, they consider whether a moral right to reproduce could justify the licensing that adoptive parents must undergo but which biological parents are spared. The argument they examine runs as follows: if people have a right to reproduce then requiring them to be licensed in order to enjoy this right would be wrong, whereas greater interference can be justified in the case of adoptive parents as they are not exercising a right to reproduce. Botterell and McLeod reject this argument on two fronts. First, they criticize the very idea that there is a general right to reproduce by calling into question the interests or autonomy-based claims that are said to ground the right. Second, they argue that the most promising ground for the right to reproduce is the interest in parenting, but they point out that this interest is one that can be satisfied via adoption as well as reproduction. Botterell and McLeod therefore conclude that either there is no right to reproduce, or the right to reproduce is grounded in an interest common to biological and adoptive parents. In either case, the right to reproduce cannot support the unequal treatment of biological and adoptive parents.

Jurgen De Wispelaere and Daniel Weinstock's chapter also highlights the asymmetry between the treatment of biological and adoptive parents. They are concerned with the ways that public policy shapes the decision whether to become a parent by adoption or by procreation. De Wispelaere and Weinstock ask how public policy can permissibly influence citizens' reproductive choices so as to encourage prospective parents to adopt. They begin by demonstrating why the interests of adults in procreative freedom make coercive interventions to encourage adoption unacceptable. The state cannot force parents to adopt rather than procreate. De Wispelaere and Weinstock also show how the interests of non-adopted children (children parented by those who created them) make many financial incentives to adopt inappropriate. If, for example, government taxes procreation, then this threatens to harm the children of parents who procreate in spite of the tax. They believe the threat of this harm renders significant financial incentives to adopt inappropriate as well.

After presenting obstacles to policies of coercion or financial incentives aimed at encouraging greater adoption, De Wispelaere and Weinstock outline three further modes of policy intervention. They argue that each of these would make headway in satisfying children's interest in being adopted, without objectionably undermining the interests of adults and children who already have parents. First, government can educate prospective parents with an eye to countering the prevalent thought that procreation is the "natural" way to become a parent. Second, government can ease the bureaucratic obstacles to adoption, with an eye to reducing privacy invasions and wasted time. Finally, government can socialize the costs of adoption, using tax revenues to compensate adoptive parents for the costs of adoptioning a child.

Colin Macleod's chapter shifts the focus away from adoption to the criteria used to judge the adequacy of parents. Macleod wants to determine how we should judge competency in parenting. He defends a dual-interest theory of child rearing, which says that the interests of both parents and children ground parental rights, and must be taken into account when determining what constitutes an adequate parent. Macleod makes it clear that it is not enough to simply avoid abusing or neglecting children. He argues that adequate parents must satisfy a host of entitlements possessed by the children in their care, which include respecting children's emerging autonomy. However, Macleod is careful to note that parents can satisfy these entitlements in many different ways, that they can share the labor with institutions like schools, and that adequate parents need not provide their children with the best possible upbringing. In other words, the standard of competency Macleod defends does not require parents to sacrifice all of their own interests for the sake of their children. He is especially interested in defending the interest that parents have in what he calls "creative self-extension," which on his view grounds a parental right to shape children's identities by exposing them to one's own conception of the good life.

The final chapter, by Matthew Clayton, elaborates on some of the themes raised by Macleod. Clayton takes up the distributive side of how we should treat the children in our care. He highlights a conflict between the interest children have in a good childhood and the interest adults possess in having resources and opportunities to pursue projects that do not relate to children. Given this conflict, Clayton is interested in how much adults—both parents and non-parents—owe to children in terms of resources. Rather than specifying exactly what or how much we owe to children, Clayton provides a framework for adjudicating the resource conflict between adults and children. People come to pay for their childhoods, in the sense that they must sacrifice as an adult to pay for the next generation of children. Because of this Clayton adopts a lifespan view, holding that the relevant question is how to distribute resources across a single life, ranging from childhood to old age. He develops a hybrid account drawing on the work of John Rawls and Ronald Dworkin. At the center of Clayton's view is a hypothetical insurance scheme. The basic idea is that in order to arrive at the just allocation of resources across a life, and thus determine what we owe children, we must ask equally placed well-informed individuals how many resources they would devote to their childhoods knowing that they had to live their lives over again as adults and children. Clayton argues that we should use the results of this thought experiment to normatively inform our policy choices about what adults owe to children.

CONCLUSION

This introduction has progressed in four sections. The first section laid out some general problems surrounding procreation and parenthood, which we are generally inattentive to in our everyday lives. The second section made the case that these problems are not merely personal, but are the appropriate subject of moral and political scrutiny. The third section offered two strategies that philosophers can use to make progress on the sorts of bearing and rearing problems highlighted in the first section: distinguishing different sorts of rights, and identifying relevant interests. I explored one way of employing each strategy. First, I offered my own view on the four sets of rights that I believe constitute parental authority, which are often run together. Second, I briefly explained how the interests of children, parents, third parties, and the state are relevant to the resolution of moral problems of procreation and parenthood. The fourth and final section briefly described the chapters contained herein and drew some connections between them.

Historically, questions about the morality of procreation and parenthood have received little philosophical attention. This is rapidly changing. This collection adds to a growing body of work on the bearing and rearing of children, contributing to the field's maturation into an important area of moral and political inquiry. The chapters gathered here attest to the richness of the issues at stake and to their fundamental importance.

NOTES

1. I thank R.J. Leland for his invaluable help and encouragement with this introduction. I thank Liam Shields and Richard Vernon for very beneficial comments, as well as Gary Edlund for design that inspired the cover art.
2. For some examples of philosophical discussion on the question of whether to become a parent, see: Christine Overall, *Why Have Children?: The Ethical Debate* (Cambridge, MA: MIT Press, 2012); and David Benatar, *Better Never to Have Been: The Harm of Coming into Existence* (Oxford, UK: Oxford University Press, 2006).
3. Overall, *Why Have Children?*, 2.
4. For discussion of the value of parenting, see, for example: Harry Brighouse and Adam Swift, "Parents' Rights and the Value of the Family," *Ethics* 117, no. 1 (2006): 80–108; and Ferdinand Shoeman, "Rights of Children, Rights of Parents and the Moral Basis of the Family," *Ethics* 91, no. 1 (1980): 6–19.
5. For a slightly dated, but still relevant discussion, see Bill McKibben, *Maybe One: A Case for Smaller Families* (New York: Simon & Schuster, 1998). For an opposing view, see Bryan Caplan, *Selfish Reasons To Have More Kids: Why Being A Great Parent Is Less Work and More Fun Than You Think* (New York: Basic Books, 2011).
6. For an edited collection with many papers touching on this topic, see Françoise Baylis and Carolyn McLeod, eds., *Family-Making: Contemporary Ethical Challenges* (Oxford, UK: Oxford University Press, 2014).
7. For a discussion of this topic, see David Archard, "What's Blood Got To Do With It? The Significance Of Natural Parenthood," *Res Republica* 1, no. 1 (1995): 91–106.

8. For a discussions on this topic, see: Michael J. Sandel, *The Case Against Perfection: Ethics in the Age of Genetic Engineering* (Cambridge, MA: Harvard University Press, 2007); Julian Savulescu, "Procreative Beneficence: Why We Should Select The Best Children," *Bioethics* 15, no. 5-6 (2001): 413–426; and Julian Savulescu and Guy Kahane, "The Moral Obligation to Create Children with the Best Chance of the Best Life," *Bioethics* 23, no. 5 (2009): 274–290.

9. See, for example, Jacque Wilson, "Boys—Like Girls—Hitting Puberty Earlier" CNN.com, October 23, 2012, accessed March 23, 2014, http://www.cnn.com/2012/10/20/health/boys-early-puberty/.

10. See, for example, Benedict Carey, "Mental Illness Risk Higher for Children of Older Fathers, Study Finds," *New York Times*, February 24, 2014, accessed March 23, 2014, http://www.nytimes.com/2014/02/27/health/mental-illness-risk-higher-for-children-of-older-parents-study-finds.html?_r=0.

11. This suggestion points to a complicated set of further questions on who should pay for the bearing and rearing of children. Many people think that we should not assume care of a child that we are unable to provide for. If this is the case, does it follow that people without certain economic means ought not to procreate or parent? This could reasonably be regarded as unfair and punishing, especially to those who are poorly off as a result of injustice. On the other hand, it also seems unjust that children should be disadvantaged by being brought up under certain conditions of scarcity, even if that scarcity is not only unintended, but the result of unfairness suffered by their parents. This problem could be resolved if society as a whole assumed the cost of raising children. Some people have argued for such a position, insisting that children are positive externalities or public goods, which all members of society benefit from and thus should foot some of the bill for. It is not entirely clear to me that children are positive externalities, and they certainly will not be when procreative levels surpass, if they have not already, the earth's carrying capacity. The question of whether children are public goods, and if so, whether their parents, society as a whole, just those with children, or children themselves should pay for their upbringing, remains an open and interesting one. For some discussion of these issues see, for example, Patrick Tomlin, "Should Kids Pay Their Own Way?," *Political Studies*, forthcoming, published online January 27, 2014. DOI: 10.1111/1467-9248.12111; Paula Casal and Andrew Williams, "Equality of Resources and Procreative Justice," in *Dworkin and His Critics: With Replies by Dworkin*, ed. Justine Burley (Malden, MA: Blackwell, 2004), 150–169; Serena Olsaretti, "Children as Public Goods?," *Philosophy & Public Affairs* 41, no. 3 (2013): 226–258; and John Stuart Mill, *On Liberty and Other Essays* (Oxford, UK: Oxford University Press, 1991), 116–117, 120. I wish to thank Richard Vernon and Mark Budolfson for independently drawing my attention to the relevant passages in Mill.

It should be acknowledged that financial readiness is only one of several candidate features that we might want people to possess before becoming parents, and perhaps even before procreating. Without going into too much detail, we generally think that people also need sufficient emotional, social, and cognitive resources, as well as certain practical capacities, and free time to successfully raise a child. I take it that this list is relatively uncontroversial because references to the importance of patience, a supportive network of family or friends, problem-solving skills, and a lot of spare time, for instance, dominate popular discussions about raising children. Moreover, unlike with financial resources, it seems that some of these deficits could not be compensated for via outside intervention or societal restructuring, though perhaps many could and should be. The point being made here is that if we think people ought to be in a certain position before procreating or assuming care of a child, there will always be some individuals falling outside of what is deemed necessary.

12. See, for example, Ki Mae Heussner, "BeautifulPeople.com Launches 'Virtual Sperm and Egg Bank,'" *ABC News*, June 23, 2010, accessed March 23, 2014, http://abcnews.go.com/Technology/beautifulpeople-launches-virtual-sperm-egg-bank/story?id=10,985,332.

13. For a discussion on this topic, see Samantha Brennan and Bill Cameron, "How Many Parents Can A Child Have? Philosophical Reflections on the 'Three Parent Case,'" *Dialogue*, published online (August, 2014): 1-17. DOI: http://dx.doi.org/10.1017/S0012217314000705

14. Dina Fine Maron, "Making Babies with 3 Genetic Parents Gets FDA Hearing," *Scientific American*, February 25, 2014, accessed March 23, 2014, http://www.scientificamerican.com/article/making-babies-with-3-genetic-parents-gets-fda-hearing/. See also Karen Weintraub "Three Biological Parents and a Baby," *New York Times* December 16, 2013, accessed March 23, 2014, http://well.blogs.nytimes.com/2013/12/16/three-biological-parents-and-a-baby/.

15. There is a relatively small but growing body of literature that addresses moral questions surrounding how to parent. See, for example David Archard, *Children: Rights and Childhood*, 2nd ed. (New York: Routledge, 2004); Harry Brighouse and Adam Swift, *Family Values: The Ethics of Parent-Child Relationships* (Princeton, NJ: Princeton University Press, 2014); Matthew Clayton, *Justice and Legitimacy in Upbringing* (Oxford, UK: Oxford University Press, 2006); and Norvin Richards, *The Ethics of Parenthood* (Oxford, UK: Oxford University Press, 2010). For recent collected editions containing many helpful papers on this topic, see: David Archard and Colin M. Macleod, eds., *The Moral and Political Status of Children* (Oxford, UK: Oxford University Press, 2002); Alexander Bagattini and Colin Macleod, eds., *The Nature of Children's Well-Being: Theory and Practice* (New York: Springer, 2014); and David Archard and David Benatar, eds., *Procreation & Parenthood: The Ethics of Bearing and Rearing Children* (Oxford, UK: Oxford University Press, 2010).

16. For a helpful discussion on parental partiality, see Harry Brighouse and Adam Swift, "Legitimate Parental Partiality," *Philosophy & Public Affairs* 37, no. 1 (2009): 43–80.

17. I have profited from many helpful discussions with Corey MacIver and Adam Swift about these distinctions, which I first outlined in my D.Phil. dissertation, *Balancing Parental Authority and Children's Autonomy Rights: A Role-Based Solution*. David Archard makes an almost identical four-part distinction in *The Family, A Liberal Defence* (Great Britain: Palgrave Macmillan, 2010). In this book, Archard distinguishes between the right to parent, the right to act as a parent, the right over a child, and the rights of a parent. These categories track the taxonomy of rights I outline here. Where our locutions differ, I prefer my own because I think they do a better job of indicating the content of the rights. For example, Archard's "right to parent" refers to a right to cause a child to exist. This name is misleading because it does not effectively signal that one may have a right to bring someone into existence without holding a right to parent, which is to say, become the guardian of the resulting child (or any other child). Given this, I prefer "right to procreate," which better illustrates that the right (or set of rights) in question can be entirely separated from custodial rights.

18. Sarah Hannan and Richard Vernon, "Parental Rights: A Role-Based Approach," *Theory and Research in Education* 6, no. 2 (2008): 173–189. This article draws a distinction between "the right to become a parent" and "parental rights." While the arguments presented in the article inform some of the distinctions drawn in this introduction, I now prefer the phrases "right to parent" and "rights of parents."

19. Harry Brighouse and Adam Swift endorse a similar view in *Family Values: The Ethics of Parent-Child Relationships* (Princeton, NJ: Princeton University Press, 2014).

20. For an explanation of the non-identity problem, see Chapter 16 of Derek Parfit's *Reasons and Persons* (Oxford, UK: Oxford University Press, 1984). For one recent attempt to resolve this problem in the context of the questions discussed in this book, see Overall, *Why Have Children?*, 150–154.

21. For a discussion on this topic, see Seana Valentine Shiffrin, "Wrongful Life, Procreative Responsibility, and the Significance of Harm," *Legal Theory* 5, no. 2 (1999): 117–148.

22. For a discussion on this topic, see S. Matthew Liao, "The Right of Children to Be Loved," *Journal of Political Philosophy* 14, no. 4 (2006): 420–440.

23. For a seminal discussion on this topic, see Joel Feinberg, "On the Child's Right to an Open Future," in *Whose Child?*, eds. William Aiken and Hugh LaFollette (Totowa, NJ: Rowman & Littlefield, 1980): 124–53. For a critical take on Feinberg's view, see Claudia Mills, "The Child's Right to an Open Future?" *Journal of Social Philosophy* 34, no. 4 (2003): 499–509.

24. Brighouse and Swift, "Parents' Rights and the Value of the Family."

25. See: Anca Gheaus, "The Right to Parent One's Biological Baby," *Journal of Political Philosophy* 20, no. 4 (2012): 432–455; Archard, "What's Blood Got to Do with It?"; and J. David Velleman, "Family History," *Philosophical Papers* 34, no. 3 (2005): 357–378.

26. See: Christina Cameron, "Debate: Clayton on Comprehensive Enrollment," *The Journal of Political Philosophy* 20, no. 3 (2012): 341–352; Matthew Clayton, "Debate: The Case Against the Comprehensive Enrollment of Children," *The Journal of Political Philosophy* 20, no. 3 (2012): 353–364; and Steven Lecce, "How Political is the Personal?: Justice in Upbringing," *Theory and Research in Education* 6, no. 1 (2008): 21–45.

27. Axel Gosseries and Lukas H. Meyer, *Intergenerational Justice* (Oxford, UK: Oxford University Press, 2009).

28. See, for example, Chapter 3 of David Archard's *Children, Family and the State* (Aldershot, UK: Ashgate Publishing Company, 2003).

REFERENCES

Archard, David. "What's Blood Got To Do With It?: The Significance Of Natural Parenthood." *Res Republica* 1, no. 1 (1995): 91–106.

——. *Children, Family and the State*. Aldershot, UK: Ashgate Publishing Company, 2003.

——. *Children: Rights and Childhood*. 2nd ed. New York: Routledge, 2004.

——. *The Family, A Liberal Defence*. Great Britain: Palgrave Macmillan, 2010.

Archard, David, and David Benatar, eds. *Procreation & Parenthood: The Ethics of Bearing and Rearing Children*. Oxford, UK: Oxford University Press, 2010.

Archard, David, and Colin M. Macleod, eds. *The Moral and Political Status of Children*. Oxford, UK: Oxford University Press, 2002.

Bagattini, Alexander, and Colin Macleod, eds. *The Nature of Children's Well-Being: Theory and Practice*. New York: Springer, 2014.

Baylis, Françoise, and Carolyn McLeod, eds. *Family-Making: Contemporary Ethical Challenges*. Oxford, UK: Oxford University Press, 2014.

Benatar, David. *Better Never to Have Been: The Harm of Coming into Existence*. Oxford, UK: Oxford University Press, 2006.

Brennan, Samantha, and Bill Cameron. "How Many Parents Can A Child Have? Philosophical Reflections on the 'Three Parent Case.'" *Dialogue*, published online (August, 2014): 1-17. DOI:http://dx.doi.org/10.1017/S0012217314000705

Brighouse, Harry, and Adam Swift. "Parents' Rights and the Value of the Family." *Ethics* 117, no. 1 (2006): 80–108.

———. "Legitimate Parental Partiality." *Philosophy & Public Affairs* 37, no. 1 (2009): 43–80.

———. *Family Values: The Ethics of Parent-Child Relationships*. Princeton, NJ: Princeton University Press, 2014.

Cameron, Christina. "Debate: Clayton on Comprehensive Enrollment." *The Journal of Political Philosophy* 20, no. 3 (2012): 341–352.

Caplan, Brian. *Selfish Reasons To Have More Kids: Why Being A Great Parent Is Less Work and More Fun Than You Think*. New York: Basic Books, 2011.

Carey, Benedict. "Mental Illness Risk Higher for Children of Older Fathers, Study Finds." *New York Times*, February 24, 2014, accessed March 23, 2014. http://www.nytimes.com/2014/02/27/health/mental-illness-risk-higher-for-children-of-older-parents-study-finds.html?_r=0.

Casal, Paula, and Andrew Williams. "Equality of Resources and Procreative Justice," in *Dworkin and His Critics: With Replies by Dworkin*, ed. Justine Burley, 150–169. Malden, MA: Blackwell, 2004.

Clayton, Matthew. *Justice and Legitimacy in Upbringing*. Oxford, UK: Oxford University Press, 2006.

———. "Debate: The Case Against The Comprehensive Enrolment of Children." *The Journal of Political Philosophy* 20, no. 3 (2012): 353–364.

Velleman, J. David. "Family History." *Philosophical Papers* 34, no. 3 (2005): 357–378.

Feinberg, Joel. "On the Child's Right to an Open Future," in *Whose Child?*, eds. William Aiken and Hugh LaFollette, 124–153. Totowa, NJ: Rowman & Littlefield, 1980.

Gheaus, Anca. "The Right to Parent One's Biological Baby." *Journal of Political Philosophy* 20, no. 4 (2012): 432–455.

Gosseries, Axel, and Lukas H. Meyer. *Intergenerational Justice*. Oxford, UK: Oxford University Press, 2009.

Hannan, Sarah, and Richard Vernon. "Parental Rights: A Role-Based Approach." *Theory and Research in Education* 6, no. 2 (2008): 173–189.

Heussner, Ki Mae. "BeautifulPeople.com Launches 'Virtual Sperm and Egg Bank.'" *ABC News*, June 23, 2010, accessed March 23, 2014. http://abcnews.go.com/Technology/beautifulpeople-launches-virtual-sperm-egg-bank/story?id=10985332.

Lecce, Steven. "How Political is the Personal?: Justice in Upbringing." *Theory and Research in Education* 6, no. 1 (2008): 21–45.

Maron, Dina F. "Making Babies with 3 Genetic Parents Gets FDA Hearing." *Scientific American*, February 25, 2014, accessed March 23, 2014. http://www.scientificamerican.com/article/making-babies-with-3-genetic-parents-gets-fda-hearing/.

Liao, S. Matthew. "The Right of Children to Be Loved." *Journal of Political Philosophy* 14, no. 4 (2006): 420–440.

McKibben, Bill. *Maybe One: A Case for Smaller Families*. New York: Simon & Schuster, 1998.

Mill, John S. *On Liberty and Other Essays*. Oxford, UK: Oxford University Press, 1991.

Mills, Claudia. "The Child's Right to an Open Future?" *Journal of Social Philosophy* 34, no. 4 (2003): 499–509.

Olsaretti, Serena. "Children as Public Goods?" *Philosophy & Public Affairs* 41, no. 3 (2013): 226–258.

Overall, Christine. *Why Have Children?: The Ethical Debate*. Cambridge, MA: MIT Press, 2012.

Parfit, Derek. *Reasons and Persons*. Oxford, UK: Oxford University Press, 1984.

Richards, Norvin. *The Ethics of Parenthood*. Oxford, UK: Oxford University Press, 2010.

Sandel, Michael J. *The Case Against Perfection: Ethics in the Age of Genetic Engineering*. Cambridge, MA: Harvard University Press, 2007.

Savulescu, Julian. "Procreative Beneficence: Why We Should Select The Best Children." *Bioethics* 15, no. 5-6 (2001): 413–426.

Savulescu, Julian, and Guy Kahane. "The Moral Obligation to Create Children with the Best Chance of the Best Life." *Bioethics* 23, no. 5 (2009): 274–290.

Shiffrin, Seana V. "Wrongful Life, Procreative Responsibility, and the Significance of Harm." *Legal Theory* 5, no. 2 (1999): 117–148.

Shoeman, Ferdinand. "Rights of Children, Rights of Parents and the Moral Basis of the Family." *Ethics* 91, no. 1 (1980): 6–19.

Tomlin, Patrick. "Should Kids Pay Their Own Way?." *Political Studies*, forthcoming (published online January 27, 2014). DOI: 10.1111/1467-9248.12111

Weintraub, Karen. "Three Biological Parents and a Baby." *New York Times*, December 16, 2013, accessed March 23, 2014. http://well.blogs.nytimes.com/2013/12/16/three-biological-parents-and-a-baby/.

CHAPTER 1

The Misanthropic Argument for Anti-natalism

DAVID BENATAR

The "most pernicious Race of little odious Vermin that Nature ever suffered to crawl upon the Surface of the Earth"
– King of Brobdingnag, in Jonathan Swift, *Gulliver's Travels*, Part II, Chapter 6.

Some arguments for the conclusion that it is (always) wrong to bring somebody into existence are what I call "philanthropic" arguments. They are rooted in a concern for the welfare of those who would be brought into existence. According to these arguments, coming into existence is such a serious harm or carries such a severe risk of serious harm to those people brought into existence that we should desist from creating them.

However, philanthropy is not the only route to anti-natalism. There are also anti-natalist arguments that we can characterize as "misanthropic." These arguments focus on the terrible evil that humans wreak, and on various negative characteristics of our species. This chapter will be devoted to advancing what I take to be the strongest of these arguments—a moral argument.[1]

Misanthropic anti-natal arguments are likely to be met with an even more hostile reaction than are philanthropic anti-natal arguments. It is not hard to see why this is the case. First, we tend to dislike those who hate us. The misanthrope is, purportedly, one who hates humans and thus it is unsurprising that the misanthrope is disliked. Second, people do not like to hear bad things about themselves and the misanthrope has lots of bad things to say.

A few comments may be offered to mitigate this instinctive response. First, the arguments that will be advanced here are misanthropic only in the sense that they point to unpleasant facts about humans. Accepting these arguments does not commit one to hating humans. Indeed, I shall argue that the misanthropic arguments are not incompatible with the philanthropic ones. Thus the characterization of the arguments as misanthropic should not be taken too literally or over-interpreted.

Second, the unpleasant claims that the misanthropic arguments make about humanity may well be true. To refuse to believe them merely because they are unpleasant would provide the misanthrope with further grounds for complaint. Failing to acknowledge one's flaws is itself another flaw.

The strongest misanthropic argument for anti-natalism is, I said, a moral one. It can be presented in various ways, but here is one:

1. We have a (presumptive) duty to desist from bringing into existence new members of species that cause (and will likely continue to cause) vast amounts of pain, suffering and death.
2. Humans cause vast amounts of pain, suffering and death.
3. Therefore, we have a (presumptive) duty to desist from bringing new humans into existence.[2]

I shall delay discussion of the first premise until later, and shall begin now by demonstrating the truth of the second premise. I do so in two stages. First, I highlight the dark side of human nature. Then I show just how harmful humans are. The two are connected because the dark side of human nature partially explains why humans are so harmful. More specifically, it explains how, in certain situations, the dark side manifests, with destructive results. I shall provide more detail than some might think necessary. I do so because some people are inclined to underestimate the extent of human destructiveness and I need to forestall that sort of glib response.

HUMAN NATURE—THE DARK SIDE

Our species is prone to a flattering view of itself. Humans have regarded themselves as the pinnacle of creation, formed by and in the image of an omnibenevolent, omniscient, and omnipotent God, and inhabiting a planet at the center of the universe—a planet around which all others revolve.[3] Science has done much to debunk some of these ideas. We now know that our planet is not at the centre of the universe: the earth revolves around the sun rather than vice versa. And we know—or at least some of us do—that we are Johnnie-come-lately products of a long, blind evolutionary process.

However, the inclination towards self-adulation is remarkably resilient, and it simply manifests differently in the scientific paradigm than it does in the religious one. Thus, in our taxonomy of species, we designate ourselves as *Homo sapiens*—the thinking human. There is, of course, *some* truth in this designation. As a species we do think more than other animals, and we have greater technical capacity than they do. The human elite has had some remarkable achievements. However, we would do well to note that these achievements are thought to be remarkable only because (1) they are not within the reach of most humans; (2) the cleverest humans typically produce them only by pushing the limits of their capacity; and (3) there are no more cognitively capable species on the planet to put our achievements into a humbling perspective.[4] There is thus something unfair about judging our entire species by the achievements of its elite. Even the cognitive capacities of the elite are massively deficient in countless ways.

We fancy ourselves as rational beings, but there is ample evidence that we regularly fall far short of thinking and acting rationally.[5] For example, we have instincts to make intuitive judgments that, on reflection, we can see to be mistaken. But we are also often too lazy to do the necessary reflection. Our decisions can be influenced by the "framing effect"—that is, our decisions are likely to differ depending on whether the *same* information is presented one way or another. In states of sexual arousal we make decisions that we know to be irrational when we are not aroused. We are willing to pay more to *retain* something than we are to *obtain* something of the same value even when there is no reason to be attached to the object we already own—the so-called "endowment effect." Humans also have a tendency to be overly optimistic and we have considerable capacity for self-deception. And these are but a few of hundreds of possible examples that could be provided.

For all the thinking that we do we are actually an amazingly stupid species. There is much evidence of this stupidity. It is to be found in those who start smoking cigarettes (despite all that is known about their dangers and their addictive content) and in the excessive consumption of alcohol—especially in those who drive while under its influence. It is to be found in the achievements of the advertising industry, which bear ample testament to the credulity of humanity. It is also to be found in the successes of political sloganeering, demagoguery, and spin, to which billions of people fall prey. The seriousness with which so many people take matters of utter inconsequence—such as sport and the vicissitudes of particular sport teams—and the popular adulation of shallow, dysfunctional sports, music, and film stars are also items of evidence.[6] Further signs are to be found in the fads and fashions and delusional obsessions that run rampant.[7]

Our cognitive and other deficiencies are troubling in their own right, but some of these deficiencies, predictably, also incline us to various moral failings. These failings explain, or partially explain, some of the terrible things humans do and thus form the basis for the strongest versions of the misanthropic argument against creating new people.

Consider, for example, the human tendency towards conformity. In one influential study[8] demonstrating this phenomenon, groups of subjects were shown a line—the "standard"—and then asked which of three other lines was the same length as the standard. The nonequivalent lines were of sufficiently different lengths that the correct answer was clear. In each group of subjects all but one were confederates of the experimenter and they were instructed, in some conditions of the experiment, to give the wrong answer. A significant number of the individuals who were the actual experimental subjects yielded to the majority's answer. Subsequent analysis has confirmed these findings but also shown that the *extent* of conformity is influenced by cultural variables.[9]

The studies have also shown that the extent of conformity is influenced by the degree to which the stimulus was ambiguous. The less clear the correct answer is, the more likely people are to conform to the majority view. We should thus expect that when we shift from simple factual matters such as the length of lines to more complicated matters, including evaluative ones, people will be even more likely to conform. That is to say, when everybody is admiring the legendary "emperor's new clothes," it is less likely that the lone individual will announce that the emperor is not wearing any clothes. We know how dangerous conformity can be in certain circumstances. One context in which it has manifested is that of witch hunts. Judging by the actual incidence of witches (where "witch" is understood the way witch hunters understand it), a witch hunt should be about as successful as a unicorn hunt. Yet tens of thousands of purported witches were "found" and killed between 1450 and 1700.[10] There have been sporadic witch hunts since then, including in our own times.[11]

Humans also have a propensity to obey authority and will often do so even when they are asked to do terrible things.[12] Most people have difficulty believing that *they* would be among those who would obey orders to commit atrocities. While it is true that there are *some* people with the strength to resist authority where it is appropriate to do so, it is not the case that everybody who thinks that they fall into that category is as exceptional as they think they are. Indeed, in the famous psychological experiments that demonstrated the tendency to obey authority, some of the subjects who had thought well of themselves were shocked to find they had followed orders. One of them began to call himself "Eichmann,"[13] a reference to Adolf Eichmann, whose defense at his trial in Jerusalem was that he was obeying orders.[14]

An even more graphic experimental example of how ordinary people can quickly descend into barbarism is that of the Stanford Prison Experiments.[15] In this experiment, twenty-four healthy student volunteers were randomly assigned to the roles of either guards or prisoners in a faux prison located in the basement of the Stanford psychology building. Both groups adapted very rapidly to their respective roles, with the authoritarian "guards" humiliating and psychologically torturing the "prisoners." The treatment of the "prisoners" got so bad that the experiment had to be terminated prematurely, after a mere six days.

I have pointed to evidence that humans are neither as clever nor as good as they often think they are. None of this is to deny that there are also positive features to human nature. For example, we can (even if we do not always) employ reason to a greater degree than other animals. And we can feel empathy and act on it (as some animals also do). I have focused on the negative, not to deny the existence of the positive, but instead to highlight what is ignored in the general self-conception of our species.[16] Moreover, the dark side is arguably the more primitive. To avoid its manifestation, considerable effort has to be expended in educating and training people and in constructing and maintaining circumstances and institutions that inhibit the dangerous lapses to which people are prone.

HOMO PERNICIOSUS

Humans may exceed other animals in their sapient capacities, but we also surpass other species in our destructiveness. Many animals cause harm, but we are the most lethal species ever to have inhabited our planet. It is revealing that we do not refer to *this* superlative property in identifying ourselves. There is ample evidence that we are *Homo perniciosus*—the dangerous, destructive human.[17]

In what follows, I shall first demonstrate how much harm humans do. I shall consider three categories of such harm: harm to other humans; harm to animals; and harm to both humans and animals via harm to the environment. While it is obviously impossible to provide a full catalogue of human destructiveness, I do plan to survey a wide range of types and provide some examples.

Inhumanity to Humans

Humans have harmed other humans for as long as there have been humans. The earliest destruction was on a relatively small scale, not least because there were so few humans at the beginning of the species' history. The harms inflicted were, most likely, assault and murder committed by individuals or small groups, with the victims being either individuals or other small groups. In other words, the totality of the destruction would have been very similar to that seen in some species of non-human primates today.

Although humans continue to inflict such harms, when we think today of the destruction that humans wreak, we are more likely to think first of much larger-scale destruction. Humans have killed many millions of other humans in war and in other mass atrocities, such as slavery, purges, and genocides.

The number has been increasing, partly because of the burgeoning number of humans that there are to kill, and partly because humans' destructive capacity has increased so significantly. That said, it is alarming just how lethal primitively armed humans can be.

Many hundreds of millions have been murdered in mass killings. In the twentieth century, the genocides include those against the Herero in German South-West Africa; the Armenians in Turkey; the Jews, Roma, and Sinti in Germany and Nazi-occupied Europe; the Tutsis in Rwanda; and Bosnian Muslims in the former Yugoslavia. Other twentieth-century mass killings were those perpetrated by Mao Zedong, Joseph Stalin, and Pol Pot and his Khmer Rouge. But these mass killings were by no means the first. Genghis Khan, for example, was responsible for killing 11.1% of all human inhabitants of earth during his reign in the thirteenth century.[18]

The gargantuan numbers should not obscure the gruesome details of the how these deaths are inflicted and the sorts of suffering the victims endure on their way to death. Humans kill other humans by hacking, knifing, hanging, bludgeoning, decapitating, shooting, starving, freezing, suffocating, drowning, crushing, gassing, poisoning, and bombing them. Sometimes the victims are killed one at a time and sometimes they are killed en masse in a single action. Although the killing is sometimes at a distance where the suffering can be obscured from the killer, at other times it is up close—the killer, covered in the blood and splattered brains of his victims, continues on his destructive path through further victims.

Mass killings are obviously not the only form of destruction wrought by humans. There are smaller scale killings and there are various barbarities other than killing. Humans rape, assault, flog, maim, brand, kidnap, enslave, torture, and torment other humans. Brutal punishments are inflicted on people, sometimes for real crimes but sometimes merely because of their religious or political views, their race or ethnicity, or their sexual orientation or practices. There are so-called "honor killings" and mutilations for perceived or suspected violations of rigid codes. And humans have performed human sacrifices to their deities.

It is hard to fathom the depth and variety of the barbarism. Consider, for example, the case of René de Permentier, a Belgian officer in the Congo in the 1890s:

> He had all the bushes and trees cut down around his house . . . so that from his porch he could use passersby for target practice. If he found a leaf in a courtyard that women prisoners had swept, he ordered a dozen of them beheaded. If he found a path in the forest not well-maintained, he ordered a child killed in the nearest village.[19]

Or consider what was done to Ahmad Qabazard, a nineteen-year-old Kuwati detained by the Iraqis. His parents were advised that he would soon be released. When they heard a car approaching, they went do the door:

> When Ahmad was taken out of the car, they saw that his ears, nose and genitalia had been cut off. He was coming out of the car with his eyes in his hands. Then the Iraqis shot him, once in the stomach and once in the head, and told his mother to be sure not to move the body for three days.[20]

Militiamen in Congo cut the flesh from living victims and force them to eat it, a practice known, macabrely, as "autocannibalism."[21] Other practices include cutting a fetus out of a woman's uterus and then making her friends eat it, and inserting the end of an AK-47 rifle into a woman's vagina and then pulling the trigger.[22] Nearly every year, fighters from the Lord's Resistance Army "club to death hundreds of people as they raid villages and kidnap children."[23]

Kidnapping of children in such contexts is the first stage in making them child soldiers. Sometimes they are forced to kill members of their own family[24] or others, typically in gruesome ways. In one case a boy was told to pound to death the baby of a woman he knew.[25] If the inductees refuse orders they are beaten savagely or even killed. Indoctrination is another component of their "training." It is estimated that there are currently about three hundred thousand child soldiers in conflicts in Asia, Africa, the Americas, and elsewhere.[26]

In other situations those who are kidnapped are sold into slavery. They are torn away from their families and sometimes shipped great distances, often in fetid, crowded conditions, in which many die. They are subjected to savage beatings, rape, and other indignities. Nor does the slave's commercial value mean that slaves were not killed. In one horrendous case, 133 live slaves were thrown overboard on the orders of the captain, who had insured them for £30 each.[27]

Some people think that slavery is no longer practiced. However, it persists even in some jurisdictions where it is illegal.[28] In some places, young girls are still sold into sexual slavery. One young Cambodian girl, Long Pross, who was kidnapped and forced into prostitution has related how she was beaten and subjected to electric shocks. Two crude abortions were performed on her. When the second left her in great pain she pleaded to be able to rest. In response her "owner" gouged out her right eye.[29]

Now, it may well be suggested that terrible though all these actions are, it is a minority of humans who actually behave in these ways. In response to this comforting thought, a few other, less-comforting ones need to be considered. First, some of the serious harms humans inflict on other humans are not as aberrational as one might think. For example, there was a time when slaveowning was widespread. Slave merchants might have been a small minority, but slave owners were far more common. Rape remains widespread today. It is probably a minority of people who are rapists, but it is not a negligible minority.

Second, even where people are not themselves perpetrators they are often facilitative of the atrocities committed by others. For example, they might support the infliction of torture and cruel punishments, or policies that discriminate against people on the basis of their race, religion, sex, or sexual orientation, and vote for governments that implement such practices and policies. Sometimes large numbers of people endorse a worldview in which "honor killings" thrive, or in which terrorists are hailed as heroes. Sometimes the facilitation of evil results not from an endorsement of the evil but from stupidity, gullibility, dogma, or some other failing. Consider, for example, so-called "useful idiots," those well-meaning people who support a cause without realizing how evil it really is. Wellintentioned people in the West who sympathized with the Soviets are common examples. Many of them would have been horrified by the brutality of and the repression within the Soviet Union, but their naïveté blinded them to the realities of the Soviet regime. Perhaps the most tragic situations are those in which well-meaning people inadvertently cause even more suffering. For example, there is some evidence that Western media attention to amputations in Sierra Leone actually encouraged further amputations by those seeking media attention.[30]

Third, we should remember how easily ordinary people can slip into contemptible behavior. One such scenario can be found in crowds of people clambering in shops for sale items or products in limited supply. In late 1998, the Furby (a stuffed toy) was the season's hottest toy in the United States, and customers were jostling to buy the limited stock. One woman in the crowd "was pushed into a door, where her arm was badly bruised."[31] In another shop a thirteen-year old girl reported that when she picked up a Furby, a woman took her "hand and chomped on it" in order to force her to let go of it.[32] The problem of shopper crowd violence is a recurring one.[33] One year a Wal-Mart employee in Valley Stream, New York, was trampled to death by shoppers who stormed into the store looking for bargains.[34]

Nor is this the worst kind of crowd behavior. Lynch mobs, whose collective intentions are to kill, are notorious examples. The members of such mobs have often been "respectable" members of society. In 1672, the De Witt brothers were lynched in The Hague. The mob's intention had been to hang them, "but they were so viciously attacked that they died before reaching the scaffold. The bodies were then hung up by the feet, stripped bare, and literally torn to pieces."[35] The philosopher, Baruch Spinoza, "was stunned by these acts of barbarity, perpetrated not by some roving band of thieves, but by a crowd of citizens that included respectable middle-class burghers."[36]

Although this particular example and some of the other evidence I have provided of atrocities is historical, it certainly cannot be claimed that the worst human destructiveness is restricted to the past. I have provided plenty of evidence of ongoing harm that humans do.[37] Second, the historical evidence is often pertinent to the present and future. What people have done in the past provides good evidence of the kinds of things people can do under certain circumstances. Sometimes relevantly similar circumstances re-emerge. One of the reasons why the Holocaust is so shocking is that it was conceived and implemented by what had been thought to be so civilized a society. It is unduly optimistic to think that civilization cannot backslide into barbarism. We saw earlier, when I described the dark side of human nature, some of the features of the human character that make this possible. It is thus altogether too convenient to assume that there are only a few evil people who do things of which the rest of humanity is incapable. Sometimes it is only moral luck that prevents somebody from becoming a genocidaire, for example.

Fourth, human destruction comes in degrees and not all of it involves the worst atrocities. There are many more minor and sometimes quotidian harms that humans inflict on others. They lie, steal, cheat, speak hurtfully, break confidences and promises, violate privacy, and act ungratefully, inconsiderately, duplicitously, impatiently, and unfaithfully. As a result people's property is lost or damaged, their feelings hurt, their confidence shattered, their trust destroyed, and their psyches scarred. These are not murder, mutilation, torture and rape but they are nonetheless deep, often life-altering hurts. In the more extreme cases the victims take their own lives as a result of the hurt, but it does not have to reach that level for it to be worthy of our moral revulsion.

Although humans do have a sense of justice, and human societies often respond to injustice in order to punish it, rectify it, and prevent future instances of it, injustice all too frequently prevails. For example, most of the perpetrators of human history's worst atrocities lived out their natural lives without penalty. Forty-nine percent continued ruling until their deaths by natural causes and a further 11% had peaceful retirements. For an additional 8% the only penalty was exile[38]. Consider, too, the number of unreported rapes, unsolved murders, and other crimes for which nobody is ever convicted. Whistle-blowers and others who refuse to countenance bad behavior by powerful people often pay a high price.[39] Evildoers often act with impunity.[40]

Nor should we lose sight of the myriad lesser injustices of human life. One such perpetrator was anatomist Henry Gray, who systematically downplayed the role of his collaborator and illustrator, Henry Carter, in the production of what, tellingly, became known as *Gray's Anatomy*.[41] Another was Selman Waksman who successfully connived to rob his student, Albert Schatz, of credit for the latter's discovery of streptomycin. As a result, Dr. Waksman and not Dr. Schatz won the Nobel Prize for the discovery.[42] Despite many attempts to rectify the injustice, Dr. Schatz went to his grave without achieving the recognition he was due.

"Bad guys" regularly "finish first." They lack the scruples that provide an inner restraint, and the external restraints are either absent or inadequate.

Brutality to "Brutes"

Humans inflict untold suffering and death on many billions of animals every year, and the overwhelming majority of humans are heavily complicit.

Over 63 billion sheep, pigs, cattle, horses, goats, camels, buffalo, rabbits, chickens, ducks, geese, turkeys, and other such animals are slaughtered every year for human consumption.[43] In addition, approximately 103.6 billion aquatic animals are killed for human consumption and non-food uses.[44]

Nor is the sum of these figures—over 166 billion animals—the total number of animals killed annually in the industries that provide humans with animal flesh. Excluded are hundreds of millions of male chicks that are culled by the poultry industry because they will be unable to produce eggs. There do not seem to be any estimates of the annual number of such kills *globally*. However, there are figures for some specific countries and regions, including the United States (260 million[45]) and the European Union (330 million[46]).

Nor do the official slaughter figures include the dogs and cats that are eaten in Asia. Reliable figures are even harder to obtain here, but one calculation puts the annual number at between thirteen and sixteen million dogs and about four million cats.[47] Similarly excluded are "bycatch"—animals such as turtles, dolphins, sharks and sea birds that are caught up in nets even when they are not the intended catch. There are no reliable figures for the numbers of animals killed in this category, but a subset of "bycatch," those discarded overboard, amounts to about a further 5 billion marine animals.[48]

The deaths of the overwhelming majority of these animals are painful and stressful. Humans kill the millions of male chicks in a variety of ways. In the United States most are killed by being sucked at high speed to a "kill" plate, which is sometimes electrified.[49] Elsewhere they are killed by suffocating or crushing, or, in the United Kingdom, by gas or instantaneous maceration.[50] Broiler chickens and spent layer hens are suspended upside down on conveyer belts and have their throats slit. Pigs and other animals are beaten and shocked to coax them to move along in the slaughterhouses, where their throats are cut or stabbed, sometimes after stunning but sometimes not.

Marine animals do not fare any better. They typically suffocate to death once out of the water, but there is suffering even on the way to the surface. Fish that are rapidly hauled by trawlers from great depths suffer barometric trauma. Gas bubbles form inside the body, causing extreme pain. Their swim bladders also become hugely inflated. "Sometimes the pressure is so great their stomach and intestines are pushed out of their mouth and anus. Eyes also become distorted and bulge out."[51] Fish caught on a smaller scale, with line and bait, suffer the trauma of the hook as they fight for their lives. Some humans would like to believe that fish do not feel pain, but this comforting fiction, once held about mammalian animals, withers in the light of the evidence.[52] The deaths of dolphins, which are highly intelligent mammals, may be even worse. When they are not bycatch but instead the intended prey of fisherman, they are driven into bays where they are butchered. Whales, also mammals, are hunted at sea where they are harpooned.

Animal suffering at the hands of humans is not restricted to the time that humans kill animals. Chickens, for example, are typically reared in the extremely confined spaces of the battery cages. They cannot spread their wings or move about. They cannot engage in any of the activities, such as dust bathing, which they would instinctually perform. They stand, with discomfort, on a sloped wire floor. Because such conditions disturb the birds and cause them to peck at one another, chicks destined for this life of suffering are de-beaked with a hot blade. When the egg yield from a battery of hens declines, the hens are shoved into crates and transported to slaughter.

Veal calves and farrowing sows are confined to such small spaces that they can barely move for the duration of their lives. Cows are fed bovine growth hormone to increase milk production, but this often causes mastitis—painful inflammation of the cows' udders. Humans mutilate various animals, including pigs and cattle, by docking their tails, castrating, dehorning, and branding them, all without anesthetic. Animals are often transported immense distances by truck and ship in cramped and foul conditions to be slaughtered at their destinations.

Producing food for humans is by no means the only context in which animals are maltreated. It is hard to know how many millions of animals are affected by scientific experiments[53] each year, but a conservative calculation suggests that it is at least 115 million.[54] Moreover, despite a commitment to the "three Rs" of animal use in science—replacement, reduction, and refinement—at least some countries are actually *increasing* the number of animals used each year.[55]

Many horrific experiments have been performed. It is hard to summarize the full range of torturous treatments to which animals have been subjected, but some examples illustrate the sorts of cruelties humans have inflicted on animals. There was a time when animals would be dissected while fully conscious.[56] As recently as the 1960s, conscious dogs were subjected to microwave blasts, resulting in the swelling of their tongues, the crisping of their skin and, if the temperatures were high enough, in death.[57] In that decade and the following one, monkeys were exposed, by the U.S. military, to massive doses of radiation, resulting in the monkeys' "going into convulsions, stumbling, falling, vomiting, twisting in an apparent endless and futile search for a comfortable position."[58]

Psychological trauma has also been inflicted. In one (in)famous set of experiments, infant monkeys were separated from their mothers, causing severe distress to both mother and infant. The infants were then deprived of any live contact. Their mothers were replaced with mannequins that blasted the infants with air, or rattled them until their teeth chattered, or catapulted them across their cages, or stabbed them with spikes.[59] Females "reared" in these ways were then forcibly impregnated. Given their own upbringing they were unable, unsurprisingly, to care for the resultant offspring, and instead assaulted, maimed, and even killed their infants.[60]

By current standards, many such experiments would not receive the approval of animal research ethics committees. However, the current standards still allow humans to inflict significant harm, including death, on animals. For example, toxicity tests (for both medicines and cosmetics) are performed where the intended or expected outcome is death, typically preceded by the suffering that accompanies the path to death by poisoning. Other animals are genetically engineered to experience motor neuron degeneration,[61] or, like the "oncomouse,"[62] to develop cancer. Humans also perform surgery on animals to produce experimental models of painful conditions, such as sciatica,[63] and they cause stroke-like symptoms in a variety of animals, including rats, rabbits, cats, dogs, and monkeys.[64] They subject animals to substances such as ethanol[65] and methamphetamine[66] and to the effects these substances have on them. Those performing such experiments receive acclaim from the majority of their fellow humans.

Even more damning of our species than cases where cruelty is inflicted as a result of indifference are cases where the cruelty is brought about for human entertainment. Consider the baiting of bulls, bears, badgers, and other animals. The baited animal is tethered to a pole and then attacked by dogs for the pleasure of human spectators. Cock fighting, dog fighting, and bullfighting continue even today.

Other "sports" also inflict suffering and death on animals even where this is not the goal. Horses are whipped on the racetrack to entice them to run faster. They are injected with performance-enhancing drugs, often illegally. They regularly break bones while racing and are then "euthanized."[67] Some horses that are too old or weak to run are sent for slaughter. Other animals that suffer for human entertainment are those confined to zoos or made to perform in circuses.

Even those animals with whom humans have the closest emotional bonds—domestic companion animals such as dogs and cats—are not immune to ill treatment on a colossal scale. Some humans confine these animals in small spaces, beat them, and fail to exercise or feed them adequately. The permutations of cruelty are endless. For example, Henry Morton Stanley, the famous nineteenth-century explorer, cut off his dog's tail, cooked it and fed it to the dog.[68] Terrible cruelty persists in our own times. In August 2006, a woman in England attempted to drown a puppy in boiling water. The puppy survived that attempt and was then left to die, which took "possibly as long as a week."[69] In other recent cases a man killed a dog by baking it in an oven,[70] and another decapitated a cat with a machete.[71] There are thousands of other such cases.

Millions of dogs and cats are abandoned each year. In the shelters to which they are sent, the overwhelming majority are killed because homes cannot be found for them.[72] It is astounding that in the context of so many unwanted domestic animals, humans actively breed more such animals, which only exacerbates the problem. Sometimes these breeding activities are informal and small-scale. A much greater problem, however, are the so-called "puppy mills" (or "kitty mills"), which produce large numbers of animals, who are often kept in poor conditions and given inadequate attention. The aim is to maximize profits for the breeders, and scant if any attention is given to animal welfare.

The human penchant for "purebreds" also leads to animal suffering. Many such animals suffer from congenital problems that impair their ability to breathe, or that render their spines vulnerable to injury, or their hips to dysplasia,[73] for example. Other bizarre human aesthetic preferences lead dogs to have their tails docked or their ears cropped, often without anaesthesia. Animals are also declawed and "debarked" for the convenience of the humans whose homes they share.

These types of human-inflicted harm on animals do not include the miscellaneous other ways in which our species spreads misery. For example, in Asia, bears are "milked" for their bile, a substance still used in traditional "medicine," even though no medicinal value has ever been demonstrated. To facilitate the harvesting of their bile, the bears are confined for the duration of their lives to "crush cages" in which they cannot stand up or move around. In these conditions their muscles atrophy and they go mad. The catheters cause pain and the wounds can become infected, often leading to death.

Even more widespread than the abuse of bears is the fur industry. Mink, foxes, rabbits, dogs, cats, and others are its victims. Many of these animals are reared on fur farms, in conditions that cause significant suffering. They are then killed so that humans can wear their furs. Some humans seem to think that fashion is a good reason to make an animal suffer and die.

Toxic to the Environment

Some of the harm that humans cause to other humans and to animals is mediated by the destructive effect that humans have on the environment. For much of human history, the damage was local. Groups of humans fouled their immediate environment. In recent centuries the human impact has increased exponentially and the threat is now to the global environment. The increased threat is a product of two interacting factors—the exponential growth of the human population combined with significant increases in negative effects per capita. The latter is the result of industrialization and increased consumption.

The consequences include unprecedented levels of pollution. Filth is spewed in massive quantities into the air, rivers, lakes, and oceans, with obvious effects on those humans and animals who breath the air, live in or near the water, or who get their water from those sources. The carbon dioxide emissions are having a "greenhouse effect," leading to global warming. As a result, the icecaps are melting, water levels are rising, and climate patterns are changing. The melting icecaps are depriving some animals of their natural habitat. The rising sea levels endanger coastal communities and threaten to engulf small, low-lying island states, such as Nauru, Tuvalu, and the Maldives. Such an outcome would be an obvious harm to its citizens and other inhabitants. The depletion of the ozone layer is exposing earth's inhabitants to greater levels of ultraviolet light. Humans are encroaching on the wild, leading to animal (and plant) extinctions. The destruction of the rain forests exacerbates the global warming problem by removing the trees that would help counter the increasing levels of carbon dioxide.

There are some people, of course, who deny that humans are having at least some of these large-scale negative effects on the environment. However, this is not the place—and I am not the person—to argue against the climate change denialists. Those who do deny that humans are having a deleterious effect on the environment may simply exclude the relevant harms. Humans are so destructive even without these harms that the second premise can easily survive their exclusion. By contrast, those who do recognize that humans are damaging the environment can simply add this to the previous list.[74]

THE NORMATIVE PREMISE

We have seen that humans cause colossal amounts of suffering and death. Having demonstrated the truth of the second premise, I turn now to consider the first premise of the moral misanthropic argument for anti-natalism:

> We have a (presumptive) duty to desist from bringing into existence new members of species that cause (and will likely continue to cause) vast amounts of pain, suffering and death.

The first thing to note about this premise is what it does not claim. It does not claim that we should *cull* members of dangerous species. Nor does it claim that we have a duty to *prevent others* from bringing new members of dangerous species into existence. The claim is a much more modest one. It says that one should oneself desist from bringing such beings into existence.

For this premise to be true it does not have to be the case that every single member of the species will cause pain, suffering and death. To see why this is so, consider another presumptive duty—the duty not to drive through red traffic lights. We have such a duty because driving through red traffic lights is dangerous, even though not every instance of such conduct results in harm.

The normative premise is neutral between whether the species in question is one's own or another. Here it is important to note how widely the premise would be accepted if the species were *not* human. Imagine, for example, that some people bred a species of non-human animal that was as destructive (to humans and other animals) as humans actually are. There would be widespread condemnation of those who bred these animals. Or imagine that some scientists replicated, and released, a virus that caused as much suffering and death as humans cause. Again, there would be little hesitation in condemning such behavior.[75]

The question, then, is whether it makes any difference whether the highly destructive species is our own. In offering an affirmative answer to this question, some people might suggest that there is something paradoxical about claiming that we have a duty to desist from bringing into existence members of a species that is harmful to itself. There is, on this view, something odd about citing the harm caused to humans by humans as a reason to desist from creating humans. In other words, the misanthropic argument seems to be in conflict with the philanthropic ones. If humans are worth protecting from harm then they are not so bad that we should not replicate the species. And if they are as bad as the second premise of the moral misanthropic argument suggests, then we should not count the harm done to them as relevant in the first premise.

This line of argument fails. First, the harm that humans do to humans is only part of the harm humans do. We are also extremely harmful to other species. Thus, even if we could not cite the harm that humans do to other humans for the purposes of the moral misanthropic argument, the argument could still be carried on the strength of the harm that humans do to animals. This does assume, of course, that animal interests count morally. However, there are very powerful arguments for this conclusion and I shall not rehearse them here.[76]

Second, it is a mistake to muddle our attitudes towards victims and our attitudes to perpetrators—even when the victims are also perpetrators. The recommendation that we should keep these attitudes separate is not uncommon. In civilized societies it is agreed that there are limits on what we may do to even the worst perpetrators, let alone lesser perpetrators. Those who torture and rape their victims before murdering them are not subjected to similar treatment by the state (at least in civilized societies). This is because the perpetrator remains morally considerable despite his perpetration and, on this view, there are limits on what we may do to morally considerable beings. The separation of attitudes is not restricted to the context of punishment. A woman may be guilty of physically assaulting her child, but that does not mean that we should be unconcerned about the physical assault her husband inflicts on her, or that we should be not be concerned about the violence he suffers at the hands of others. We should be concerned about the harm inflicted even on those who inflict harm on others. This point is even more important when greater harms are inflicted on lesser perpetrators. Thus, the philanthropic and misanthropic arguments are not incompatible. We can believe both that it would be better if humans never suffered the harms of existence and that it would be better if there were no humans to inflict harms.

Now, it may be suggested that what is odd about the moral misanthropic argument is the particular way it recommends preventing harm. It seeks to prevent harm to humans by preventing humans. This objection would have more force than it does if there were reasonable prospects of reducing human destructiveness to negligible levels fairly promptly and then ensuring that they do not rise again. If that were the case then it could be argued that instead of preventing humans we should rather reduce their destructiveness. In fact, however, we cannot expect that human destructiveness will *ever* be reduced to such levels. Human nature is too frail and the circumstances that bring out the worst in humans are too pervasive and are likely to remain so. Even where institutions can be built to curb the worst human excesses, these institutions are always vulnerable to moral entropy. It is naïve utopianism to think that a species as destructive as ours will cease, or all but cease, to be destructive.

Am I being overly pessimistic here? After all, it has been argued that rates of violence have been steadily diminishing and are now much lower than they were in prehistoric times.[77] This trajectory does not supplant the pessimism implicit in the misanthropic argument. Insofar as violence has decreased it is only the *rate* of violence that has declined. People are now less likely to suffer violence than they were before.[78] However, the total *amount* of suffering and death that is inflicted has increased, primarily because there are now many more people to inflict harm and to suffer harm at the hands of others. Desisting from creating new humans would mean that there would be fewer humans to be harmed and thus less total harm. While rates of violence are important, the total amount of violence is at least as important a consideration in deciding whether to create new people. There would be less violence if there were fewer people.

Even if we restrict our attention to the rate of violence, the rate could still increase. Given human nature, we cannot assume that the trend towards reduced rates is inexorable. However, even if we set that concern aside, the current rates are far from negligible despite the reduction. Even if it were not naïve to think that in the very long term, human destructiveness could be reduced to negligible levels, it would still be indecent to create beings that in the interim would cause massive pain, suffering and death.

A PRESUMPTIVE DUTY

If my argument so far is correct, then we have a presumptive duty to desist from bringing new humans into existence. Can the presumption be defeated?

Those who think it can might suggest that while the destructiveness of humans does create a presumption, the presumption can be defeated because of the good that humans do. One version of this view maintains that the good is sufficiently widespread that the presumption can *regularly* (even though not always) be defeated, and I shall consider this version first.

The more regularly a presumption can be defeated, the less clear it is that the presumption really is a presumption. However, the presumption against creating new members of a species that is as destructive as ours must surely be a strong one. Thus, those who would suggest that it is regularly defeated must bear the burden of proof and demonstrate that humanity does enough good to outweigh all the harm it does. I am not optimistic that this burden can be met.

Certainly in the case of the treatment of animals, the scales are heavily weighted against us. Although it is true that some humans do some good for animals, much of this is merely rescuing animals from the maltreatment of other humans. At the level of the human species such benefits cannot be used to offset the harms. If there were no humans to inflict the harms, these benefits would not be necessary. Of course, humans do bestow some other benefits, such as veterinary care for their companion animals. However, the number of animals affected and the amount of good done is massively outweighed by the harm the human species does to non-human animals.

Humans do bestow more benefit on other humans than they do on animals. Nevertheless, it seems clear to me that the good humans do is not sufficient to outweigh the presumption against creating new people. There may well be no definitive argument to prove this to those who think otherwise. However, there are a number of considerations that can be offered in support of my assessment. At the very least, these considerations show that those who think that the presumption is defeated cannot demonstrate that it is.

First, the benefits humans provide to other humans have to offset not only the harms done to humans but also those done to animals, and these harms are colossal. When the levels of destruction are this great, the amount of benefit one is going to have to demonstrate in order to defeat the presumption is immense. If pro-natalists think that the good humans do does indeed outweigh the terrible destruction I have described, then we need to hear some explicit details. Approximately how much good outweighs the dismemberment of a living being? How much outweighs mass rape? How much outweighs the Rwandan genocide or Joseph Stalin's purges? It is when one actually keeps the atrocities in mind rather than speaking about them abstractly as "the evil humans do" that the claim that these atrocities are outweighed is shown to be indecent.

Second, we need to understand what it means for the good to outweigh the bad. This may not be as straightforward as it sounds. For example, imagine you knew that if you conceived a child it would later, as an adult, murder somebody. How many lives would that potential person have to save during the course of his life (that would not otherwise be saved) in order to override the presumption against bringing him into existence? I doubt that that number is 2 or even anything close to that.

What this case suggests is that the notion of "good outweighing bad" is more complicated than may first appear. Now, perhaps it will be suggested that this particular case is a poor analogy for the matter at hand. Whether or not that is true, the very same point can be made about the case at hand. Thus, a species that kills n-billion humans and animals over some specified period would not redeem itself by saving n-billion + 1 lives over that same period.

Perhaps there are some utilitarians who would, in each of the cases just mentioned, assert that saving an additional life would indeed be sufficient to offset the lives taken. However, utilitarians are not committed to such a view and any form of utilitarianism that did adopt it would be a simplistic one. A more nuanced view would recognize that taking lives typically (even if not always) has worse secondary effects than failing to save lives. A murderer, for example, arouses more fear than a person who fails to save some lives that he could otherwise have saved.

Non-utilitarians would have further reason for accepting the more complicated conception of what it takes for good to outweigh bad. For them, considerations such as the violating of rights could be a moral cost that is not offset by saving a few more lives than are lost by the violation of rights. On at least some non-utilitarian views, there could be a threshold of harm beyond which no amount of benefit can compensate. If there is any such threshold then human destructiveness arguably exceeds it.

Third, some benefits will be moot in determining whether the presumption is defeated. To understand which these are, consider two intersecting distinctions:

1(a) benefits to those humans who already exist; and
  (b) benefits to those future people who will be brought into existence only if the presumption against creating them is defeated.
2(a) benefiting by preventing harm; and
  (b) benefiting by bestowing some (intrinsic) good.

At least those benefits at the intersection of 1(b) and 2(a) are moot.[79] This is because the benefits that fall in this intersection can be achieved in two ways: (1) by overriding the presumption and creating the people who will prevent the harm; and (2) by deferring to the presumption and not creating the people who will suffer the harm. Because of this, these benefits are not net benefits of creating new humans. That is to say, they are not an advantage over the situation that would result from following the presumption against creating new humans. Thus, they should not be factored into a decision whether or not the presumption is defeated.

Fourth, at least under current conditions the creation of each new human or each new cohort of humans does not produce benefits at the same rate that it produces harms. Given the current size of the human population and the current levels of human consumption, each new human or cohort of humans adds incrementally to the amount of animal suffering and death and, via the environmental impact, to the amount of harm to humans (and animals). The additional harm caused by each additional human may be imperceptible but it is nonetheless an addition that, when aggregated with other imperceptible additions, becomes perceptible. However, it is not the case that the addition of every new human or cohort of humans adds benefits. Much of the good that humans do could be done by fewer rather than by more humans. Thus, even if it is not always the case that creating additional humans is a net harm, it certainly is a net harm when the human population is sufficiently large (and destructive).

For these reasons I reject the suggestion that the presumption against creating new people can *regularly* be defeated. In response, those who think that the presumption can be defeated could fall back on a less ambitious version of this view—namely, that the presumption can *occasionally* be defeated. Thus, particular potential procreators might agree that humanity is in general a very dangerous species. However, they might suggest that the odds are that their own potential offspring are much more likely to do enough good and little enough bad to defeat the presumption.[80]

Depending on what we take to be "enough good and little enough bad," this may well be true of *some* (small number of) potential people. However, we can fully expect that most potential procreators will be very poor judges of whether their potential offspring are likely to fall into this category. The optimism bias, coupled with a tendency to rationalize that the action one wants to perform will serve the greater good, will lead the vast majority of potential procreators (or at least the vast majority of those who think before procreating) to the conclusion that the presumptive duty of the misanthropic argument is defeated in their case. The overwhelming majority of them will be wrong. Those who doubt this should consider the average person's destructive effect on, at least, animals and the environment.

We saw earlier that well in excess of 166 billion animals are killed every year for human consumption or in industries providing for this consumption. The overwhelming majority of humans on the planet are contributing to this killing and the prior suffering. With the exception of India, where a significant proportion of the population is vegetarian,[81] only a very small proportion of people in other countries are either vegetarian or vegan.[82] This suggests that, on average, each flesh eater is responsible for the deaths (and suffering) of at least twenty-seven animals per year[83]—which amounts to at least 1690 animals over the course of a lifetime.[84] This is an underestimate, but it is nonetheless a lot of destruction for a single individual.

Each new person also has an impact on the environment and thereby on those sentient beings affected by environmental damage. In developed countries, the impact of each person is massive. In the United States, for example, the average person produces 28.6 tons of CO_2 emissions per year.[85] In developing countries the per capita emissions are typically lower, but they are not zero. In Bangladesh and India, the annual average emissions of CO_2 per person are, respectively, 1.1 and 1.8 tons.[86] Thus each new child contributes to environmental damage. Perhaps a pronatalist will want to argue that we cannot expect the production of new people to have *no* impact on the environment and that some such impact is acceptable. However, whatever force this argument has is weakened as the number of people increases. The more people there are, the less justifiable it is to add further increments of environmental damage. Developing countries often have higher birthrates than developed ones. Individuals within such countries are going to have a difficult time justifying their repeated procreation.

Humanity is a moral disaster. There would have been much less destruction had we never evolved. The fewer humans there are in the future, the less destruction there will still be.

CONCLUSION

Anti-natalist arguments vary in the scope of their conclusions. At its most extreme an anti-natalist conclusion opposes all procreation, but milder versions oppose only select cases of procreation.

The philanthropic arguments generate an extensive conclusion. They suggest that coming into existence is always a harm. Because that harm is actually severe, it is, at least on some views, always wrong to have children. (Other views might allow some procreation as part of a plan to phase humans out of existence.[87])

The conclusion of the moral misanthropic argument is that it is presumptively wrong to have children. It is possible that this presumption could sometimes be defeated. I have argued that people will think it is defeated much more often than it actually is and that it is very difficult, if not impossible, to know when the presumption is indeed defeated. However, it remains possible that there are some circumstances in which a new human would produce sufficient good to offset the harm that that particular human would cause.

When the misanthropic argument is considered in conjunction with the philanthropic ones we find that the case against procreation, and especially in our current circumstances, is almost always over-determined.

APPENDIX

From the Bad to the Ugly: (Un)aesthetic Considerations

People tend to regard the birth of a child as something beautiful. However, there are good reasons for thinking that the opposite is true—that creating new people is an aesthetic disaster. These (un)aesthetic considerations do not ground a strong argument against procreation. However, these thoughts—which are in some sense misanthropic[88]—can be added to the moral arguments that I have already advanced. At least a number of them seem to provide some reason for having *fewer* children even though they do not support the conclusion that one should have no children.

Childbirth itself is hardly attractive. It does not feel good: the woman herself typically is not having any fun, and it is not pleasant for the baby either. Nor does it look very good. Here is Plutarch's description:

> For there is nothing so imperfect, so helpless, so naked, so shapeless, so foul, as man observed at birth, to whom alone, one might almost say, Nature has given not even a clean passage to the light; but, defiled with blood and covered with filth and resembling more one just slain than one just born, he is an object for none to touch or lift up or kiss or embrace except for someone who loves with natural affection.[89]

Saint Augustine of Hippo (or, on some accounts, Bernard of Clairvaux) reminds us that "Inter faeces et urinam nascimur"—we are born between feces and urine (or, more colloquially, between shit and piss). Our passage into the world is located between the orifices from which feces and urine are voided. Rabbi Akavya ben Mahalalel traces the ugliness back to conception or before. He says that one should remember that one came "from a putrid drop" [of semen].[90]

Moreover, each new child created will produce massive quantities of effluvia during the course of his or her lifetime. The average person produces about 2066 mL of urine[91] and at least 100 g of feces[92] each day. This amounts to about 754 liters of urine and at least 36.5 kg of feces per year. Over the course of a lifetime, the average person[93] excretes approximately 50,969 liters of urine and more than 2467 kg of feces.

Given the current human population[94] the annual human production of urine is well in excess of 5 trillion liters. Human bowels currently contribute more than 256 billion kg of feces annually. These amounts increase each year as the human population grows. In the light of these figures, the total lifetime contribution of each new human may seem paltry. However the thirteen-figure annual totals are, of course, an aggregation of many individual decisions to create more producers of urine and feces.

Nor are these the only effluvia. The average woman expels 14.97 liters of menstrual blood over her reproductive life,[95] and the average man ejaculates 11.08 liters of semen between puberty and death.[96] Harder to calculate are the amounts of nasal mucous and saliva, only some of which is expelled. Vomit, sweat, pus, and vaginal discharge are highly variable. Accompanying human excretion are billions of sheets of soiled toilet paper, tissues, tampons, and sanitary pads. Not all human emissions are either solid or liquid. Some are gaseous, as in the case of eructation and flatulence. From puberty onwards, human bodies tend to smell bad and have to be deodorized to prevent olfactory repugnance. And the ugly facts of human waste have to be hidden from polite society. The acts themselves are typically closeted to varying degrees, depending on the effluvia concerned. (Far too many people feel free to expectorate onto sidewalks and other public places, but the rest of us have a dim view of them.) What emerges from the various human orifices has to be discretely disposed.

Physical beauty is statistically abnormal. A minority of people are beautiful even if the vast majority are not repulsive. But nature ensures aesthetic entropy. Acne, an aesthetic scourge in its own right, manifests chiefly, by a cruel irony, on the part of the body most visible to all—the face. Hair is lost where it looks best—on the top of the head—and it sprouts in places it looks least attractive—from the nostrils and the ears, for example. Fat accumulates. Breasts and buttocks sag. Skin wrinkles. Advancing decrepitude is not a pleasant sight. Finally, decomposing bodies are so repulsive, both visually and olfactorily, that we meticulously have to hide these facts from our senses by careful disposal of the dead.

Human waste and remains are not our only aesthetic assaults. Our species litters and makes noise. It produces fumes from factories, cars, and cigarettes, and generates masses of rubbish. The fewer humans there are, the less such ugliness there is.

In response to these aesthetic considerations, it might be said that ugliness, just like beauty, is in the eye of the beholder and that for this reason the aesthetic considerations are far too subjective to be invoked in support of anti-natalism. Aesthetic judgments do differ, of course. However, the degree of disagreement varies, depending on the aesthetic domain. In the domains of effluvia, bodily decline, and decomposition, there is widespread agreement, at least among non-infants. Effluvia are waste—matter to be discarded, not aesthetically admired. Nobody yearns for or celebrates the sight of acne or bodily disfiguration or putrefaction. There seem to be good reasons for a negative rather than a positive or even a neutral reaction to such sights (even though aesthetic responses in some other domains are often inapt). However, even if we could not fault those few people who do not have a negative aesthetic reaction to human bodily waste, we could still acknowledge that for the vast majority who find it ugly, the facts of this voluminous waste provide aesthetic considerations against creating more people.

A second possible response to the (un)aesthetic considerations might be to concede them but to deny that the overall picture is an ugly one. In other words, it could be agreed that humans do produce a lot of filth but that their net aesthetic contribution is a positive one. This is not entirely implausible in a minority of cases—some artists and composers, for example, whose creative works produce significant positive aesthetic value. However, it is very difficult to see how the average human could be thought to produce enough positive aesthetic value to outweigh the buckets of effluent each one produces.

Creating ugliness is not always wrong but the more humans there are fouling the earth, the more heavily the aesthetic considerations weigh against creating even more filth. Sometimes the aesthetic considerations merge into moral ones. For example, where societies are too poor to provide sanitation facilities for, and to process waste from, an excessive number of people, there may actually be moral reasons to desist from creating new generators of waste because their creation would impose undue burdens on those who already exist.

Few prospective procreators consider the aesthetic impact of their potential children. But how many more producers of excrement and urine, flatulence, menstrual blood and semen, sweat, mucus, vomit, and pus do we really need? How much more human waste do we need to process? How many more corpses do we need to dispose of? It would be an aesthetic improvement if there were fewer people.[97]

NOTES

1. In the appendix at the end of this chapter, I offer some aesthetic considerations against procreating.
2. A variant of this argument would focus on human nature rather than on what humans do. There is obviously a close connection between these two versions.

Human behavior could be taken as evidence of humanity's flawed nature, and its flawed nature partially explains its bad behavior. Thus the difference between the two versions is primarily one of focus or emphasis.

3. This is not to deny that the religious worldview also recommends species humility—but typically only relative to God.

4. Some animals may surpass us in *some* cognitive capacities, but none do all things considered.

5. See, for example, Dan Ariely, *Predictably Irrational* (Revised and Expanded Edition) (New York: HarperCollins, 2009); Daniel Kahneman, *Thinking, Fast and Slow* (London: Penguin, 2011).

6. Consider the case of Joe DiMaggio, of whom it has been asked how he, "a high school dropout whose favorite reading material was Superman comics, a man who was a lousy father, an unfaithful husband and a wife beater . . . someone who never did a meaningful day's work in the last 47 years of his life, who was monumentally vain and cheap and mistrustful – became an American hero?" The answer, we are told, is simple: "He could hit and throw and run with a gliding grace, and when he could no longer do those things he . . . well, he looked great in a suit." (Daniel Okrent, "Say It Ain't So, Joe," *Time*, November 20, 2000, 74.)

7. At the time of writing, the latest instance is the doomsday hysteria from those who feared that the world would come to an end on December 21, 2012. Russia's government resorted to issuing a statement, saying that it "had access to 'methods of monitoring what is occurring on the planet Earth,'" and that it "could say with confidence that the world was not going to end in December." See Ellen Barry, "In Panicky Russia, It's Official: End of World Is Not Near," *New York Times*, December 1, 2012, accessed December 2, 2012, http://www.nytimes.com/2012/12/02/world/europe/mayan-end-of-world-stirs-panic-in-russia-and-elsewhere.html?pagewanted=print.

8. Solomon E. Asch, "Studies of Independence and Conformity: I. A Minority of One Against a Unanimous Majority," *Psychological Monographs* 70, no. 9 (1956): 1–70.

9. Rod Bond and Peter B. Smith, "Culture and Conformity: A Meta-Analysis of Studies Using Asch's (1952b, 1956) Line Judgment Task," *Psychological Bulletin* 119, no. 1 (1996): 111–137.

10. Steven T. Katz, *The Holocaust in Historical Context, Vol 1: The Holocaust and Mass Death Before the Modern Age* (New York: Oxford University Press, 1994), 403–404.

11. Sharon LaFraniere, "African Crucible: Cast as Witches, Then Cast Out," *New York Times*, November 15, 2007, accessed November 15, 2007, http://www.nytimes.com/2007/11/15/world/africa/15witches.html?_r=2&th=&oref=slogin&emc=th&pagewanted=all&.

12. Stanley Milgram, *Obedience to Authority* (New York: Harper Torchbooks, 1974).

13. Ibid., 54.

14. Hannah Arendt, *Eichmann in Jerusalem: A Report on the Banality of Evil* (New York: Penguin Books, 1965).

15. Philip Zimbardo, *The Lucifer Effect: Understanding How Good People Turn Evil* (New York: Random House, 2007).

16. Of course, psychologists and others who have studied the human mind are aware of the flaws to which I have pointed. The problem is that their findings have not shaken the dominant self-congratulatory view of humanity.

17. We are in denial about our destructive capacities. When humans behave in all the appalling ways I shall describe, we characterize them as "inhuman." Yet such behavior is so rampant in human history that the negation signalled by the prefix "in" in "inhuman" is, in fact, a negation of our pretensions (or, more charitably, our aspirations) about what it means to be human. It does not signal a deviation from the way the species actually conducts itself. It is similarly ironic that when humans behave badly—and even when they behave badly towards animals—we say they are behaving like animals, namely *brutally*. When I use the terms "inhuman" and "brutal", I am using them ironically.

18. "Population Control, Marauder Style," *New York Times*, November 6, 2011, accessed November 7, 2011, http://www.nytimes.com/imagepages/2011/11/06/opinion/06atrocities_timeline.html?ref=sunday.

19. Adam Hochschild, *King Leopold's Ghost* (Boston: Houghton Mifflin Company, 1998), 234.

20. Julie Flint, *Observer*, March 3, 1991, cited in Jonathan Glover, *Humanity: A Moral History of the Twentieth Century* (New Haven, CT: Yale Nota Bene, 2001), 32.

21. Nicholas Kristof, "The Grotesque Vocabulary in Congo," *New York Times*, February 11, 2010, accessed February 11, 2010, http://www.nytimes.com/2010/02/11/opinion/11kristof.html?th=&emc=th&pagewanted=print.

22. Jeffrey Gettleman, "The World's Worst War," *New York Times*, December 15, 2012, accessed December 16, 2012, http://www.nytimes.com/2012/12/16/sunday-review/congos-never-ending-war.html?pagewanted=2&pagewanted=print&_r=0.

23. Ibid.

24. Neil G. Boothby and Christine M. Knudsen, "Children of the Gun," *Scientific American*, June 2000, 43.

25. "Midnight's Children," *Harper's Magazine*, August 2004, 23.

26. Boothby and Knudsen, "Children of the Gun," 40–45.

27. Adam Hochschild, *Bury the Chains: The British Struggle to Abolish Slavery* (London: Macmillan, 2005), 79–80. (One of the slaves survived by grabbing onto a rope from the ship and getting himself back on board without being noticed.)

28. Lydia Polgreen, "Court Rules Niger Failed by Allowing Girl's Slavery," *New York Times*, October 28, 2008, accessed December 24, 2012, http://www.nytimes.com/2008/10/28/world/africa/28niger.html?_r=3&pagewanted=print.

29. Nicholas Kristof, "If This Isn't Slavery, What Is?," *New York Times*, January 4, 2009, accessed December 24, 2012, http://www.nytimes.com/2009/01/04/opinion/04kristof.html?pagewanted=print.

30. Sierra Leone Truth and Reconciliation Commission, *Witness to Truth*, 2004, 17.

31. Jo Thomas, "What's Furry, Literate and, Judging by Events, Indispensable?," *New York Times*, December 11, 1998, accessed December 25, 2012, http://www.nytimes.com/1998/12/11/us/what-s-furry-literate-and-judging-by-events-indispensable.html?pagewanted=print&src=pm.

32. Ibid.

33. Michael Barbaro, "Attention, Holiday Shoppers: We Have Fisticuffs in Aisle 2," *New York Times*, November 25, 2006, accessed November 27, 2006, http://www.nytimes.com/2006/11/25/business/25shop.html?_r=0.

34. Robert D. McFadden and Angela Macropoulos, "Wal-Mart Employee Trampled to Death," *New York Times*, November 29, 2008, accessed December 1, 2008, http://www.nytimes.com/2008/11/29/business/29walmart.html?_r=0.

35. Steven Nadler, *Spinoza: A Life* (New York: Cambridge University Press, 1999), 306.
36. Ibid.
37. For an example of a more recent mob killing, see "Murder Most Pointless," *Time*, July 5, 1999, 14.
38. The balance (32%) were imprisoned, executed, assassinated, killed in battle, or took their own lives. Matthew White, *The Great Big Book of Horrible Things* (New York: W. W. Norton & Co., 2012), 534.
39. See, for example, Nicholas Kulish, "Speculation Surrounds Case of Albanian Whistle-Blower's Death," *New York Times*, October 8, 2008, accessed October 8, 2008, http://www.nytimes.com/2008/10/08/world/europe/08albania.html?ref=europe&_r=0; "Deaths in Moscow," *The Economist*, January 24, 2009, 57.
40. For example, Simon Romero and Taylor Barnes, "In Brazil, Officers of the Law, Outside the Law," *New York Times*, January 9, 2012, accessed January 10, 2012, http://www.nytimes.com/2012/01/10/world/americas/in-parts-of-brazil-militias-operate-outside-the-law.html?pagewanted=print.
41. Ruth Richardson, *The Making of Mr. Gray's Anatomy: Bodies, Books, Fortune, Fame*, (New York: Oxford University Press, 2008).
42. Peter Pringle, "Notebooks Shed Light on an Antibiotic's Contested Discovery," *New York Times*, June 11, 2012, accessed June 14, 2012, http://www.nytimes.com/2012/06/12/science/notebooks-shed-light-o...mentors-betrayal.html?_r=1&partner=rss&emc=rss&pagewanted=print.
43. This data is from the Food and Agriculture Organization (FAO) of the United Nations. According to its statistics for 2010, the number of animals in these and related categories that were slaughtered numbered 63,544,184,849. See faostat.fao.org, accessed December 4, 2012.
44. This figure is for 2009 and is based on the FAO's estimate that 145.1 million tons of aquatic animal life was "harvested" that year (*The State of the World Fisheries and Aquaculture* [Rome: FAO Fisheries and Aquaculture Department, 2010], 3) and assumes that the "average marine animal's weight" is about 1.4 kg (see http://adaptt.org/killcounter.html, accessed December 4, 2012). It is noteworthy that official agencies such as the FAO do not calculate the number of animals, but estimate only the weight of the catch. Aquatic animals, on this view, are not individual sentient beings but rather mere biomass.
45. Michael C. Appleby, Joy A. Mench, and Barry O. Hughes, *Poultry Behaviour and Welfare* (Wallingford, UK: CABI Publishing, 2004), 184.
46. This figure is cited in a European Union Memo: "Questions and Answers on the proposal for the protection of animals at the time of killing," MEMO/08/574, Brussels, September 18, 2008, accessed December 19, 2012, http://europa.eu/rapid/press-release_MEMO-08-574_en.htm.
47. "How Many Dogs and Cats Are Eaten in Asia?" *Animal People*, September 2003, accessed December 19, 2012, http://www.animalpeoplenews.org/03/9/dogs.catseatenAsia903.html.
48. *The State of the World Fisheries and Aquaculture*, 83–84, cites a figure of 7 million tons. On the average marine animal weight cited, this amounts to about 5 billion animals.
49. Appleby, Mench, and Hughes, *Poultry Behaviour and Welfare*, 184.
50. Ibid., 184–186.
51. Victoria Braithwaite, *Do Fish Feel Pain?* (Oxford: Oxford University Press, 2010), 177.
52. Ibid. For the pain inflicted by hooks, see 164–168.

53. I am skeptical about the value of animal experimentation, but even if one thought that this practice were justifiable on account of a benefit to humans, it would still be the case that if there were no humans these harms would not be inflicted on animals.

54. Katy Taylor, Nicky Gordon, Gill Langley, and Wendy Higgins, "Estimates for Worldwide Laboratory Animal Use in 2005," *Alternatives to Laboratory Animals*, 36 (2008): 327–342.

55. Ingrid Torjesen, "Animal Experiments Rose in 2011 Despite Coalition Pledge to Reduce Them," *British Medical Journal*, 345 (2012): e4728.

56. See, for example, Kathryn Shevelow, *For the Love of Animals: The Rise of the Animal Protection Movement* (New York: Henry Holt, 2008), 144.

57. Deborah Blum, *The Monkey Wars* (New York: Oxford University Press, 1995), 82.

58. Ibid., 83.

59. Ibid., 90.

60. Ibid., 91.

61. Mark E. Gurney et al., "Motor Neuron Degeneration in Mice that Express a Human Cu,Zn Superoxide Dismutase Mutation," *Science* 264, no. 5166 (1994): 1772–1775.

62. Alun Anderson, "Oncomouse Released," *Nature* 336, no. 6197 (1988): 300.

63. See, for example, Peter M. Grace, Mark R. Hutchinson, Jim Manavis, Andrew A. Somogyi, and Paul E. Rolan, "A Novel Animal Model of Graded Neuropathic Pain: Utility to Investigate Mechanisms of Population Heterogeneity," *Journal of Neuroscience Methods* 193 (2010): 47–53.

64. Juliana Casals et al., "The Use of Animal Models for Stroke Research: A Review," *Comparative Medicine* 61, no. 4 (2011): 305–313.

65. See, for example, Kathryn L. Gatford, Penelope A. Dalitz, Megan L. Cock, Richard Harding, and Julie A. Owens, "Acute Ethanol Exposure in Pregnancy Alters the Insulin-like Growth Factor Axis of Fetal and Maternal Sheep," *American Journal of Physiology—Endocrinology and Metabolism* 292 (2007): E494—E500.

66. See, for example, Kelly J. Clemens, Jennifer L. Cornish, Glenn E. Hunt, and Iain S. McGregor, "Repeated Weekly Exposure to MDMA, Methamphetamine or their Combination: Long-term Behavioural and Neurochemical Effects in Rats," *Drug and Alcohol Dependence* 86 (2007): 183–190.

67. See, for example, Walt Bogdanich, Joe Drape, Dara L. Miles, and Griffin Palmer, "Mangled Horses, Maimed Jockeys," *New York Times*, March 24, 2012, accessed March 25, 2012, http://www.nytimes.com/2012/03/25/us/death-and-disarray-at-americas-racetracks.html?_r=2&hp=&pagewanted=print.

68. Hochschild, *King Leopold's Ghost*, 196.

69. http://www.pet-abuse.com/cases/10007/EN/UK/, accessed December 17, 2012.

70. http://www.pet-abuse.com/cases/16982/WI/US/, accessed December 17, 2012.

71. http://www.pet-abuse.com/cases/16970/WA/US/, accessed December 17, 2012.

72. It is very difficult to determine how many millions of dogs and cats are killed each year by animal shelters because those animals cannot be homed. The American Humane Association estimates that the number in the United States is about 3.7 million animals per year and says this "number represents a generally accepted statistic that is widely used by many animal welfare organizations, including the American Society for the Prevention of Cruelty to Animals (ASPCA)." (http://www.americanhumane.org/animals/stop-animal-abuse/fact-sheets/animal-shelter-euthanasia.html, accessed December 4, 2012.) However, these figures, which are based on a 1997 survey conducted by the National Council on

Pet Population Study and Policy explicitly notes that it "is not possible to use these statistics to estimate numbers of animals entering animal shelters in the United States, or the numbers euthanized on an annual basis" because the "reporting Shelters may not represent a random sampling of U.S. Shelters." (http://www.petpopulation.org/statsurvey.html, accessed December 4, 2012).

73. Nicola Rooney and David Sargan, *Pedigree Dog Breeding in the UK—A Major Welfare Concern?* (RSPCA, 2009).

74. There are some environmental ethicists who believe that damage to the environment is morally relevant in its own right, independent of the effects on humans and animals. That is a controversial position, which I do not accept. Those who do endorse it can, again, add to the list of (morally relevant) harm that humans cause.

75. Some might argue that these other species do not do as much good as humans do and are thus not analogous. I shall later consider whether the good that humans do can defeat the presumption against creating more of them.

76. These arguments are advanced in dozens of books and articles. See, for example, Peter Singer, *Animal Liberation* (New Revised Edition) (New York: Avon Books, 1990), and David DeGrazia, *Taking Animals Seriously* (New York: Cambridge University Press, 1996).

77. The evidence and arguments for this have been presented in impressive detail in Steven Pinker, *The Better Angels of our Nature: The Decline of Violence in History and its Causes* (London: Allen Lane, 2011).

78. The same may not be true of animals. Although some kinds of animals, such as dogs and cats, are now treated better than they were in the past, other animals, most notably farm animals, are treated worse today than they were before. The intensive farming and associated suffering is a product of the last few decades.

79. If one accepts the basic asymmetry, then the benefits at the intersection of 1(b) and 2(b) are also moot.

80. It is curiously rare for people to think that chances are that their own children would produce a net harm but that the children of others would produce a net benefit.

81. There are varying estimates of the number of vegetarians in India. Here I shall assume a generous estimate of 42% of the population (R. Mehta et al., "Annex II: Livestock, Industrialization, Trade and Social-Health-Environment Issues for the Indian Poultry Sector," Food and Agricultural Organization, June 2002, accessed January 15, 2013, http://www.fao.org/WAIRDOCS/LEAD/X6115E/x6115e0c.htm.)

82. There are not data for the proportion of vegetarians worldwide. There are data for some developed countries, where the proportions are between around 1% and 9%. [See Matthew B. Ruby, "Vegetarianism: A Blossoming Field of Study," *Appetite* 58 (2012): 142.] For my purposes, I shall assume that 5% of the world (outside of India) is vegetarian or vegan. This is likely an overestimate as the rate of vegetarianism in the developing world (outside of India) is likely to be lower.

83. This calculation assumes a world population of 7,021,836,029 and the population of India as 1,205,073,612 [*The World Fact Book*, Central Intelligence Agency, accessed January 15, 2013, https://www.cia.gov/library/publications/the-world-factbook/geos/xx.html]

84. This assumes an average life expectancy of 67.59 years, which is the current average globally (https://www.cia.gov/library/publications/the-world-factbook/geos/xx.html, accessed December 27, 2012), with meat consumption beginning

at age 5. (Of course omnivorous humans begin eating meat earlier than age 5, but their consumption levels are low at the earliest stages.)

85. Edgar G. Hertwich and Glen P. Peters, "Carbon Footprint of Nations: A Global, Trade-Linked Analysis," *Environmental Science and Technology* 43, no. 16 (2009): 6416.

86. Ibid.

87. For more on this, see David Benatar, *Better Never to Have Been* (Oxford: Oxford University Press, 2006), 182–193.

88. Like the philanthropic argument, this aesthetic misanthropic argument could also be applied to animals. There is much that is aesthetically unappealing about animals. However, there are some ways in which humans are aesthetically worse. This is partly a function of the number and impact of humans.

89. Plutarch, "On Affection for Offspring," in *Moralia*, vol. VI, trans. W. C. Helmbold, (London: William Heinemann Ltd., 1939), 349.

90. *Ethics of the Fathers*, 3:1.

91. Obviously the amount depends in part on water intake and on other variations between people, including whether the person is an adult or a child. The figure I cite here is from a careful study of adults: Dick Parker and S. K. Gallagher, "Distribution of Human Waste Samples in Relation to Sizing Waste Processing in Space," in *The Second Conference on Lunar Bases and Space Activities of the 21st Century*, ed. W. W. Mendell (NASA Conferences Publication 3166, Vol. 2, Part 6, 1992), 564.

92. This is very likely an underestimate as those in the study did not eat fresh fruit and vegetables, which, the authors of the study note, would increase stool volume. See Parker and Gallagher, "Distribution of Human Waste Samples in Relation to Sizing Waste Processing in Space," 563 and 566.

93. This assumes an average life expectancy of 67.59 years.

94. Estimated as 702,183,6029 in July 2012. Ibid.

95. This assumes 36.7 mL per menstruation (http://ebm.rsmjournals.com/content/32/9/1458.short, accessed December 27, 2012); that the average ages for menarche and natural menopause are 14 and 50 respectively (Alfredo Morabia, Michael Costanza and the World Health Organization Collaborative Study of Neoplasia and Steroid Contraceptives, "International Variability in Age at Menarche, First Livebirth, and Menopause," *American Journal of Epidemiology* 148, no. 12 [1998]: 1195–1205); that the average woman has 2.47 children (https://www.cia.gov/library/publications/the-world-factbook/geos/xx.html, accessed December 27, 2012), yielding 408 months of menstrual cycles per woman.

96. This assumes 1.5 mL per ejaculation (Trevor Cooper et al., "World Health Organization Reference Values for Human Semen Characteristics," *Human Reproduction Update* 16, no. 3 (2010): 231–245), mean age of first ejaculation as 13.5 years (http://europepmc.org/abstract/MED/6106006/reload=0;jsessionid=raWEbqG5dSAVKzRoikTM.14, accessed December 27, 2012), average male life expectancy as 65.6 years (https://www.cia.gov/library/publications/the-world-factbook/geos/xx.html, accessed December 27, 2012) and 142 ejaculations per year (based on Michael Leitzmann et al., "Ejaculation Frequency and Subsequent Risk of Prostate Cancer," *Journal of the American Medical Association* 291, no. 13 (2004): 1578–1586).

97. I am grateful to Anna Hartford for research assistance, and to participants in the "Permissible Progeny" workshop (London, Ontario, June 2013) for their comments.

CHAPTER 2
Procreative Ethics and the Problem of Evil

JASON MARSH

Many people see the evil and suffering in our world as important if not decisive evidence against the claim that a loving God created our world and yet these same people typically see no real moral problem with human procreation. This chapter argues that these attitudes are in tension. More accurately, although it might turn out that the facts of evil and suffering threaten theism without also threatening human procreation, it would take philosophical work to show that this is the case. In the meantime we are left with two basic options—at least those of us who take global arguments from evil seriously.[1] First, we can grant the tension and revise our beliefs about the severity of the problem of evil in order to make procreation more justifiable. Second, we can grant the tension and acknowledge that human procreation raises important ethical problems. Although both possibilities are worthy of consideration, I will primarily explore the latter possibility in this chapter. My goal, to clarify, will not be to argue that procreation is in fact impermissible on account of the problem of evil, but to motivate the idea that procreation may be in need of a systematic justification. Whatever one makes of my particular aims, however, I hope it becomes clear that thinking about procreative ethics and the problem of evil in tandem is fruitful because it unveils important connections between the two areas and reveals new challenges for each side.

THE CONTEXT

According to a recent survey,[2] the vast majority of professional philosophers self-identify as nontheists—more than 85% self-identify as atheists, agnostics, or something other than theists. If you ask these philosophers why they are nonbelievers or lean toward nonbelief, one response you're likely to get is that the problem of evil justifies their stances, at least in part. It is not just nonbelievers who take the problem of evil seriously, though. Many believers do as well. Indeed, another survey suggests that atheists, agnostics, and theists agree that the argument from evil represents the single strongest argument for disbelief.[3]

Of course, there are various versions of the argument from evil (logical, evidential, local, global, etc.) and various lines of response to those different arguments (the free will defense, the soul-making defense, and skeptical theism, etc). The relevant surveys naturally do not track these various distinctions. But it is interesting that although we survey people about their general views concerning the problem of evil, no one feels the need to survey philosophers about whether human procreation is permissible. This is almost certainly because almost all philosophers think that procreation raises no real problems, at least in the vast majority of cases. Actually, most philosophers along with most people think that procreation is obviously justified, and as a result fail to really reflect on the matter.

Now, as one might expect, the situation is slightly different among the experts in procreative ethics. Here the question of whether bringing persons into existence is permissible has recently begun to be taken very seriously. On the one hand, there are the anti-natalists. These thinkers, though they remain in the minority,[4] have argued that procreation is rarely if ever justified, given certain facts about harm, risk, and consent, and given certain empirical facts about how we overestimate the quality of our lives. On the other hand, there are the pro-natalists. These thinkers, though they do not normally seek to explain why procreation is justified, occasionally try to answer anti-natalist challenges.[5] In addition to pro-natalism and anti-natalism there is a third, and almost entirely neglected, option called procreative skepticism.[6] According to this view we should be uncertain or agnostic about the moral status of procreation, at least in many cases. Such a view is worth mentioning because it is weaker (and intrinsically more plausible)[7] than anti-natalism, and because it might have similar practical consequences to anti-natalism.

If you look to the literature in procreative ethics, then, you might be inclined to think that we are already in need of a more robust justification of procreation. My task will be to argue that this need is confirmed if common ways of reasoning about God and evil are thought to be on track.

HOW THESE PROBLEMS DO AND DO NOT RELATE

In response to my thesis, some might claim that the problem of evil and the problem of procreation are too different to really speak to one another. After all, goes the thought, the problem of evil is supposed to be an argument against the existence of God, but nobody is arguing that human parents do not exist. This claim misconstrues the connection we are exploring, however. Our question is not whether the problems of evil and procreation have an identical logical structure or conclusion. Our question is rather whether certain features of these problems, or ways of reasoning about them, speak to one another.

For instance, if we had notably different attitudes about evil and optimism when reasoning about the problem of evil than we do when reasoning about human procreation, consistency would force us to revise our views in at least one of these two domains. Similarly, if we drew on notably different evidence when evaluating people's well-being, depending on which problem we are working on, this would be significant and could reveal the presence of a bias. Unfortunately, however, few philosophers have appreciated these possibilities, which shall soon be developed in detail.[8]

This is not to say that every version of the problem of evil, if endorsed, will generate problems for human procreation. For instance, according to the classic version of the problem of evil—the logical version—any amount of evil logically entails the non-existence of an all-perfect God. On this view, often attributed to J. L. Mackie,[9] the bare existence of evil establishes atheism; it wouldn't matter if the world were fantastic overall. More precisely, this argument states that the following claims are logically inconsistent: (1) God is omnipotent (that is, all powerful), (2) God is omniscient (that is, all knowing), (3) God is omnibenevolent (that is, all loving), (4) Evil exists.[10] If such an argument were successful, goes the thought, then the problem of evil and the problem of procreation would reasonably be thought to be entirely independent. For it does not seem, on the face of it, that the bare existence of evil poses a moral problem for human procreation.

There are problems with endorsing this version of the argument to escape the tension that I am exploring, however. Most notably, the logical problem of evil has largely fallen out of fashion among philosophers of religion. Indeed, according to one common narrative,[11] most writers now acknowledge that it is very hard to show that God and evil are in logical tension and prefer instead to see the evil and suffering we observe as providing *evidence* against God's existence. In light of the evidential or probabilistic turn in philosophy of religion, it seems unwise to appeal to the logical problem of evil to escape problems about human procreation.

Another complication for the above escape route concerns recent developments in axiology. Some moral philosophers deny that the bare existence of evil lacks procreative significance. David Benatar, for instance, argues that even a single harm in a human life, if notable, would render starting that life impermissible. I am referring here to Benatar's asymmetry argument against human procreation.[12] According to this argument, existence in our world can never really be in anyone's interest in light of the following four claims that Benatar thinks most people implicitly accept: (1) the presence of pain is bad, (2) the presence of pleasure is good, (3) the absence of pain is good, even where no one exists to appreciate its absence, and (4) the absence of pleasure is not bad unless some existing person is deprived of this absence.

Though rarely encountered by philosophers of religion, Benatar's argument supports an idea that could seriously alter discussions of theism and evil: namely that unpopulated worlds are always preferable to populated worlds that include some evil. (To clarify, I do not endorse the asymmetry argument.[13] My claim is merely that those who wish to draw upon the logical argument from evil to escape the problems raised here ought to at least engage Benatar's argument.)

In addition to logical arguments from evil, it may be that certain local arguments from evil—e.g., those based on seemingly isolated and gratuitous natural evils, such as a fawn burning in a forest fire—have no significance for procreation. It would be a basic misunderstanding to think this undermines my thesis, however. For leaving aside problems with local arguments from evil,[14] our question is not whether all arguments from evil must always have procreative significance. Our question is whether some of the most widely held and most forceful versions do. This is hardly a trivial possibility. It would be very interesting if some of the most common and forceful arguments from evil implicated people's beliefs about procreation.

HOW GOOD IS THE WORLD? GLOBAL ARGUMENTS FROM EVIL

So what are these widely discussed versions of the problem of evil? Like many, I suspect that the best and most discussed arguments from evil are global and evidential in nature; they concern how much evil there is and whether this evil notably disconfirms, or perhaps even falsifies, theism. Indeed, it is precisely because there is so much horrible evil around the world that these global evidential arguments from evil are thought to have evidential traction. Consider, for instance, the following remarks from Alvin Plantinga:

> Our world contains an appalling amount and variety both of suffering and of evil.... I'm thinking of suffering as encompassing any kind of pain or discomfort: pain or discomfort that results from disease or injury, or oppression, or overwork, or old age, but also disappointment with oneself or with one's lot in life (or that of people close to one), the pain of loneliness, isolation, betrayal, unrequited love; and there is also suffering that results from awareness of others' suffering ... [15]

Consider, too, the following words from Michael Peterson:

> Something is dreadfully wrong with our world. An earthquake kills hundreds in Peru. A pancreatic cancer patient suffers prolonged, excruciating pain and dies. A pit bull attacks a two-year-old child, angrily ripping his flesh and killing him. Countless multitudes suffer the ravages of war in Somalia. A crazed cult leader pushes eighty-five people to their deaths in Waco, Texas. Millions starve and die in North Korea as famine ravages the land. Horrible things of all kinds happen in our world—and that has been the story since the dawn of civilization.[16]

The above authors, being theists, do not think that evil defeats theism. Their claims do, however, suggest that extremely bad things happen very frequently and appear to raise a question about the basic goodness of the world. In saying this, I do not mean to deny that the authors of these passages are themselves optimistic—perhaps they are and perhaps their religious outlook helps them.[17] The claim is only that their words may tell a different story. And the story is that, at least in the absence of some kind of redemption or way of dealing with all of this evil, our world is not obviously good and can sometimes even look bad.

Further evidence of this worry shows up in the works of many non-theists as well. According to Paul Draper, for instance, the fact that so many sentient beings never flourish because they suffer for much or even "most or all of their lives" is much more likely on metaphysical naturalism than on theism.[18] Draper realizes that there is also cooperation in the world and that some sentient beings get lucky.[19] But he claims that "countless living organisms", including many human beings, still fail to live good lives. Philip Kitcher draws on similar data to issue a direct challenge to the divine. He states, "had the Creator consulted me at the Creation, I think I could have given him some useful advice."[20] Kitcher of course does not literally believe that there exists a creator for him to advise. But his claim about natural evil remains relevant to our discussion all the same. For Kitcher seems to imply that even limited and minimally decent beings like ourselves, never mind a perfect Anselmian creator, would not design this world with all of its competition, suffering, disease, and death. The worry generated by such a claim should be apparent. We bring people into the very same world, with the very same patterns of suffering, all of the time.[21] Rarely do we ask whether this makes us less than minimally decent creators.

Other examples could be cited as well. For instance, Ken Taylor mentions that 'of the roughly 106 billion human beings who have so far lived on the earth it seems fair to estimate that an extraordinary percentage have lived in circumstances of considerable material, political, and/or spiritual deprivation.'[22] Taylor adds that even the 'providential theist' cannot rule out that 'many more millennia of moral darkness do not still await us.'[23] In addition, Julian Savulescu, now a philosopher, describes how his experiences as a physician helped to undermine his former faith.

> I saw for the first time the reality of death and suffering. I did some hard jobs like Haematology and Oncology, and Intensive Care. I saw completely innocent ordinary young people die agonizing deaths, their skin peeling from their body as they were narcotised to death. I saw horrible burns and amputated limbs from utterly meaningless accidents. I saw people screaming as they died and others silent with terror. . . . While there is a voluminous theological literature spanning millennia on the problem of suffering, and great writers like Dostoyevsky and Tolstoy propose solutions, the idea that there was any value or meaning in suffering and death evaporated for me. What I saw and heard just killed a belief in God for me, for no special philosophical reason. This was a phase of existential senselessness. I bought a safe car, went surfing and skiing a lot and decided to do philosophy. . . . That was my response to the value of suffering.[24]

To be sure, Savulescu also acknowledges experiential moments of "exquisite beauty" and points to his children as his greatest joy in life. I can appreciate that. But it rather helps to make my point: the reader is left with the sense that he is more optimistic when describing his children than when describing theism.

In light of these claims, a question facing many philosophers is this: are we notably more pessimistic about the basic goodness of the world when reasoning about the problem of evil than we are when reasoning about human procreation? I think the answer is yes. And although I haven't done detailed empirical analysis, I can give my impressions. I can also make predictions. For instance, I'd be willing to bet that those who write on global evidential arguments from evil, including those who claim that evil defeats theism, do not have many less children on average than other academics. I also bet that they are no less likely to celebrate the birth of a child than others.

Even if you disagree with me about the empirical issues, however, there remains a normative question worth asking. Should the kinds of pessimistic claims we are talking about, claims which regularly show up in debates about the problem of evil, be more consistently factored into our thoughts and claims about the morality of human procreation? You do not have to be an anti-natalist to raise this question. After all, the passages we have been considering seem to show that suffering is extremely pervasive.

Perhaps some philosophers will wish to resist an overly gloomy interpretation of their claims. Hopefully the present discussion, whatever else it accomplishes, will encourage more philosophers to become clearer on what they mean to imply about the world's overall value or about the value or meaning of the average life. In some cases little clarification is required, however. This is because some authors are explicit about the relationship between evil and optimism. Most notably, Marilyn McCord Adams acknowledges that horrendous evils "challenge a believer's faith." But she adds that evil represents a problem for everyone, including nonbelievers. She states,

> The world is riddled with what I have called horrendous evils. They're not a rare thing. And it's easy to become a participant in them. And thousands, millions of people, are participating in them now even as we speak. And so what I want to say to people who don't believe in God is this: if you're optimistic and idealistic, if you think life is worth living and you have high purposes in your life, this is not a rational posture unless you think that there is some superhuman power who is capable of making good on the many and various horrors that human beings perpetuate everyday on one another, and which could befall you tomorrow, even in the next half hour.[25]

Adams intends to set up a pragmatic argument for belief in God, a so-called argument from the conditions of optimism.[26] I will not address this argument here. For present purposes, Adams' more basic claims about whether optimism is rational in the absence of faith are my target.

Adams' claims are highly relevant to procreative ethics since, although the point seems to escape her notice, they arguably commit her to two forms of anti-natalism. The first form of anti-natalism arises if we endorse a widely held view about what justifies procreation. According to Jeff Mc-Mahan, "What makes procreation morally permissible in most cases is the reasonable expectation that the bads in a possible person's life will be out-weighed, and significantly outweighed, by the goods."[27] When combined with McMahan's claims about what justifies procreation, Adams' claim that secular persons cannot justify an optimistic outlook suggests that secular persons should not procreate, at least if they are informed of their predicament.

Perhaps Adams will respond by rejecting McMahan's claim that rea-sonable expectation about how one's child will fare (expected utility) as opposed to her actual future (actual utility) are what matter to procreative decision-making. Perhaps she will further remind the reader that, given her theological framework, everyone will fare well, at least in the long run. Indeed, since Adams believes that there will be a final victory over evil, culminating in the salvation of all persons, she may think that procrea-tion is always objectively safe.

I think that this theistic defense of pro-natalism, which makes use of universal salvation and consequentialism, would be an interesting move. I am surprised that no one has made it. But such a move is also risky. Recall that Adams admits that evil poses a problem for the believer and could objectively undermine theism. Such an admission is risky now since it introduces a second form of anti-natalism. In particular, if Adams is wrong about God's existence and right about the world's present value, then her claims would seem to imply that nobody should, objectively speaking, procreate.[28]

The most obvious way to generate a problem for procreation, then, is to explicitly claim that the world risks being bad or to claim that optimism is irrational, at least if theism is false. But there are other, less explicit ways to generate a problem for procreation. Some authors might implicitly com-municate that the world is bad or extremely mixed, whether or not God exists. Others might implicitly communicate that the world's value, or at least the value of many lives, is ambiguous, neither clearly good nor clearly bad. Any of these claims should trouble us, since if it is anything short of clear that the average life is quite good it might also seem clear (given McMahan's claim) that informed persons, at least, are not well positioned to start the average life.

In my experience, few seem to notice that their claims about God and evil have procreative significance. Of the authors discussed so far, only Julian Savulescu comes close to being an exception, which is perhaps unsurprising since he works in procreative ethics. In another article, co-written with Guy Kahane, he states: "parents are exposing children to risks of suffering, hardship and frustration simply by bringing them into existence. If procreative choices were constrained in this way, there could be strong presumptive reasons to abstain from procreation altogether."[29] Savulescu never explains why procreative choices aren't so constrained, but his earlier claims about God and evil make this silence puzzling. After all, if God's creative choices are constrained by suffering, why doesn't something similar apply to human parents? If God ought to create beings that suffer less than us, or not create at all, why doesn't something similar apply to us?[30]

I will soon explore some possible answers to these questions and why they fail. In the meantime, we seem to be left with the following problem. The premises of many evidential arguments from evil, if endorsed, may challenge the existence of a perfect God or even a minimally decent creator. But these premises equally appear to challenge the value of many human lives and by extension many acts of human procreation. If we convey, whether explicitly or implicitly, that the world risks being bad or far less than good then we make procreation risky in general. If we communicate, less strongly, that the value of many but not nearly all lives is negative or ambiguous, we still raise important local challenges to procreation, according to which many shouldn't procreate.

This last claim about local procreative worries reveals something important about the nature of our challenge. In particular, it would be inadequate to respond to my claims by pointing out that defenders of arguments from evil are themselves typically well positioned to procreate, given their privileged place in society. Even if such a claim were beyond dispute, it would be highly significant if the arguments of many philosophers of religion implied that very many people should not create.

OBJECTION 1: GOD AND HUMANS ARE DIFFERENT

The most obvious objection to my claims is that there are serious differences between humans and the divine, differences that generate asymmetrical moral responsibilities in the context of creation. In particular, a perfect God, it might be argued, could easily create far better off creatures than us and could easily improve our environments. By contrast, we humans do not have nearly as much control over the kinds of being we create or the amount of natural evil there is. This means that we should be held to a much less demanding creation ethic than God, given our limitations.

I think that this objection, which points to differences between God and humans, is not ultimately helpful to the pro-natalist defender of arguments form evil. For one thing, even if we grant that a theistic God, being perfect, can be held to a higher creative standard than we limited human beings, it hardly follows that human procreation is problem-free. For it may be that no truly loving being, whether human or divine, would create persons who suffer or who seriously risk suffering in the ways outlined earlier. Pointing out that a powerful God could eliminate more suffering than us, in other words, won't get us off the hook if there is a serious problem with anyone's placing sentient creatures in a world like this one. In fact, if the world risks being bad, or if its value is ambiguous, it doesn't really matter if God could have easily created a far better world than this one. Procreation will still raise serious moral problems for us.

There is another problem with the current objection. Showing that a perfect God would have a more difficult time justifying creating than we limited beings do, in some respects, is not tantamount to showing that a perfect God would have a more difficult time justifying creation than we do in all respects. In fact, when it comes to the decision to make persons, it may be that we humans have the larger justificatory burden, all things considered. This is because, a perfectly powerful God could plausibly defeat any evil that arises in the lives of our children in ways that we humans, left to our own devices, could not hope to. Most notably, a perfectly powerful God could radically extend our natural life span, say in the hereafter, ensuring that present evils are radically overcome, even to the point that they no longer seem significant. By contrast, we limited human beings lack the resources to defeat horrendous evil or to offer our children maximal levels of well-being. This fact alone would arguably make God better positioned to place persons in *this* world than humans, or at least humans who deny the existence of God.

It is not just that we lack the power to make good on horrendous evils should they arise in our child's life. It is also that we cannot foresee whether these (or less severe but still serious) evils will arise in the first place and cannot always see how they might be justified, should they arise. Put another way, an all-knowing God might be aware of moral justifications for creating persons who suffer that we finite beings lack, assuming there are such justifications.

What all of this means is that our lack of power and knowledge can work against us when it comes to creation ethics. Pointing to differences between divine and human attributes to escape the problem we are raising can easily backfire. It can show that we should not create at all, or at least that we should create beings who experience less harm than we do.[31]

OBJECTION 2: BEING IS INHERENTLY GOOD

Another possible objection to my claims is axiological. Benatar, recall, draws on axiological claims to argue that coming into existence is always a net harm, at least in this world. This strikes many people as way too strong. But some philosophers of religion I have spoken with have appeared to endorse a comparably strong claim: namely that existence is always a net benefit. Now such a claim might be interesting if based on Marilyn Adams' universalist outlook, described earlier. But the philosophers I have in mind did not base their claims about the goodness of existence on the universality of salvation. They rather based them on the Medieval doctrine, according to which being is inherently good and is indeed to be identified with goodness.

Perhaps these philosophers misspoke. And no doubt there are different interpretations of the doctrine in question, some of which might be extremely sophisticated. But if the "being is goodness" doctrine is literally interpreted such that coming into existence is always a net good—and a net good for a conscious agent no matter what happens in this life or the next—then I find it highly dubious. I am not exactly sure how to argue for this judgment. I suspect that almost no one would agree that an existence that was literally full of misery, with no hope of relief, is good for an agent all things considered. In fact many people would commit suicide under less harsh conditions, which testifies to their beliefs on these matters. I suppose I am largely assuming with most moral philosophers that a life could fail to be worth living, if it goes badly enough. For those who share this assumption, the present objection will not provide a good basis for severing the connection between procreative ethics and the problem of evil.

OBJECTION 3: THERE CAN BE OPTIMISTIC ARGUMENTS FROM EVIL

Perhaps a better response to the current tension would be for philosophers to simply tone down their pessimistic claims when reasoning about religion in order to make it easier to justify human procreation. Here it might be said that many arguments from evil, whether on account of emotion or rhetoric or both, overstate how bad the world is. It might be added that once we factor in all of our evidence, including our evidence for life's many goods things look pretty darn decent overall. According to this view, if a divine creator does exist, our response to this fact (pace Kitcher and others) should be not one of complaint about suffering and evil, but one of great thanks and acknowledgement of the gift of life. In addition, on this view, if there is a global normative challenge for theism, it will not be that the world risks being bad or that its value is unclear. It will rather go something like this:

1. The world is clearly good all things considered, well worth celebrating, but it could be even better and indeed far better.
2. If there were a perfect God, premise 1 would be false. That is, if there were a perfect God, the world would likely not be such that it could be radically improved upon. (This is because a perfect God would likely not satisfice or at least would likely not satisfice very much in creating or sustaining the world)
3. Therefore a perfect God likely doesn't exist.

The anti-satisficing argument acknowledges that human life is generally quite good and yet still manages to raise a global and evidential problem for theism. That said, the anti-satisficing approach raises difficult questions of its own (questions that should lead anyone to think twice before abandoning standard global arguments for the present one to get out of the pickle).

For instance, how good would a world, or a life, have to be before it is worthy of creation? Does the anti-satisficing approach imply that there shouldn't be any squirrels, if theism is true, since these creatures cannot enjoy maximal levels of well-being? Or does it merely imply that squirrels should be as happy as possible relative to their natures? What are the cut-off points for "good enough"? I, for one, am not sure what to say about these matters. Moreover, that few philosophers nowadays think that there is a best possible world, or a best possible life, further complicates matters.[32]

Perhaps, contrary to first appearance, these questions can be answered. But even if they can, another problem emerges. The more we stress how good the world is, in order to save optimism and procreation, the less plausible, in general, evidential arguments from evil will become. To put the point another way, evidential challenges from evil carry notably less force under more optimistic assumptions than under more pessimistic ones. This is because pessimistic arguments from evil can easily, and almost always do, incorporate the thought that a perfect God could create a better world than this one. Pessimistic arguments from evil will just add that this is only half the story; the other half is that the world has not just some, but many, terrible features; features that leave many in depression and despair. It is the evidence of these evils, and the thought that sadness might often overcome gladness, that gives the argument from evil much of its normative flavor and force.

In fact, it is a little bit misleading to imply that evidential arguments from evil should be equally concerned with maximizing good as they are with minimizing evil. This is because our reasons against causing or allowing suffering, as many moral philosophers have noted, are stronger than our reasons for causing or allowing benefits. For instance, it seems more important to prevent a happy person from experiencing something terrible (like suffering a car accident) than it is to ensure that that same person experiences even more happiness (like winning a lottery). Turning to creation ethics, a similar asymmetry appears to hold. It seems more important to prevent a miserable person from existing than it is to cause an abnormally happy person to exist.[33] These claims about the relative priority of preventing suffering, though interesting in their own right, further confirm optimistic arguments from evil have less force than pessimistic ones.

Now theists will presumably welcome the idea of a weakened challenge from evil—and if procreation is literally on the line, then non-theists and even anti-theists might as well. But there is another question about whether this anti-satisficing option is even available anyhow. It is one thing, after all, to *want* to become more optimistic in response to a quandary. It is quite another thing to literally show that one's optimism is justified in the face of evil. This is not to say that I am not optimistic about the world or about the lives of future people. It is rather to say that optimism about the world hasn't exactly been established and that establishing its reasonability, as I have argued elsewhere, could be rather hard.[34]

Suppose, however, that we were up to the task. That is, suppose that a fairly optimistic outlook could literally be shown not just to be of prudential interest, but uniquely reasonable. Would this be sufficient to show that procreation is problem-free? Is a life that is reasonably expected to be quite good, all things considered, a life that we are automatically justified in starting?

IS GOODNESS ENOUGH TO JUSTIFY CREATION? SOME KANTIAN COMPLEXITIES

In this last part of the chapter, I will explain why answering these questions affirmatively is trickier than many realize. Many, after all, agree with Kant that there are important deontic constraints on obtaining good outcomes. This explains, in part, Kant's claim in his 1791 essay "On the Miscarriage of all Philosophical Trials in Theodicy" that there is no successful theodicy or known explanation "of the highest wisdom of the creator against the charge which reason brings against it for whatever is counterproductive in this world."[35] As Derk Pereboom points out, Kant's endorsement of the Categorical Imperative, and in particular the formula of humanity, leaves him with little tolerance for greater-good theodicies, which attempt to justify evils in our world in light of the greater goods they make possible.[36]

Part of the worry here stems from interpersonal aggregation or trade-offs between different persons (for instance, killing one person to save two others). Eleonore Stump does justice to this worry when she argues that a perfectly loving and powerful divine creator would cause or permit undeserved, involuntary human suffering only if such suffering produces a net "benefit for the sufferer" and if the benefit couldn't be gotten except through the suffering.[37] Interestingly, some philosophers of religion find Stump's constraint too strong, even when applied to a perfect being.[38] Also interestingly, some moral philosophers would find it too weak, even when applied to human beings. Most notably, Seana Shiffrin, a contemporary Kantian, worries about intrapersonal aggregation or trade-offs within a single life (for instance, harming someone in order to benefit that same person).[39] Shiffrin's views imply that even when all of Stump's conditions are satisfied, some benefits should not be bestowed on persons.

Let us call this the problem of impermissible benefits. To see the problem it is helpful to consider an example. Suppose, that the only way to get college money for your daughter is to break her arm while she is ten years old. We might question whether breaking your daughter's arm is permissible in this case even if all of Stump's conditions are satisfied. That is, even if the act benefits the child more than it harms her, and even if the harm is required to get the benefit, the act might still seem wrong and even disturbing. In fact, even if the child later comes to be glad about your decision, that decision still might seem questionable.

This is not to say that every benefit that is mixed with severe suffering is impermissible. To borrow an example from Shiffrin, if you have to break an unconscious person's arm in order to save his life, then in the absence of reasons to think he wouldn't consent to your actions, saving the life seems justified and perhaps obligatory. This is because you do not merely improve an agent's well-being in such a case. You further save him from suffering a far greater harm or loss. But Shiffrin's point is that creation is not like this. If you fail to create someone, nothing bad happens to her and none of her interests are set back. This explains why even the most optimistic people don't feel bad for not creating even more happy people than they do. It also explains why creation is not analogous to the rescue case. For unlike the rescue case, the creation case amounts to bestowing a pure benefit: it involves harming someone in order to benefit them as opposed to harming them in order to prevent them from experiencing an even greater harm.

If there is a general lesson here, it is this. Even if it is often permissible to harm a nonconsenting person in order to prevent her from suffering an even greater harm, it is not in general permissible to harm a nonconsenting person to secure a pure benefit.[40] Such an asymmetrical view explains why it would be wrong to break your child's arm to get her funds for college (or if you prefer, to get her a new sports car) but it would not be wrong to break her arm to save her life. But such a view also implies that creating is more questionable, in some respects, than breaking your child's arm to secure her college funds. This is because although there is a clear sense in which an already-existing child is made worse off if she doesn't get a good education, there is no clear sense in which a possible person is made worse off if she never exists to begin with. In a word, if we go with Shiffrin's normative outlook, then procreation raises real moral concerns, pace Jeff McMahan, even where a future life is reasonably expected to be good overall.[41]

I confess that Shiffrin's reasoning can seem somewhat plausible, particularly when one doesn't see where it leads. In fact, a related Kantian worry, made explicit by Elizabeth Harman, is whether "some harms are such that nothing could justify them."[42] Hopefully, for the sake of procreation, there aren't any such harms; or hopefully if there are, no one actually suffers them. Even if these absolutist worries can be set aside, though, it's difficult to deny Shiffrin's claim that a typical life contains severe harms.[43] We still need to ask whether causing (or allowing) all of this harm is permissible.

To be sure, not everyone likes this way of putting the problem since not everyone thinks that we can benefit or harm in creating. In particular, the non-identity problem and related problems have led some ethicists to abandon talk of procreative harm.[44] A chief worry here concerns whether acts that make no one worse off can be wrong; it can seem strange to say that you harm somebody by giving her a life that is, on balance, worthwhile, particularly where the only alternative for that person was never existing.[45] Some, in response to these worries, defend a noncomparative account of harm, according to which you need not make someone worse off in order to harm her.[46] Others claim that we can speak of harms within a life without saying that a life as a whole is harmful. We need not resolve these normative disputes here, however, for we can use different language to communicate Shiffrin's basic worry about creation ethics.

Consider, for instance, David Velleman's explanation for why procreation is morally equivocal.[47] As Velleman sees it, the problem with procreation is not that it involves harming anyone; the problem is that it involves tossing persons, without their consent, into a risky "predicament", where the "stakes are high, both for good and for ill."[48] Since failure, and not just opportunity, comes easily, and since serious burdens and suffering befall even the best lives, Velleman appears to agree with Shiffrin that "being brought into existence is at best a mixed blessing" and that "those who confer it are not entitled to walk away congratulating themselves on a job well done."[49]

Perhaps the best response to the problem is not to refrain from creating but to help one's child to flourish by giving her as good an upbringing as is feasible. This is Velleman's suggestion. The reader, however, is still left with the impression that there is a problem with creation.

CONCLUSION

By way of conclusion, all of the previous arguments lead me to find the following asymmetrical principle puzzling.

> EVIL ASYMMETRY: The amount and kinds of suffering we see provide strong, and many will say decisive, evidence against the very idea that our world is the product of divine creation. But this same suffering does not have any bearing on the general morality of human procreation whatever.

Though implicitly held by many philosophers, I find it difficult to motivate EVIL ASYMMETRY. This is not to say that no good justifications of EVIL ASYMMETRY could ever be developed, only that some of the most obvious candidates fail. In particular, if we're too pessimistic about the human condition then problems for procreation emerge. By contrast, if we're too optimistic, then standard global arguments from evil become less plausible.

This does raise the possibility that defenders of EVIL ASYMMETRY might seek to construct a middle position, somewhere in between optimism and pessimism. But the question is whether this is really a safe place to be. In particular, a mediocre world where lives are highly mixed might be thought to pose problems for procreation. In fact, until the problem of impermissible benefits can be resolved, then even under somewhat more optimistic assumptions, some will doubt that creation is problem-free.

To be sure, there may be other defenses of EVIL ASYMMETRY that I have failed to consider. But there also may be other reasons for rejecting EVIL ASYMMETRY that warrant exploration. For instance, I have not even mentioned that the people we create are very likely, not just to themselves suffer, but also to cause others to suffer. The harm we cause to others (discussed by David Benatar in Chapter 1) might reveal further connections between procreative ethics and the problem of evil: can anyone justify creating persons who will not only suffer but who will also almost certainly cause, and we might add allow, other sentient beings to suffer in fairly severe ways?

These are interesting questions. Instead of exploring them here, though, let me conclude by simply reminding the reader of my goal in raising these issues. My goal is not Benatar's goal. I am not trying to convince people that pessimism and anti-natalism are the correct ways to go, nor am trying to make ultimate pronouncements about the problem of evil or whether a loving God exists. My goal has rather been to encourage more people to see a tension in their own beliefs about these matters, and to be motivated by the tension to develop a systematic defense of procreation. There needn't be anything incoherent about these goals. Just as many philosophers of religion take the problem of evil seriously without abandoning their religious outlooks, something similar might apply to pro-natalists. Pro-natalists might take the problem of procreation seriously and be motivated to address it. More generally, all of us who have interests in ethics and philosophy of religion might put our heads together to try to better defend human procreation. Along the way we might make some interesting discoveries about the argument from evil.[50]

NOTES

1. I will focus on global arguments from evil here, which, as we shall see, concern the vast amount of horrendous evil in the world—and whether all of this evil would occur if God existed. I realize that some will deny that any version of the problem of evil is worrisome to begin with and so will not face the tension I am highlighting. But this chapter is not written with such persons in mind, who are at any rate in the clear minority in philosophy. It is rather written for those who feel the problem of evil in their bones.
2. David Bourget and David Chalmers, "What do Philosophers Believe?" *Philosophical Studies*, no. 3 (2014): 465–500. To be fair, the survey focused mainly on analytic departments at secular schools.

3. Though they disagree about how much force the argument has. Helen De Cruz, "Preliminary Results of My Survey on Natural Theological Arguments," Academia.edu, https://www.academia.edu/1438058/Results_of_my_survey_on_natural_theological_arguments (August 7, 2014).

4. Most notably there is David Benatar. David Benatar, *Better Never to Have Been: The Harm of Coming into Existence* (Oxford: Clarendon, 2006).

5. Elizabeth Harman, "Critical Study of David Benatar. *Better Never to Have Been: The Harm of Coming into Existence*," Noûs 43, no. 4 (2009): 776–785; Ben Bradley, "Benatar and the Logic of Betterness," *Journal of Ethics & Social Philosophy* (2010): 1–5.

6. Jason Marsh, "Creating and Raising Humans: Essays on the Morality of Procreation and Parenting," PhD dissertation, University of Western Ontario, 2012. Here I seek to explain and ultimately weaken the case for procreative skepticism. I also argue for a view I call "qualified pro-natalism." See also my "Quality of Life Assessments, Cognitive Reliability, and Procreative Responsibility," *Philosophy and Phenomenological Research*. 89, no.2 (2014): 436–466.

7. It is in general easier to show that we lack knowledge that some claim is true (like the claim that the external world exists) than it is to establish the falsity of that same claim. My explanation of this claim is as follows. Since knowledge is factive (i.e. requires true belief) any argument that P is false will also amount to an argument that we lack knowledge that P. By contrast, not nearly all arguments for the claim that we lack knowledge that P will also be arguments that P is false. This claim about the many ways that knowledge can fail explains why Benatar's metaphysical approach is harder to defend than a more skeptical epistemological approach.

8. Robert Adams is one of the exceptions. He argues that common complaints about evil could commit us to to morally regretting our own existence and the existence of our loved ones. Robert Adams, "Existence, Self-interest, and the Problem of Evil," *Noûs* 13 (1979): 53–65. Adams also argues that our views about the ethics of divine creation might be connected to certain controversial views about genetic selection. Robert Adams, "Must God Create the Best?" *Philosophical Review* 81, no. 3 (1982): 317–332.

9. John Leslie Mackie, "Evil and Omnipotence," *Mind* 64, no. 254 (1955): 200–212.

10. More acccurately, these claims, when combined with common assumptions about the nature of omnipotence, the nature of love, and the badness of evil, are supposed to generate an explicit contradiction between God and evil, rendering God's existence impossible.

11. Daniel Howard-Snyder, *The Evidential Argument from Evil* (Bloomington: Indiana University Press, 1996). Trent Dougherty, "Recent Work on the Problem of Evil." *Analysis* 71, no. 3 (2011): 560–573

12. See David Benatar, *Better Never to Have Been: The Harm of Coming into Existence*, 38.

13. I will mention one overlooked consequence of Benatar's view that seems to me very difficult to endorse. Imagine three worlds. In world A everyone experiences only pleasure, but they live for only 20 years. In world B everyone experiences infinite pleasure in heaven, but only after a very serious needle prick on earth (suppose this one harm will help them to better appreciate infinite bliss). In world C there are no sentient creatures at all, only space and rocks. Benatar's asymmetry argument implies that A and C are tied in value *and* that B is the least preferable option. This latter claim seems especially difficult to accept.

14. See Peter van Inwagen, *The Problem of Evil* (Oxford: Oxford University Press, 2006), 95–112.
15. Alvin Plantinga, *Warranted Christian Belief* (New York: University of Oxford Press, 2000), 372.
16. Michael Peterson, *God and Evil: An Introduction to the Issues* (Boulder, CO: Westview Press, 1998), 9.
17. Alvin Plantinga, for instance, is clearly optimistic and tells me that the best worlds on his view require suffering, incarnation, and atonement. He seems to be presupposing a consequentialist normative framework.
18. Paul Draper, "Natural Selection and the Problem of Evil," in *God or Blind Nature? Philosophers Debate the Evidence*, ed. Paul Draper (The Secular Web, 2007–2008), http://www.infidels.org/library/modern/paul_draper/evil.html
19. Draper is also himself a very cheery fellow and no doubt one of the lucky ones.
20. Philip Kitcher, "The Many-Sided Conflict Between Science and Religion," in *The Blackwell Guide to Philosophy of Religion*, ed. W. E. Mann (Wiley-Blackwell, 2004), 268.
21. True, humans can do more than non-human animals to minimize suffering, but we should not overestimate our abilities here.
22. Kenneth Taylor, "Without the Net of Providence: Atheism and the Human Adventure" in *Philosophers without Gods: An Anthology of Original Essays*, ed. Louise Antony (New York: Oxford University Press, 2007), 150.
23. Ibid., 150.
24. Julian Savulescu, "Three Stages of Disbelief," in *50 Voices of Disbelief: Why We Are Still Atheists*, ed. Blackford & Schüklenk (Malden:Wiley-Blackwell, 2009), 169–170.
25. This passage comes from an interview entitled, "Marilyn McCord Adams on Evil," accessed August 7, 2014. http://philosophybites.com/2009/07/marilyn-mccord-adams-on-evil.html
26. For more details on Adams' argument, see her "God Because of Evil: A Pragmatic Argument from Evil for Belief in God, " in *The Blackwell Companion to the Problem of Evil*, ed. Justin P. McBrayer and Daniel Howard-Snyder (Chichester: Wiley-Blackwell, 2013), 160–173.
27. Jeff McMahan, "Asymmetries in the Morality of Causing People to Exist," in *Harming Future Persons: Ethics, Genetics and the Nonidentity Problem*, ed. Melinda A. Roberts and David T. Wasserman (Springer, 2009), 61.
28. I am assuming here, with most moral philosophers, that objective moral values and obligations do not require the truth of theism.
29. Julian Savulescu and Guy Kahane, "The Moral Obligation to Create Children with the Best Chance of the Best Life," *Bioethics* 23, no. 5 (2009): 282.
30. To be fair, Savulescu, although he fails to discuss anti-natalism thinks that prospective parents have strong moral reasons to create the best-off children they can.
31. Caspar Hare agrees that even minimally decent and minimally rational agents can have serious moral obligations to create better off, beings. See *The Limits of Kindness* (Oxford: Oxford University Press, 2013).
32. Then again, some may wish to defend the Leibnizian idea that there is a best possible world or a best possible best life. After all, presumably God's life is the best life, given theism, and perhaps it could be argued that a world with only perfect beings would be the best world.
33. See Jeff McMahan, "Asymmetries in the Morality of Causing People to Exist."

34. "Quality of Life Assessments, Cognitive Reliability, and Procreative Responsibility," *Philosophy and Phenomenological Research*. doi: 10.1111/phpr.12114

35. Cited in Derk Pereboom, "Kant on God, Evil, and Teleology," *Faith and Philosophy* 13, no. 4 (1996): 508.

36. Ibid.

37. Eleonore Stump, "The Problem of Evil," *Faith and Philosophy* 2, vol. 4 (1985): 411. Although Stump seems most concerned with the question of whether allowing evil is permissible, she also discusses how natural evil could be good for people, which looks more like a case of doing than allowing. Of course, not everyone thinks there is a significant moral difference between doing and allowing.

38. T. J. Mawson, "Theodical Individualism." *European Journal for Philosophy of Religion* 3, no. 1 (2011):139–159.

39. Seana Shiffrin, "Wrongful Life, Procreative Responsibility, and the Significance of Harm," *Legal Theory*, 5 (1999): 117–148. In contrast to Stump, Shiffrin's moral outlook stems not from the nature of divine love, but from the nature of duty.

40. This is not to say that Shiffrin is a full out anti-nalist, though she comes close to such a position. She states: "I am not advancing the claim that procreation is all-things-considered wrong. It is consistent with these arguments to regard nonconsensual, burden-imposing actions as morally problematic but not always impermissible, or to regard procreation as a special case. All I mean to advance is the claim that because procreation involves a nonconsensual imposition of significant burdens, it is morally problematic and its imposer may justifiably be held responsible for its harmful results." (Ibid., 139). Benatar, by contrast, clearly thinks that procreation is always objectively wrong.

41. There are other possible standards of procreative responsibility too. According to the zero-line view, for instance, all that it takes to justify starting a life is the expectation that this life will be worthwhile or even barely worthwhile. Many procreative ethicists seem to reject the zero-line view.

42. Elizabeth Harman, "Can We Harm and Benefit in Creating?" *Philosophical Perspectives* 18, no. 1 (2006):102.

43. In Shiffrin's words, "Even though procreators may benefit their progeny by creating them, they also impose substantial burdens on them. By being caused to exist as persons, children are forced to assume moral agency, to face various demanding and sometimes wrenching moral questions, and to discharge taxing moral duties. They must endure the fairly substantial amount of pain, suffering, difficulty, significant disappointment, distress, and significant loss that occur within the typical life. They must face and undergo the fear and harm of death. Finally, they must bear the results of imposed risks that their lives may go terribly wrong in a variety of ways." Seana Shiffrin, "Wrongful Life, Procreative Responsibility, and the Significance of Harm," 136–137.

44. Derek Parfit. *Reasons and Persons* (Oxford: Clarendon Press, 1987).

45. The teen parent case, often discussed in procreative ethics, is a good example of this. After all, had the parents waited until they were older to have a child, a non-identical child would have existed instead. Of course, we want to say that the parents wrong the original child in some sense, if she has a bad start in life, not just that there has been impersonal wrongdoing, thus the problem.

46. Elizabeth Harman, "Can We Harm and Benefit In Creating?" *Philosophical Perspectives* 18 (2004): 89–113.

47. David Velleman, "II. The Gift of Life." *Philosophy & Public Affairs* 36 (2008): 245–266.
48. Ibid., 251.
49. Ibid., 246.
50. Thanks to David Benatar, Andrew Botterell, Samantha Brennan, Dan Groll, Sarah Hannan, Meena Krishnamurthy, Micah Lott, Colin Macleod, Jon Marsh, T. J. Mawson, Carolyn McLeod, Matthew Clayton, Alvin Plantinga, Alexander Pruss, Seana Shiffrin, Anthony Skelton, Adam Smith, Eleonore Stump, Charles Taliaferro, John Thorp, David Velleman, Richard Vernon, and Daniel Weinstock for helpful discussion. The views discussed here do not implicitly or explicitly represent official positions of any institution that I am affiliated with.

REFERENCES

Adams, Robert. "Must God Create the Best?" *Philosophical Review* 81, no. 3(1972): 317–332.

———. "Existence, Self-Interest, and the Problem of Evil." Noûs 13, no. 1 (1979): 53–65.

Adams, Marilyn. "God Because of Evil: A Pragmatic Argument from Evil for Belief in God." In *The Blackwell Companion to the Problem of Evil*, ed. Justin P. McBrayer and Daniel Howard-Snyder, 160–173. Chichester: Wiley-Blackwell, 2013.

———. Marilyn McCord Adams on Evil – Philosophy Bites podcast. Accessed December 3, 2014. http://philosophybites.com/2009/07/marilyn-mccord-adams-on-evil.html.

Beatar, David. *Better Never to Have Been: The Harm of Coming into Existence*. Oxford: Clarendon Press, 2006.

Bourget, David, and David Chalmers. "What Do Philosophers Believe? " *Philosophical Studies*, no. 3 (2014): 465–500.

Bradley, Ben. "Benatar and the Logic of Betterness." *Journal of Ethics & Social Philosophy, Discussion Notes* (March 2010): 1–5.

De Cruz, Helen. "Preliminary Results of My Survey on Natural Theological Arguments," Academia.edu, https://www.academia.edu/1438058/Results_of_my_survey_on_natural_theological_arguments (December 3, 2014).

Dougherty, Trent. "Recent Work on the Problem of Evil." *Analysis* 71, no. 3 (2011): 560–573.

Draper, Paul. "Natural Selection and the Problem of Evil." In *God or Blind Nature? Philosophers Debate the Evidence*, ed. Paul Draper. The Secular Web, 2007–2008. http://www.infidels.org/library/modern/paul_draper/evil.html

Hare, Caspar. *The Limits of Kindness*. Oxford: Oxford University Press, 2013.

Harman, Elizabeth. "Critical Study of David Benatar. *Better Never to Have Been: The Harm of Coming into Existence*." Noûs 43, no. 4 (2009): 776–785.

———. "Can We Harm and Benefit In Creating?" *Philosophical Perspectives* 18, no. 1 (2004):89–113.

Howard-Snyder, Daniel. *The Evidential Argument from Evil*. Bloomington: Indiana University Press, 2008.

Kitcher, Philip. "The Many-Sided Conflict Between Science and Religion." In *The Blackwell Guide to Philosophy of Religion*, ed. W. E. Mann, 266–282. Oxford: Blackwell, 2004.

Mackie, J. L. "Evil and Omnipotence." *Mind* 64, no. 254 (1955): 200–212.

Marsh, Jason. "Quality of Life Assessments, Cognitive Reliability, and Procreative Responsibility." *Philosophy and Phenomenological Research*. 89, no.2 (2014): 436–466.

———. "Creating and Raising Humans: Essays on the Morality of Procreation and Parenting." PhD dissertation, University of Western Ontario, 2012.

Mawson, Tim. "Theodical Individualism." *European Journal for Philosophy of Religion* 3, no. 1 (2011): 139–159.

McMahan, Jeff. "Asymmetries in the Morality of Causing People to Exist." In *Harming Future Persons: Ethics, Genetics and the Nonidentity Problem*, ed. Melinda A. Roberts and David T. Wasserman, 49–68. New York: Springer, 2009.

Parfit, Derek. Reasons and Persons. Oxford: Clarendon Press, 1987.

Pereboom, Derk. "Kant on God, Evil, and Teleology." *Faith and Philosophy* 13, no. 4 (1996): 508–533.

Peterson, Michael. *The Problem of Evil: Selected Readings*. Notre Dame: University of Notre Dame, 1998.

Plantinga, Alvin. *Warranted Christian Belief*. New York: Oxford University Press, 2000.

Savulescu, Julian. "Three Stages of Disbelief." In *50 Voices of Disbelief: Why We Are Still Atheists*, ed. Russell Blackford and Udo Schüklenk. Malden: Wiley-Blackwell, 2009.

Savulescu, Julian, and Guy Kahane. "The Moral Obligation to Create Children with the Best Chance of the Best Life." *Bioethics* 23, no. 5 (2009): 274–290.

Shiffrin, Seana. "Wrongful Life, Procreative Responsibility, and the Significance of Harm." *Legal Theory* 5, no. 3 (1999): 117–148.

Stump, Eleonore. "The Problem of Evil." *Faith and Philosophy* 2, vol. 4 (1985): 392–423.

Kenneth Taylor, "Without the Net of Providence: Atheism and the Human Adventure" In *Philosophers without Gods: An Anthology of Original Essays*, ed. Louise Antony. New York: Oxford University Press, 2007.

Van Inwagen, Peter. *The Problem of Evil*. Oxford: Oxford University Press, 2006.

Velleman, David. "II. The Gift of Life." *Philosophy & Public Affairs* 36, vol. 3 (2008): 245–266.

CHAPTER 3

Could There Ever Be a Duty to Have Children?

ANCA GHEAUS

INTRODUCTION

Could there ever be a duty to have children? I explore the case for a positive answer and advance the suggestion that there is a collective responsibility[1] to procreate and raise (enough) children—in short "to have children"—in order to avoid great harm to a potential last generation of childless people. By collective responsibility I mean the duty owed by a group of people to individuals who are vulnerable to how the respective group of people act (or fail to act) collectively.[2] I also address the question whether such a responsibility can, under certain circumstances, translate into individual and enforceable duties. My interest is not in the related discussion about whether there are reasons to bring into existence children whose lives are very likely to be good, and about the weight of these reasons. Rather, I consider the possibility that a general duty to help others can, under certain circumstances, entail a duty to have children in order to avoid dramatic depopulation and its material and psychological consequences on the last generations. If it exists, such a duty would be grounded in the interests of already existing persons rather than in the interests of the prospective children. Therefore, I avoid the contentious assumption that a state of affairs can be better even if it is not better for any person; my line of reasoning is compatible with a person-affecting view of ethics.

I consider the possibility of a collective responsibility to have children and the conditions under which it could generate in a *pro tanto* individual duty only given certain assumptions. First, that the prospective children will have adequate lives[3] which are not worse, on average, than those of their parents' generation.[4] Second, that procreation is not, in general, morally wrong. Thus, I start from the background common-sensical view that having children is morally permissible: under normal conditions (including normal demographic and environmental conditions), most individuals[5] have a liberty right, but no duty, to have children.

Even qualified, the idea that people may ever have a duty to have children is unpopular in secular, liberal, and cosmopolitan circles. We are used to hear from religious and nationalist leaders that people have a duty to procreate in order to accomplish the plans of a deity or in order to contribute to a strong, resourceful nation. Communitarians may argue that the value of particular traditions and ways of living can provide weighty moral reasons for members of the respective communities to have children. But these claims do not sit well with a liberal view that respects individuals' autonomy. Societies worldwide are committed to individuals' freedom to decide whether or not to have children, and how many. This freedom is protected by legal rights encoded in widely endorsed—if not always binding—international conventions.[6] Not only is there no legal duty to have children, but philosophers discussing the matter generally believe that there is no such enforceable moral duty either.[7] Christine Overall, for instance, thinks that "[P]eople's rights to control their reproductive functions 'militate against any supposed duty or obligation to reproduce in any way"[8] where she takes "'militate against'" to mean something like "rules out." Like many others who hold liberal convictions about autonomy and bodily integrity, Overall thinks there cannot be an enforceable duty to have children because this would come into conflict with those convictions. Finally, there are philosophers who endorse a more fundamental reason against a possible duty to have children. According to David Benatar, it is always morally wrong to procreate—which rules out the possibility of a duty to have children.[9]

Not only is the idea of a duty to have children unpopular amongst liberals, but it also seems out of sync with our times. The context in which I discuss a possible duty to have children is that of a world facing the risk of dramatic depopulation due to a lack of interest of people in having children. But, worldwide, we currently fear overpopulation rather than depopulation; philosophical work on procreation and parenting starts to reflect this fact. It is far from clear that the natural environment can sustain the current population growth, at least at existing levels of consumption.

True, in some countries fertility has been declining, and birth rates are below the replacement level. But these tend to be countries with some of the highest consumption levels (and therefore a population decrease is in this case good environmental news), and undesirable population deficits in these countries can be avoided by means that do not increase the overall population of the world—such as international adoption or migration. Therefore it is not clear that we—especially in highly consumerist societies—have a *liberty right* to procreate, or to procreate unrestrictedly, since overpopulation is likely to put future generations as well as our contemporaries who live in geographically disadvantaged locations at the risk of great harms. If it is doubtful that there is a right to unrestricted procreation under current circumstances, what is the point of reflecting on a *duty* to procreate?

Third, there is a pressing egalitarian worry that thinking about a duty to have children—which includes procreation—neglects the interests of existing children in need of parenting. Even without the risk or reality of overpopulation putting into question the morality of procreation, the large number of existing children without parents is enough to make one turn one's attention away from a possible duty to have children. Perhaps we should think, instead, about the duty to look after the children who already exist and are in need of adequate parenting—and, indeed, some philosophers argue that there is a duty to adopt rather than procreate.[10]

Finally, it may seem otiose to enquire into a possible duty to have children: it seems useless to theorize a duty to procreate and rear children, given people's widespread desire to do it anyway. Why use the bigger hammer of moral reasons if the friendly touch of inclination can do the job alone? To sum up, liberal egalitarianism provides several good reasons to resist the idea that there is a duty to procreate.

WHAT DIFFERENCE DOES A COLLECTIVE RESPONSIBILITY TO HAVE CHILDREN MAKE?

I nevertheless raise this question because a moral requirement to have children will make a significant difference in how liberal egalitarians should think about parenthood. The motivation that drives my enquiry comes from outside the area of reproductive ethics, from its close neighbor, child-rearing ethics. Here, one of the fundamental issues is who should shoulder the significant—and ever mounting!—costs of child rearing[11]: parents alone, or parents and non-parents together? And, if the latter, how should the costs be split between these two social groups?

I will not take the time to recapitulate this complex debate in detail,[12] but merely indicate the main positions within the liberal egalitarian discussion. Following Serena Olsaretti,[13] I call the view that child-rearing costs should be shared by parents and non-parents "the pro-sharing view," and the opposite view "the anti-sharing view." Various liberal egalitarians argue that, in an ideally just world, the costs of child rearing should be borne by their parents, on two different grounds: First, because parents are causally and morally responsible for the existence of children, assuming that procreation is informed and intentional. (This may not be true of all or even the majority of real-world parents, but the discussion is set at the ideal level.) Child rearing is costly, and it would be unfair to impose the costs on non-parents, who have no say about children's existence in the first place. Second, because having children is a lifestyle that some people value while others—including the voluntary non-parents—do not; child rearing is to be understood by analogy with expensive tastes, or perhaps with creating something valuable, like a beautiful painting. Since neither the satisfaction of expensive tastes, nor the funding of creative pursuits in general are required by justice, it is only fair that the costs of child rearing be taken by those who also enjoy the benefits of child rearing: parents.

However, it seems clear that not only parents enjoy the benefits of children's existence. Some of the defenders of the pro-sharing view note that, by having children and raising them well, parents make an important contribution to future public and collective goods. In a few decades, the argument goes, today's adults will have to rely on today's children for their welfare; the sustainability of a pension system, which requires new workers, is the example given most often.[14] The view that children are sources of public and collective goods entails, according to some defenders of the pro-sharing view, that it is unfair that parents alone should carry the costs of bringing up children.

The public and collective goods argument has so far failed to convince the proponents of the anti-sharing view.[15] They note that people do not have children with the intention of benefiting others, nor do they see their having and rearing children as some kind of cooperative venture in which parents and non-parents engage together, but rather as a private enterprise from which non-parents merely happen to benefit. In arguing that there is a collective responsibility to have children, I intend to challenge the last type of defense of the anti-sharing view.

An important question, then, is how the members of a community *ought to* see the cooperative aspect of child rearing, rather than how they in fact see it. Suppose that non-parents *should* have a say about whether there will be a future generation although they are not willing to contribute by procreating or by doing the hands-on work necessary to raise that generation themselves. Then non-parents are likely to have a duty of fair play to contribute financially to the effort of raising an optimal number of members of that generation. If there is a collective responsibility to have children in order to avoid future harm to both current parents and non-parents, then having children—up to the number that is required to meet the responsibility—*is* in fact a cooperative enterprise between parents and non-parents. In this case, it is plausible that individuals who volunteer to parent and thus meet the collective responsibility are owed financial support from those who do not want to take part directly in meeting the responsibility. True, parents are not likely to be motivated to parent by a desire to discharge a collective responsibility (and they may not see their parenting primarily—or at all—as an activity aimed at meeting a collective responsibility). Contributing to a public good is not their primary intention in raising children. Yet, in this context, intentions alone do not seem to make a difference. Consider the analogy, often used to help us think about the social nature of the burdens of child rearing, between going to war and having children: I may enroll in an army of volunteers because I want to partake in the glory of war rather than to do my duty in defending my people. I will not, for this reason, be expected to fund alone my participation in the army; rather, fairness seems to require that I be given the goods necessary for subsistence during service, possibly a salary, and medical care resulting from injuries during service. That I am motivated by an intention to acquire glory rather than live up to my responsibility does not take away from the fact that the people I defend have a duty to help defray the costs of my enrollment in the army.

In fact, if there is a collective responsibility to have children, the foundation of the anti-sharing view is shaken: in this case having children is not akin to either an expensive taste or to the creation of something valuable but morally supererogatory. Nor is the fact that procreation is intentional and informed relevant for the question of who should pay the costs of childbearing and child rearing, up to an optimal population size. Even if current parents did not want to have children, either they or others ought to have some of them. One way or another, the costs of having children *should not* be collectively avoided.

A COLLECTIVE RESPONSIBILITY?

But is there such a responsibility? Consider the following story: the inhabitants of a certain state have always depended on a complex system of welling for water; everybody has a well in their garden, and a system of cleaning the water to make it drinkable is maintained through some form of spontaneous social cooperation. A number of individuals voluntarily work in well digging and water well maintenance, support the costs of providing everyone with clean water and are fairly rewarded for their work. But at some point in time no new people are interested in working as well diggers or in water well maintenance. Unless collective action is taken, the reserves of clean water will start to dry out. Without enough people being trained and convinced to maintain the supply, there will be increasing shortages of clean water and, in twenty years' time, everybody will die of thirst. Suppose that some of the people who will suffer are, at the present moment, still children.

Do the members of this state have a collective responsibility to ensure that those of them who will still be around in twenty years will continue to be provided with clean water? And, if so, ought the state authorities adopt policies that nudge some individuals to work as water providers? Should nudging fail, ought the state to adopt more coercive policies that result in new people taking up this essential kind of work? More generally, do we have a collective responsibility to ensure that goods and services essential to the satisfaction of basic needs are being socially produced? And, if market mechanisms fail to result in their production, ought states to meet the collective responsibility through policies that translate it into individual, and possibly enforceable, duties?

The most promising ground for a positive answer is to point to a general duty—be it of justice or of beneficence—to avoid the frustration of basic needs.[16] More specifically, if some persons are vulnerable for the satisfaction of their basic needs to the way in which others, taken as a group, act or fail to act, the latter bear collective responsibility for the first.[17] People need clean water if they are not to die prematurely, and if they are not to suffer unnecessarily. It is plausible that, if nobody *wanted* to work towards the provision of clean water, the state authorities ought to either provide special incentives to some to engage in this kind of work, or, failing that, to find the least problematic means of coercing individuals to cooperate in ensuring a sufficient supply of drinkable water. (For simplicity, assume the option of bringing guest workers from a different country is unavailable.)

One tempting way to resist the idea that there is a collective responsibility to ensure the future production of clean water is by noting that, in the imagined case, it is not clear that there would be any victims and perpetrators should the alleged duty remain unmet. If citizens failed to organize their own future water supplies, they would only have themselves to blame. Moreover, if they are well informed, perhaps they have the authority to trade the future satisfaction of basic needs for present occupational freedom and make an informed, and legitimate, decision to go without water in twenty years. Yet, there are several reasons that support the existence of a collective responsibility in the case of the drying-out threat. Each of these reasons may be enough to dispel the objection; their conjunction makes the case stronger. First, in this imagined case no single individual can ensure a continuous supply of clean water for herself or her own family. Clean water is a type of collective good for the existence of which people cannot be held individually responsible. Second, some of the people who will suffer are now too young to make a responsible and authoritative decision to let their future basic need for water be frustrated. And third, more contentiously, it is not clear that in situations like this *even adults* have the authority to trade the satisfaction of essential future interests for the sake of less important current ones; we know that people are inclined to discount future well-being, at very high rates if the future is sufficiently distant, and that in most cases this is a failure of rationality.

It is even more tempting to resist the idea that, even if a collective responsibility to prevent the frustration of basic needs exists, it can never translate into state policies that coerce (some) individuals into particular jobs. Many liberal egalitarians believe that individuals have a freedom-right to occupational choice, and that it is unjust for states to take coercive measures aimed at ensuring that particular jobs get done, even when these measures are necessary for reaching equality, or an adequate minimum, or an improvement in the situation of the worst-off.[18] While I do not have the space to discuss this important issue here, let me only mention three reasons why appeal to freedom of occupational choice does not make the present enquiry a non-starter. First, it is unclear that freedom of occupational choice is consistent with an adequate liberal egalitarian theory of justice.[19] Second, in spite of the widespread view that justice is the *first* virtue of a society, it is not implausible to think that moral considerations other than justice can sometimes trump requirements of justice; a duty of humanity to prevent extreme and generalised suffering is likely to be such a consideration. In fact, many states do infringe on their citizens' freedom of occupational choice if this is needed to secure the avoidance of great harm, for instance in the context of providing health care. Over seventy countries have used compulsory service programs in recent times to recruit health workers for the provision of essential health care services in deprived areas.[20] Third, and related to the previous point, it is not obvious that the situation under consideration—a society that is at risk of breaking down due to lack of basic resources—meets the conditions that some philosophers consider necessary in order for concerns of justice to arise in the first place. Rawls has famously, and controversially, argued that justice is a virtue of societies where certain conditions or "circumstances of justice" hold, and one of these is moderate, rather than extreme, scarcity of resources. But a world without drinking water, or with an economy on the brink of massive breakdown, looks more like one in which resources are extremely scarce and which therefore is not characterized the usual "circumstances of justice." So states may be justified in adopting coercive policies that would be unjust under normal conditions, if this is what it takes to avoid a situation in which considerations of justice would become obsolete.

There is a close analogy, for the purpose of this chapter, between having children and working to create future water supplies as in the example—only that children make possible a larger number of public and collective goods. The benefits that everybody, including people who do not want to raise children, enjoy as a result of there being children are hard to overestimate. Some of them are indeed material, but not restricted to pensions, while others are not material, and possibly just as important. To see this, consider what it would mean if everybody stopped having children.

One consequence would be immense physical suffering for many members of the last generation. A new generation is needed in order to avoid people dying from unnecessarily painful and probably premature deaths. Without a new generation, the economy would collapse. It is unavoidable that many people end their lives in a state of dependency (the old, the ill, the disabled) and if there was no one to care for them they would die hungry, thirsty, and without pain relief and other palliative care. Not only services, but also material goods would become extremely scarce if everybody stopped having children. A working pension system is a good made possible by rearing children, but a focus on pensions alone is too narrow. Some people—who are independently wealthy, or who save enough—can survive without pensions. But they cannot survive without a minimally working economy, and most people cannot do without some hands-on care during times of temporary illness. Therefore, taking a wide view of the economic benefits of rearing children can show that having a working economy itself is a cooperative venture not only between contemporaries, but also diachronically between generations—and hence, indirectly, between parents and non-parents.

More contentiously perhaps, all of us—old *and* young, parents *and* non-parents—depend psychologically on the existence of future people: our motivation to accomplish things, and probably even our zest for life, are possible because we take for granted the existence of future generations. We need to believe in their existence if all, or almost all of our activities are to have meaning and if we are to avoid a state of perpetual apathy and gloom. At least this is what Samuel Scheffler—drawing on others—has recently argued.[21] If he is half right, then future generations—or rather their parents—benefit us by providing the background, inconspicuous, motivational conditions for life as we know it.

Even more contentiously, one may think that there is a collective responsibility to have sufficient children in order to ensure the continuation of political society. This line of reasoning can be found, in nuce, in Rawls who wrote that: "[P]olitical society is always regarded as a scheme of social cooperation over time indefinitely; the idea of a future time when its affairs are to be concluded and society disbanded is foreign to the conception of political society. Thus, reproductive labor is socially necessary labor."[22] One aspect of the undesirable consequence of an entire citizenry stopping to have children is impersonal: the disappearance of the political society, which may be as such regrettable. But there is also a person-affecting aspect of the disappearance of the political society: the last people to be alive will be deprived of the good of living in an institutionally organized society that can regulate and legitimize the uses of power.

There is a collective responsibility to avoid all these bads. Of course, the responsibility is not merely to bring into existence sufficient children in order to make all these present and future goods possible. The responsibility goes well beyond a duty to procreate, to include a duty to raise a new generation of individuals who, at the very least, are ready to cooperate in order to prevent the avoidable frustration of basic needs.

ENFORCEABILITY

The next question, to which I now turn, is whether a duty to have children can ever be enforceable. Ought state authorities to incentivize or even coerce people to have children, if too many people stopped doing so voluntarily? A positive answer is more likely than a negative one to shed some light on the sharing of the costs of child rearing under present circumstances. If a collective responsibility to have children can generate enforceable duties, it is hard to see how some may legitimately opt out of supporting those who discharge it on their behalf.[23] If, by contrast, the duty is not enforceable, then perhaps people should be allowed to opt out just like they are granted other "rights to do wrong."[24]

The claim that there is an enforceable duty to have children will confront immense theoretical obstacles stemming from widespread beliefs about autonomy and good parenting. Even if one disagrees that individuals always have a freedom-right to occupational choice, one may think that procreation and child rearing are kinds of activities that should never be coerced or even actively promoted through state policies. I shall look at those reasons I find most compelling in favor of this position, and suggest some tentative answers.

I shall consider, in turn, adults-centred and children-centred arguments against the idea that states may ever promote or enforce a duty to have children. The first set of arguments has to do with the importance of the potential parents' autonomy and with their rights in their own bodies. Separate concerns will be discussed with respect to procreation and child rearing. The second set of arguments is about the potential children: would they be impermissibly used as means rather than ends in themselves, and would they necessarily be deprived of adequate parenting, if raised by people who have not chosen parenthood voluntarily?

Some of the reasons against enforceability are more powerful than others, and I am not sure they can all be satisfactorily met but, at the very least, they are not as compelling as usually assumed.

Adults

One objection to an enforceable duty to have children is that there cannot be a duty to have children because both procreation and child rearing are highly intimate activities. A plausible system of enforceable duties cannot regulate the most intimate aspects of human beings with burdening positive duties because this would jeopardize autonomy. The thought here is that the most intimate aspects of our lives are closely connected to our moral and rational agency; thus, to protect our agency—including moral agency—we need a significant degree of freedom when deciding how to act with respect to these aspects of our lives.[25] I will not question here the truth of this general principle, nor resist the liberal endorsement of the value of autonomy. I assume that the important issues are (1) whether an enforceable duty to have children is compatible with personal autonomy under any circumstances, and (2) whether values other than individual autonomy, such as for instance an egalitarian commitment to avoid the frustration of basic needs, can have sufficient weight to generate the enforceability of the duty under consideration even when enforcing that duty is inimical to autonomy.

I disentangle the two separate questions of whether, and to what extent, autonomy is compromised by a duty to have children. First, would the enforcement of a duty to procreate necessarily be a serious infringement on autonomy? And second, would the enforcement of a duty to rear children necessarily be a serious infringement on autonomy?

It is not uncommon to believe that people have duties to help others that involve the use of their body and bodily parts. We think that sometimes we owe others personal services and many think that people have a moral duty to donate body parts—most often blood. The really contentious issue is whether such duties can ever be enforceable. It is quite obvious that an enforceable duty to procreate does not sit well with respect to individual autonomy, as long as gestation is necessary for procreation. Pregnancy is a long-term, labor- and emotion-intensive experience.[26] It comes with health risks—which are sometimes significant—and it often involves discomfort and pain. Giving birth naturally can also be painful, even extremely so, even if painkillers are used, and caesareans are a type of major surgery. And we know that women perceive forced pregnancy as extraordinarily intrusive. In short, coerced pregnancy is incompatible with respect for autonomy; moreover, the violation of autonomy in this case is so serious that it is difficult to see how it could be outweighed by other moral considerations. This means that, at most, states can legitimately create certain incentives for individuals to bear children—making sure they do not make pregnancy the only acceptable choice for any particular individual.

However, technological development may render pregnancy optional for procreation. If and when this happens, the most formidable autonomy-based argument against an enforceable duty to procreate will disappear. The use of people's bodies will still be necessary for procreation, but a much more modest level of interference will be required. Gamete donation is not the most trivial medical procedure, but perhaps it will become possible to create artificial gametes using skin. Unlike in the case of pregnancy, it is less clear that a one-off requirement that individuals serve as gamete or skin donors necessarily infringes on their autonomy. Or, if some autonomy infringement is involved, this appears to be an acceptable price to pay for making possible a new generation.

Separate from how the process of gamete donation may infringe on autonomy, there is the question of whether individuals own their gametes, and therefore nonconsensual gamete extraction amounts to theft. An enforceable duty to procreate is incompatible with an unqualified right to bodily self-ownership. But egalitarianism (with the possible exception of left-libertarian egalitarianism) seems to rule out an unqualified right to either personal integrity or bodily self-ownership. Cecile Fabre argued that a consistent egalitarian theory of justice should recognize that the worse-off have rights to other people's personal services and bodily organs, if these are necessary to meet their needs.[27] (Moreover, she argued that respect for these rights is compatible with respecting a qualified right to personal integrity and to autonomy.)

Like childbearing, child rearing can limit parental autonomy. It is a very intimate, emotionally intense, labour- and time-demanding commitment. Because one of children's most important needs is continuity in the relationship with their parents, parenting is also a particularly long-term endeavour, one which has no or very difficult exit options. Indeed, the combination of all these features led Anne Alstott to argue that (proper) parenting entails a very significant diminution of parents' autonomy, one for which parents are being owed some compensation.[28] But, of course, exactly how intensive and resource demanding child rearing is depends a lot on how it is socially organized. Parenting a particular child could be more socialised than it is currently in societies where nuclear families are dominant. Studies indicate that spending significant time in child-rearing institutions such as day care and kindergartens is not necessarily detrimental to children's well-being.[29] If the hands-on aspect of child rearing was partly socialized—by putting in place adequate child-rearing institutions and/or other communal ways of bringing up children—rearing a child would be a lot less inimical to parents' autonomy than the current status quo in many Western societies. Moreover, to the extent to which child rearing takes place in the family it need not be the job of only one or two individuals. Currently, several societies are moving towards a practice of sharing child rearing between more than two related adults; having a larger number of parents—say three or four—need not be detrimental to children's well-being, nor to other central values of the family such as intimacy and love.[30] Child care could be reorganised such that it conflicts with parents' autonomy to a much lesser extent than it currently does.

However, no matter to what extent we were to socially reorganize child care, the sacrifice in parental autonomy would be considerable, especially if children's need for continuity in care is to be met. I don't know whether this means that a duty to rear children can never be enforceable. Accepting this conclusion would also mean to accept that, should a society's children tragically lose their parents, and should the remaining adults be unwilling to parent, these adults could not be legitimately coerced into parenting the orphans. I find this implication implausible. At the very least, it seems, the orphans' needs would generate an enforceable duty for the adults to organize decent child-rearing institutions and divide the child-rearing work between themselves in a way that ensures that children's needs are met (including the need for continuity of care, if it is as important as developmental psychology suggests it is). In the orphans' case—as well as in the real-life case of orphaned children—it seems that states may and should provide incentives for adoption and, if that fails, incentives for low staff turnover in full-time institutional care.

To conclude this section, enforcing a duty to procreate would entail a massive infringement of autonomy by imposing childbearing. If, however, childbearing was to become obsolete, an enforceable duty to procreate would not raise major worries concerning the gamete donors' autonomy. In contrast, enforcing a duty to rear children is likely to unavoidably entail some loss of autonomy; yet, in other situations—such as the orphans' example—we are likely to judge such an infringement of autonomy as legitimate, if it is the only way to meet the children's basic needs. If the meeting of some people's basic needs justifies the infringement of autonomy in the case of the orphans, why would the meeting of other people's basic needs not justify the infringement of autonomy in the case of imminent depopulation?

Children

A second group of worries concerns the potential children who would be born as a result of states encouraging, or possibly coercing, individuals to have children: would these children be thereby subjected to impermissible treatment?[31]

Before addressing these worries, let me reiterate the assumption that a duty to have children is explicitly constrained by adults' ability to give the prospective children a good chance to lead acceptably good lives. This means that, for instance, in a world afflicted by natural disasters, extreme shortage of resources, or endless wars, we would have no duty to procreate and rear children in order to alleviate future suffering (and possibly no right to procreate for any other reason).

Even so, the creation of children with the intention to meet other people's basic needs has been thought to be morally wrong, as the discussion of savior siblings shows. Savior siblings are children born as a result of their parents selecting, from several zygotes, the ones that will result in a child who can provide an organ or cell transplant to a sibling that is affected with a fatal disease. The creation of savior siblings has been criticized for treating the prospective children as mere means to an end. As several authors pointed out, this criticism is unconvincing.[32] Savior siblings are not treated as mere means, if, once they exist, they are also cherished for themselves, loved by their parents, and given the same respect and care due to all human beings.

There is, however, a significant difference between savior siblings and the prospective children discussed here—a difference which may, but need not, make the mere means charge more difficult to address. Savior siblings are raised by parents who are willing to have that particular child, not by people who see themselves as acting on duty, much less people who are acting under an enforced duty. As far as respect and being treated justly are concerned, it need not make a difference whether or not children are raised by people nudged or coerced into parenting. However, things may be different with respect to love and emotional attachment between parents and children. If love and attachment are very difficult to achieve unless parenting is freely chosen, there are two grounds on which one should resist the enforcement of a duty to have children. First, because it would lead to the existence of children who are unwanted for themselves, and hence more likely to be treated as mere means to an end. Second, because it is possible that a serious failure of emotional attachment between parents and children is incompatible with ensuring an adequate life for the child.

Therefore, a lot depends on what is parental love and under what conditions it is likely to develop. Do most people really need to voluntarily assume the rearing of a child in order to form a deep and committed emotional bond with them? Some may think that good parenthood must be both non-moralized (that is, not done out of duty) and freely chosen (that is, not done out of a promoted or enforced duty). In this case, the charge of using the unwanted children as mere means, and of letting them be harmed, is more credible.

Or, by contrast, will most people spontaneously and unavoidably bond with children whom they see as their responsibility to rear? The latter situation is not implausible: as parents look after their children, children respond emotionally to their parents, and for most people this may be enough to create the initial bond. It is likely that most children have not been brought into the world intentionally, at least until recently; yet, we do not tend to worry that parents who had their children thrust upon them by chance failed, for this reason, to love them.[33]

SOME TENTATIVE CONCLUSIONS

The question raised here is whether, given liberal egalitarian assumptions, individuals can ever have a duty to have children—that is, to procreate and rear children. A subsequent question is whether, in case there is such a duty, states can be justified in policy-making to induce individuals to satisfy the duty or even to coerce them to do so.

I assumed that there is a duty to prevent basic needs from being frustrated, that basic needs will be frustrated if everybody stopped having children, and that making possible a new generation requires collective action. Since cooperation is necessary to avoid the harms of being the last people, the state is responsible to take action to see that harm be averted. The only way to bring about a new generation is to have people procreate and rear children. I suggested that, just like a state whose citizens are at high risk of running out of clean water has a duty to encourage citizens to become water-providers, a state whose citizens stop procreating has a duty to encourage procreation. But can states ever be justified in nudging or even conscripting their citizens into procreation and child rearing?

The reason for asking if there can be a duty to have children is that the answer bears on the fair way of sharing some of the costs of childbearing and child rearing between parents and non-parents. To provide a powerful argument in favor of the pro-sharing view, it is not enough to show that each generation has a duty to have up to a (certain number of) children; the duty should be such that individuals cannot claim state protection for a freedom to act against it. When individuals claim a right to do wrong, they claim a freedom from interference with doing what they have a moral duty not to do, or with not doing what they have a moral duty to do. Many are puzzled by the thought that people can have rights to do wrong and there are several ways of making sense of such rights; I find most plausible the understanding that there is a right to do wrong only when there are no legitimate ways of interfering with individuals' failing to do their duty. It follows that an adequate discussion of the enforceability of a duty to have children would need to examine the legitimacy of particular possible pronatalist policies. This is an issue I did not attempt to discuss here; instead, I pointed out which policies are very unlikely to be ever legitimate, such as coerced pregnancy. The most convincing argument against the possibility of an enforceable duty to have children—that forced pregnancy seriously violates women's autonomy—could in theory be made obsolete by technological development. I have also attempted to dispel the worry that consideration of adult autonomy and child welfare make all pro-natalist policies in principle illegitimate.

The existence of a collective responsibility to have children in order to prevent great harm has consequences for other issues. Most immediately, it bears on the question of whether there is not merely a right, but also a duty to bring into the world "savior children" if this is necessary for the satisfaction of the basic medical needs on an existing individual. I started this chapter by suggesting that a collective duty to have children can help us think about the question of who should shoulder the burdens of child rearing. It is to that question that I now return. What, if any, difference does a collective responsibility to have enough children make to how we should decide who should pay for children? In the world as it currently is people volunteer to have enough—or more than enough—children and therefore live up to the collective responsibility without much incentive, let alone coercion. However, the existence of a collective responsibility to have enough children indicates one reason why it is inadequate to model child rearing (up to an optimum population) as a form of expensive taste or a hobby. If volunteering to have children is more like volunteering to defend your community against aggression than like indulging in fine wines or producing beautiful sculptures in your spare time, then there is a stronger case that having children is a form of social cooperation. And if having children is a form of cooperation, then fairness requires that some of its costs be socially shared. The interesting question, then, is which of the costs of childbearing and child rearing should be socialized. A plausible suggestion is that we should socialize, on grounds of fairness, the morally mandatory costs of childbearing and child rearing, up to an optimum number of children. These are likely to include the costs of providing children with proper nutrition, clothing, homes, safety, health care, education, and non-overworked parents, but are not identical with the full costs of child rearing. Parents also tend to spend money for goods that are not necessary to ensure an adequate level of well-being to their children.[34]

However, to capture the spirit of the anti-sharing view, it is essential to note that rearing children represents, for most people, a benefit as well as a source of financial and non-financial burden, and this seems crucial for determining what is a fair distribution of the costs of child rearing between parents and non-parents. If there is no shortage of children this is precisely because parenting is so valuable to many people that they are keen on having children, in spite of the significant (non-shared part of the) cost of raising them in developed countries. The next questions, then, are whether and how the intrinsic valuing of parenting should be factored in determining what fairness demands in terms of sharing the costs of having children. Whatever the correct answers to these questions, it is highly unlikely that they will entail that parents should shoulder alone the morally mandatory costs of childbearing and child rearing. Remember the analogy with ensuring an adequate water supply; before the threat of shortage, people were organizing the provision of water through voluntary cooperation, without the intervention of the state. This is the right analogy for a situation in which enough people volunteer to have children.

The task is to determine what is the fair amount of support, if any, that they should be socially given for rearing children. In the imagined story, the exact form of cooperation was intentionally left unspecified: perhaps it was through a free market exchange, perhaps it was a more communal way of organization, such as a services co-op. Similarly, the motivation of the workers supplying water was left unspecified: perhaps supplying water was, for them, a mere job, or perhaps it was (also) done from a sense of pride in providing an essential good to their community. Even if we imagine that the water was provided via market mechanisms, and free market exchanges should determine the level of fair compensation, and even if we imagine that workers were motivated by pride, such that they were ready to do their work without pay, it would be highly implausible to think that fair compensation for providing water could be less than the costs of production. Indeed, a case in which some people provide an essential good to their community *and* support the costs of production themselves without getting *any* compensation looks a lot more like exploitation than like a fair market exchange. If such a practice was ongoing on any significant scale— if, say, some people voluntarily supplied clean water, supporting themselves the costs of production and without any financial compensation from their community—we would rightly suspect that the water suppliers are exploited. We would suspect that something in their motivational dispositions, or perhaps a structural aspect of their relationship with the rest of the citizens makes them vulnerable to an obviously unbalanced social exchange.

Similarly, assume that the fair level of financial support that non-parents owe to parents should be sensitive to the level of incentive that some people demand in order to parent, and that people in fact need very low incentives in order to parent: they value parenting enough to happily put in all the time, effort, and foreclosed opportunities without compensation. If indeed having (enough) children is a matter of social responsibility, then it is very implausible to think that fairness will demand from non-parents to share with parents less than the morally mandatory costs of childbearing and child rearing. It is perhaps not impossible to imagine that some individuals would want to have children even if they had to support themselves all the costs of bearing and rearing them—in terms of money, time and effort—without *any* societal help. But the most plausible explanation of why they would want to do this is that the desire to have children is so overpowering and hence unresponsive to reasonable assessment that it makes individuals who have it vulnerable to exploitation.[35]

NOTES

1. In this chapter I take "duty" and "responsibility" to be the same thing. I use the first to refer to individual duties and the second to refer to collective ones.
2. See Robert Goodin, *Protecting the Vulnerable. A Reanalysis of Our Social Responsibilities* (Chicago: Chicago University Press, 1985).
3. I intentionally avoid the discussion of the threshold of well-being of a prospective person below which it is plausible that bringing that person into existence is impermissible. At least, the threshold is at the level where the life is worth living—that is, the well-being of the life offsets its badness.
4. And so I avoid, as well, the question of which principle of distributive justice should regulate relationships between successive generations—that is, whether parents owe their children equality or sufficiency.
5. Because "having children" includes, for the purposes of this chapter both procreation and child rearing, I assume that only those individuals who would make adequate child rearers have this right.
6. Reproductive rights figure as a subset of human rights since the 1968 *Proclamation of Tehran*, which stipulates that "Parents have a basic right to decide freely and responsibly on the number and spacing of their children and a right to adequate education and information in this respect." The same right is reiterated by the *Cairo Programme of Action*, a document adopted in 1994 recommending that governments prioritize the respect of individuals' reproductive freedoms over demographic targets.
7. For an exception, see Saul Smilansky, "Is There a Moral Obligation to Have Children?" *Journal of Applied Philosophy* 12, no. 1 (1995), 41–53.
8. Christine Overall, *Why Have Children? The Ethical* Debate (Cambridge, MA: MIT Press, 2012), 76.
9. David Benatar, *Better Never to Have Been: The Harm of Coming Into Existence* (Oxford: Oxford University Press, 2006).
10. See Daniel Friedrich, "A Duty to Adopt?" *Journal of Applied Philosophy* 30, no. 1 (2013): 25–39; and Tina Rulli, "The Unique Value of Adoption," in *Family-Making: Contemporary Ethical Challenges*, ed. Francoise Baylis and Carolyn McLeod (Oxford: Oxford University Press, 2014).
11. Strictly speaking, the argument here bears both on the costs of child rearing and on the costs of childbearing. But since the former are much greater, and since they—rather than the costs of childbearing—are the object of a heated dispute concerning who should shoulder them, I often refer only to "the costs of child rearing."
12. Good summaries can be found in Serena Olsaretti, "Children as Public Goods?" *Philosophy and Public Affairs* 41, no. 3 (2013): 226–258, and Patrick Tomlin, "Should Kids Pay Their Own Way?" *Political Studies*. DOI: 10.1111/1467-9248.12111, 2014 (forthcoming).
13. Olsaretti, "Children."
14. The best-known proponent of this argument is Nancy Folbre; for instance, "Children as Public Goods,"*The American Economic Review* 84, no. 1 (1994): 86–90.
15. Paula Casal, "Environmentalism, Procreation, and the Principle of Fairness," *Public Affairs Quarterly* 13 (1999); Paula Casal and Andrew Williams, "Equality of Resources and Procreative Justice," *Dworkin and His Critics*, ed. Justine Burley (Oxford: Blackwell, 2004).

16. I take basic needs to be especially powerful interests. They include, uncontroversially, needs for clean water and other things necessary for physical survival, as well as relief from physical pain. I see no reason why they would not also include relief from intense psychological suffering.

17. According to Goodin, *Protecting the Vulnerable*.

18. John Rawls, for instance. See the discussion in Lucas Stanczyc, "Productive Justice," *Philosophy and Public Affairs* 40, no. 2 (2012): 144–164.

19. See Stanczyc, "Productive Justice." For a liberal egalitarian theory of why states are permitted to require that citizens provide personal services and even body parts, see Cecile Fabre, *Whose Body Is It Anyway? Justice and the Integrity of the Person* (Oxford: Oxford University Press, 2006).

20. Seble Frehywot, Fitzhugh Mullan, Perry W. Payne, and Heather Ross, "Compulsory Service Programmes for Recruiting Health Workers in Remote and Rural Areas: Do They Work?" *Bulletin of the World Health Organization* 88, no. 5 (2010): 364–370.

21. Samuel Scheffler, *Death and the Afterlife*, ed. Niko Kolodny (Oxford: Oxford University Press, 2013).

22. John Rawls, "Idea of Public Reason Revisited," in *The Law of Peoples, with "The Idea of Public Reason" Revisited* (Cambridge, MA: Harvard University Press, 1999), 157.

23. At least if one accepts the principle of fair play. One of its best-known defenders, George Klosko, sees the principle of fair play as restricted to goods that "can be presumed to be necessary for an acceptable life." In the previous section, I showed that children are necessary for a bearable life. See George Klosko, "Presumptive Benefit, Fairness, and Political Obligation," *Philosophy & Public Affairs* 16, no. 3 (1987): 247.

24. Liberals tend to agree that certain individual duties should not be enforceable; for instance, people should be free not to donate any money even if they have a duty of charity, and should be free to vote for parties with morally problematic agendas.

25. Williams Bernard and J. J. C. Smart, *Utilitarianism: For and Against* (Cambridge: Cambridge University Press, 1973); Seana Shiffrin, "Moral Autonomy and Agent-Centred Options," *Analysis* 51, no. 4 (1001): 244–254.

26. An excellent, book-length discussion of the philosophical relevance of pregnancy is Amy Mullin's *Reconceiving Pregnancy and Childcare: Ethics, Experience, and Reproductive Labor* (Cambridge: Cambridge University Press, 2005).

27. Fabre, *Whose Body*.

28. Anne Alstott, *No Exit: What Parents Owe Children and What Society Owes Parents* (Oxford: Oxford University Press, 2004).

29. Jane Waldfogel, *What Children Need* (Cambridge, MA: Harvard University Press, 2006).

30. Daniela Cutas, "On Triparenting: Is Having Three Committed Parents Better Than Having Only Two?" *Journal of Medical Ethics* 37, no. 12 (2011): 735–738. Samantha Brennan and Bill Cameron, "How Many Parents Can a Child Have?" DOI: http://dx.doi.org/10.1017/S0012217314000705

31. I leave to one side, for the purpose of this work, the easy solution made available by the non-identity problem: given that the children in question would not exist at all without the state promoting or enforcing a duty to have children, they cannot be said to be harmed by the enforcement of such a duty (unless their lives would be so bad as to be not worth living).

32. See, for instance, SallySheldon and Stephen Wilkinson, "Should Selecting Saviour Siblings Be Banned?" *Journal of Medical Ethics* 30, no. 6 (2004): 533–537.
33. I am grateful to Lindsey Porter for pointing this out.
34. For this distinction between morally mandatory costs of child rearing and costs of child rearing that are not morally mandatory, see Olsaretti, "Children."
35. For helpful feedback on previous drafts, I am grateful to Christine Bratu, Lindsey Porter, and the participants in the "Permissible Progeny" conference that took place at Western University in London, Ontario in July 2013. While writing this chapter I have benefited from a De Velling Willis Fellowship at the University of Sheffield. Work towards this article was also supported by the Swedish Research Council, grant no. 421-2013-1306.

CHAPTER 4

Procreation or Appropriation?

COREY MACIVER

Contemporary discussions of environmental ethics and green political theory are surprisingly reticent about issues of population or human reproduction.[1] Although modern environmental movements emerged in part as a response to unprecedented and exponential increases in global population over the course of the twentieth century, procreation has largely disappeared from normative dialogue about human ecology and environmental degradation. There are a number of likely causes for this conspicuous absence, some better-grounded than others.[2]

To some extent, viewing procreation through the lens of environmental politics has become taboo simply by association with some of the discursive and political choices made by those with concerns about population. Broadly environmental discussions of population have, at times, gone down fairly questionable paths with respect to claims about the developing world, immigration, and the status of women.[3] Politically, of course, state intervention in reproductive decisions has come to be inextricably linked in the popular imagination with coercive population control policies pursued in China and India, the consequences of which have included forced sterilization, infanticide, and sex-based selective abortion. For many, this association alone is sufficient to put procreative decisions firmly outside the scope of reasonable political discussion.

A second reason for diminished interest in reproduction and population in discussions of human ecology and environmental politics is that initial predictions about the ecological consequences of overpopulation have proven at least somewhat overblown. Although world population is still increasing at a rapid rate, the increase is mostly confined to a few regions of the world.[4] The overall rate of population growth has slowed consistently since peaking in the late 1960s, and political discourse in much of the global North has been re-focused on the social and economic consequences of *under*population as domestic fertility rates dip below replacement levels.[5] Moreover, the worldwide ecological and social collapse predicted by early, neo-Malthusian accounts failed to occur (or at least failed to occur on schedule). Mass starvation and resource scarcity of the sort commonly predicted in the 1970s was avoided, or at least forestalled, by increased agricultural yields and technological innovation. Although our numbers have risen considerably since global population became a cause for concern, our ability to meet human needs in the short term has largely kept up or even improved.

It is also widely assumed that the overall fertility rate will continue to decline, leveling off at some point in the coming century.[6] As infant and child mortality decline, women are increasingly afforded access to education and social empowerment, and access to modern methods of contraception becomes more widely available, the assumption is that women will voluntarily limit their fertility to a level at or below the rate of replacement, as they largely have in societies in which these conditions obtain.

Although these first two points are empirically sound, neither of them, in my view, constitutes a compelling basis for omitting procreation from discussions of sustainability. On the first point, the stigma of negative associations with real-world phenomena is a poor reason to shy away from discussing a potentially important topic. While I would certainly not defend the *content* of much of the early discourse around global population, it presented a set of questions that are still worth asking—particularly given ongoing (and worsening) environmental degradation. The value of the discussion persists quite apart from specific policies undertaken by particular states or specific positions held by non-state actors, no matter how questionable those may be.

On the second point, it is undeniable that global population growth has slowed and that in some parts of the world reproduction has fallen well below replacement level. What we can and should question is the assumption that this trend will simply continue of its own accord, resulting in a gradual and painless leveling-off (let alone a manageable decline) of the global population. Widespread access to contraception is both a recent and hard-fought right even in the global North, and as recent controversy around the inclusion of contraception in federally funded health insurance in the United States shows, powerful opposition to this access is still very active. Moreover, projected decreases in the rate of population growth are estimates, not certainties. As Diana Coole points out in her recent account of green population discourse, the current fertility rate is still quite high. A business-as-usual projection of global population leads to the shocking prospect of a 27-billion-person world by 2100, rather than the 10.1 billion currently projected.[7] In such a scenario, there is almost certainly a point at which human ingenuity will be trumped by natural limits, with catastrophic results.

Finally, and crucially, even if we opt for complacency about the rate of population growth, we are not thereby absolved from thinking about population as such, or about the morality of procreation in general. It is far from clear that the eventual plateau of human population, whatever that number may be, is either desirable or sustainable—particularly given the ecological havoc already being wrought by our current numbers.

A third (and better) reason for the absence of procreation from contemporary discussions of environmental ethics and politics is that their focus has shifted from population to a more nuanced and accurate consumption-based account of anthropogenic environmental degradation. The mere fact of our existence is not, in itself, particularly informative about our ecological impact. What matters is our so-called "ecological footprint"—the sum total (often expressed in spatial terms) of the resources and ecological processes appropriated or consumed or destroyed as a means to or a consequence of our existence.[8] It is a truism that ecological footprints vary enormously on the basis of affluence and lifestyle; in practical terms an average American and an average Bangladeshi (for example) are not even remotely ecologically interchangeable. Nor, for that matter, are an American in the top economic quintile (of Americans) and one in the bottom quintile. In general, the ecological footprint of the relatively affluent will typically dwarf that of the relatively impoverished based on the kinds of demands that their respective lifestyles and consumption patterns have on the natural world.[9] As such, it is just empirically false to treat ecological impact as a function of mere population. If our concern is with the material impact of human beings upon the natural world, it makes a great deal more sense to focus on what and how people are consuming rather than merely on how many of them there happen to be.

This chapter takes it as given that a focus on consumption, rather than on population as such, is entirely appropriate if we are interested in drawing normative conclusions about human ecology. What I will argue here is that thinking about human ecology in consumptive terms in no way entails that we should stop thinking about procreation. Rather, we should collapse the dichotomy between consumption and procreation, and acknowledge procreation as one of the most significant ways in which individual human beings lay claim to the natural world. When we assess the ecological impact of a given individual (or, perhaps more appropriately, a given set of potential biological parents), this assessment should include not only their demands upon the natural world, but also their contribution to the creation of new demands upon the natural world through procreative means.[10] That is, a narrowly consumption-based assessment of individual ecological impacts is fundamentally incomplete, and hopelessly inaccurate, if it fails to take what we might call "procreative consumption" into account—that is, consumption (or other material impacts) arising as a consequence of procreative behavior. The point is not merely conceptual; it may have significant practical consequences. I will argue that if the dichotomy between procreation and consumption is collapsible, it follows that the notion of unlimited procreative rights cannot be sustained—and further, that we should reject the widespread belief that procreative decisions are (or should be) exempt from moral scrutiny or political intervention.

This section will present an argument for the material and moral equivalence of consumption and procreation, building to the conclusion that procreative decisions should be incorporated into ecological footprint analysis, and as such cannot be considered private. To the extent that procreation can infringe upon the legitimate interests of others, it should not be treated differently than other, similarly infringing behaviors. As such, under some conditions it may be appropriate to apply moral suasion or even intervention aimed at curtailing the procreative behavior of others.

It should go without saying that this is a conclusion with which many will disagree. Procreative behavior is widely held to be in a kind of separate category from (other) consumptive behavior, as well as being fundamentally private and pre-political. Because my conclusion is at odds with prevailing beliefs about procreation, the argument will be set out here as a series of explicitly stated premises. This style of argumentation may strike some readers as tedious, but the aim is to make it as easy as possible for opponents of the argument to discern exactly where it has (on their view) gone wrong. Due to space constraints, some premises will be merely stated rather than argued for at length; I will endeavour to argue for the premises that seem the most likely to generate controversy or misunderstanding. As the discussion progresses, I will try to anticipate and respond to objections to some of the more contentious points.

The argument is divided into three sub-sections, each advancing a conclusion. The first is that human claims to natural goods cannot reasonably be understood as unlimited; we inhabit a finite world and our claims impact the ability of others to make claims of their own. The second is that procreation is materially and morally equivalent to other types of claims to the natural world, and as such it should be included in our assessment of individuals' environmental impact. The third point, following from the the first two, is that our ability to exercise procreative autonomy cannot be understood as unlimited. Decisions about procreation thus cannot reasonably be understood as private.

NO UNLIMITED RIGHTS TO NATURAL GOODS

P1: Human existence is fundamentally material; that is, human beings have a number of objective interests that can only be met through the appropriation, use, transformation, or destruction of the natural world.[11] These include both physical stuff (food, water, and so on) as well as ecological processes and services, and their use is both direct and indirect. I will refer to these, broadly, as "natural goods." Human existence is only tolerable, let alone conducive to flourishing, when a certain threshold of natural goods can be reliably obtained and used.[12]

P2: Human existence is predicated on complex ecological relationships and is subject to the same natural limitations as all other species on Earth. A key limit faced by all species is the availability of (species-specific) natural goods. While our ability to exploit the natural world to our advantage fluctuates and has historically increased over time, it remains finite by virtue of the fact that the world in which we live is finite. Ecological decline, moreover, is not merely a theoretical concern for human beings. As uncomfortable as it may make us to acknowledge it, human existence is ecologically precarious. Human history is littered with examples of ecological overreach and collapse, some of which have had profound and lasting impacts on the societies in which they occurred.[13]

P3: Natural goods are limited. Some natural goods are nonexclusive; they can be enjoyed without any discernible impact upon the ability of others to enjoy them. Many, perhaps most, of the natural goods necessary for a decent human life are not like this, however. Their appropriation or use is rivalrous—that is, use or enjoyment by one agent diminishes the supply or quality of those goods available to others, either because the good in question is altered or destroyed through use or because it is the sort of good that can only be enjoyed by a limited number of agents.

P4: No person has any inherent claim or entitlement to a greater share of (rivalrous) natural goods than any other.[14] A full theory of just appropriation is well beyond the scope of this chapter, but in general I assume the (broadly left-libertarian) premise that the natural world is either commonly owned (by humanity, for our purposes) or that it is wholly and permanently unowned. In either case, individuals may be afforded an unequal share by force or by convention, but there is no non-arbitrary basis on which any given individual can reasonably claim more natural goods than any other with similar basic needs.[15]

P5: Each morally considerable entity (a category that I assume includes human beings, at minimum, and may include a great many other species) has a natural or negative right to the natural goods necessary for a decent life. That is, there is no reasonable basis on which others can permissibly deny or withhold access to necessary natural goods except to protect or secure their own basic interests. Note that this is not an argument for *positive* rights to the natural goods necessary for a decent life. I am not claiming here that anyone should provide these to anyone else where they are lacking.[16] I am making the (considerably less-demanding) claim that we cannot reasonably stand in the way of others obtaining these goods for themselves, and that they can legitimately take whatever measures are necessary to obtain such goods against those who would deliberately withhold them.

P6: If human beings have valid claims to some quantity of natural goods in either of the senses suggested in P4 and P5—that is, if they are entitled to a share of natural goods roughly equal to that of others, or to a sufficient quantity to ensure their well-being, or both—infringing those claims constitutes a wrong, a harm, or both. To claim the share of another in whole or in part is to wrong them, even if they are unharmed by the infringement.[17] Infringing the claim of some other person to the subset of natural goods that they require in order to fulfill their basic needs not only wrongs them in the first sense, but harms them.[18]

P7: *Ceteris paribus*, we ought not wrong or harm others.

C1: It follows from premises 1–7 that no individual (in a world populated by more than one person) can legitimately lay claim to an unlimited quantity of natural goods. The scope of what we can legitimately claim is limited by the ability of others to make similar claims, to meet their basic needs, or both.

PROCREATION AND CLAIMS TO NATURAL GOODS

P8: Insofar as all people make claims to natural goods by virtue of existing, creating new people is functionally equivalent to creating new claims to natural goods.

As established earlier, human existence is inseparable from a predictable set or bundle of claims to natural goods, with predictable impacts upon the natural world. Thus, to procreate is to act in such a way as to bring about de facto claims to some quantity of grain, plants, or meat; to so much freshwater, coal, iron, cadmium, lumber, or rubber; to the emission of foreseeable quantities of liquid, solid, and atmospheric waste; to the exploitation of a number of biochemical and ecological processes; and so on.[19] The precise demands of any given person will of course depend on the specific cultural context into which they are born, as well as the level of affluence they attain within that context. The basic conceptual point remains, however: whatever else it is, the act of creating a new person is also and always an act of creating a new set of claims to natural goods.[20]

P9: No person has an interest in being brought into existence. I remain neutral here on the question of whether coming into existence is a benefit conferred upon those who receive it or, as David Benatar suggests, a burden.[21] Even if being created is a benefit, however, it is not a benefit that anyone can choose to accept or reject (nonretroactively) by virtue of the fact that they do not exist.[22]

P10: Parents owe their children whatever natural goods are necessary for or constitutive of a minimally decent life. This follows from P8 and P9; new people have no interest in being brought into existence, but their existence will invariably require a significant quantity of natural goods if it is to be in any way tolerable. Assuming the additional premise (P7) that we ought not expose others to undue harm, procreation should be understood to include or imply a claim by procreators to whatever additional natural goods are required in order for the lives of newly created people to meet some minimal threshold of decency.[23]

At the very least, procreation generates a duty upon parents to *intend* to ensure the basic material well-being and flourishing of their offspring.[24] The alternative would be that the role of parents is merely to provide the opportunity for new people to struggle for existence—perhaps pledging to assist them where they can, but not taking full responsibility for meeting their needs.[25] This would be to expose children to an unjustifiable level of risk.

Of course, parents might fail (for a variety of reasons, at least some of which will not be wholly their fault) to secure the natural goods necessary for their children to enjoy a minimally decent life. Children may, upon reaching adulthood, make decisions that inhibit their ability to meet basic needs. These contingencies should not affect our understanding of the kinds of duties and claims conceptually associated with procreation, however. In the morally relevant sense, the decision to have children is, or should be, understood as a claim to the natural goods necessary for their well-being over their life span. This claim should be understood as being fundamentally of and by parents, rather than children, for the reasons already discussed.[26]

P11: The creation of new claims to the natural world by biological parents is not qualitatively distinguishable in any morally significant way from non-procreative claims to the natural world. While they may have a specific and distinct function in the lives of parents, from the vantage point of affected parties procreation-related claims are indistinguishable from other sorts of claims. That is, there is no morally relevant distinction between an individual claiming a large quantity of natural goods for her own personal use, and an individual claiming a large quantity of natural goods for the use of her offspring. There is nothing inherently special or defensible about the latter.

This is not to say that *all* claims to natural goods (procreative or non-procreative) are normatively identical. Some of the natural goods we make claims to are necessary for meeting our basic needs, while others are superfluous. Some of our claims are consistent with the ability of others to make similar claims, and others are not. In general, how we assess the moral (and hence the political) standing of material claims will depend on what is being claimed, as well as whether those claims can be understood as meeting fundamental interests, mere preferences, or something in between. Procreation may or may be the sort of activity that constitutes an interest; I will discuss this further later. The point for the time being is simply that procreative claims ought not be exempted from the scrutiny to which we subject other sorts of claims merely because they are procreative.

P12: Each individual has an "ecological footprint," a metric representing the overall ecological impact of that individual's activities, arising through the direct and indirect use of natural goods.[27] Ecological footprint analysis (conventionally measured in hectares of biologically productive land and sea) is a reasonably straightforward method of quantifying the impact of people or objects on the planet—and, by extension, their contribution to and moral responsibility for environmental degradation. The concept of an ecological footprint is also useful as a means of quantifying entitlements to natural goods, and of comparing claims and impacts made by individuals.[28] So, another way in which we could frame these premises is that we are at minimum entitled to a large enough ecological footprint to meet our basic needs. At maximum, we are entitled to a footprint no larger than is consistent with not subjecting others to harmful deprivation, however we define this.

C2: The natural goods necessary for or constitutive of a minimally decent life for newly created people should be understood as part of the ecological footprint of procreators. Like other claims to natural goods, the claims associated with procreation should be understood both as part of the ecological impact for which the procreator is responsible, and as subtractable from any entitlement the procreator may have. Or, to put it in more tangible terms, the decision to procreate should not be understood as qualitatively distinct from any other (optional) decision to use natural goods.[29] Moreover, and more importantly from a normative perspective, the *quantitative* consequences of procreation far outweigh virtually all other claims to natural goods that a given individual will make over the span of a life.[30] Because the claims associated with procreation are so significant, it can singlehandedly cancel out other efforts at mitigating environmental impacts. For example, adopting a range of standard greenhouse gas emission-reducing measures (reducing gasoline consumption, improving home energy efficiency, and so on) may generate a reduction of—at best—a few hundred metric tons of GHGs.[31] Each new (American) child, conversely, is foreseeably likely to emit several thousand metric tons over their life span. This not only negates the benefits associated with taking harm-reducing measures, but arguably undermines them by an order of magnitude.

The argument that the ecological footprint of one generation encompasses some of the claims or impacts associated with another raises a number of interesting practical and conceptual puzzles about how to allocate responsibility between them. One obvious issue is the question of how best to attribute some, but not all, of a given person's impact to their parents. None of the impacts associated with my existence would occur had my parents not decided to bring me into existence, but it is important to acknowledge that I bear responsibility for making better and worse choices (including my own procreative choices) as I go through life. Any allocation of ecological footprint, and hence of moral responsibility for environmental impact, should reflect the agency of both parents and children (or rather, of the adults that children will become). Wherever we draw the line, however, it is clear that the status quo (in which parents are understood as blameless conduits through which additional human beings appear) is woefully inaccurate.

My proposal for redrawing the boundary of ecological footprint analysis is this: insofar as we have no role or interest in being brought into existence, at minimum the *unavoidable* impacts and claims associated with our existence should be understood as belonging to our parents—at least for the purposes of assigning responsibility or weighing entitlements. Thus, whatever ecological footprint is necessary to ensure a minimally decent life (per P10) is attributable to parents rather than to children, since children have no reasonable option but to claim those goods.

As noted, each of us has control over our impact to some extent, and it would be unreasonable to assign responsibility for my voluntary actions to my parents in perpetuity. Whatever metric we devise must reflect the agency that can be exercised once we develop the capacity for autonomous choice. But we cannot meaningfully exercise agency over the meeting of our basic material needs, because these are not optional in any real sense. Given that the meeting of basic needs is not reasonably within the purview of our agency, moral responsibility for any harms or wrongs visited upon third parties in the process of meeting those basic needs rightly rests with those who could (reasonably) have acted otherwise (i.e., our parents).

It seems plausible to me that we could take a stronger approach and attribute not only the unavoidable but also the *foreseeable* claims of a second generation to the first, even though many foreseeable claims are in principle avoidable (in the sense of not being strictly necessary for a minimally decent life). That is, where children are born into conditions in which the status quo involves use of the natural world at a level over and above that necessary for a minimally decent life, there is a case to be made that responsibility for those impacts rightly belongs with their parents. There are certain impacts that children born in contemporary North America are virtually certain to have, for example, simply by participating "normally" in that society.

To the extent that it would impose hardship for them to refrain from the activities that generate those impacts, it seems inappropriate to hold them responsible—even if we still believe that they ought not, on balance, engage in those activities.

So, for example, one of the most significant environmental impacts associated with life in contemporary North America is the emission of greenhouse gas. It is, strictly speaking, possible to live and even to flourish in North American society while emitting substantially less-than-average quantities of greenhouse gas. One can use public transport, live in a modestly sized home, consume a plant-based diet, and so on. However, there will almost certainly be a point at which a lifestyle conducive to greenhouse gas emissions that are *much* lower than average will be excessively demanding within the social and institutional context that presently prevails. A North American *can* go entirely "off the grid" in order to achieve more drastic reductions, but the individual consequences of doing so are so (contingently) onerous that it seems inappropriate to hold them morally responsible for failing to do so. We might therefore plausibly argue that parents are responsible not only for emissions that are literally unavoidable, but also for the foreseeable emissions that contingent circumstances make it very difficult or excessively demanding to avoid.

However we divide up responsibility for impacts, what is more important for our purposes here is the underlying conceptual point—that procreative decisions are by far the most ecologically significant decisions that individuals will make in their lives, and that causal and moral responsibility for much of our individual ecological impact rightly rests with our parents. When we are calculating environmental impacts, therefore, we cannot reasonably exclude procreation from our analysis.

PROCREATIVE AUTONOMY AND PRIVACY

Thus far, the discussion has focused on the relationship between procreation and (limited) natural goods. I have argued that procreation should be understood as a kind of consumptive or appropriative claim by (would-be) parents, but have said little about what, if anything, might follow from this conceptual argument. The main point of this final section is that procreative decisions cannot reasonably be understood as private. As such, they are potentially subject at least to moral scrutiny, and potentially to political intervention.

P13: In general, we distinguish between private and public spheres of activity. Very roughly, the private sphere is the domain within which our actions are not legitimately subject to scrutiny or to intervention by those "outside." The liberal tradition (within which this discussion is broadly situated) typically assumes that activities are private unless otherwise demarcated, but that the boundary of the private sphere stops where an activity negatively and unduly affects the interests or life prospects of another without their consent.[32]

P14: Where an activity is likely (or certain) to cause harm by infringing upon the legitimate claims or interests of others (without their consent), it prima facie ceases to be private. Those affected by an activity or behavior, or those acting on their behalf, may reasonably intervene.[33] Activities in the public sphere are at minimum potentially subject to moral censure where appropriate. Under serious enough conditions they may also be subject to preventative or corrective intervention.[34] By intervention I mean a range of possible behaviors ranging from the mildly discouraging to the overtly coercive, the common theme being that the interaction is intended to change behavior rather than merely to comment upon it.

There are some key exceptions to this premise. An action may be subject to intervention but not to moral scrutiny if it is involuntary or unintentional. We might physically prevent an absent-minded pedestrian from stepping into the path of another, but when it comes to assigning blame we typically differentiate between careless walking and deliberate assault.

Alternatively, an action may be exempt from both moral scrutiny and from intervention if it is undertaken in order to fulfill or protect a fundamental interest.[35] The paradigmatic case here is action undertaken in self-defense, but as noted in P5, we have a more general set of negative rights to the conditions necessary for a minimally decent existence.

P15: Appropriation and use of the natural world (in the broad sense) is almost certainly not private much of the time, by virtue of the fact that our interactions with the natural world can and often do have significant negative consequences for morally considerable others. If the ecological sciences have taught us anything, it is that the natural world is interconnected in often unimaginably complex ways. Seemingly isolated actions can have causes and consequences that reach far beyond what may be immediately apparent. Whether any particular instance of natural resource appropriation or use can be legitimately considered private is an empirical matter, of course, and the question of whose (or of which) interests should be taken into consideration is hotly contested, but the basic point stands.

P16: As a kind of voluntary claim to natural goods made by procreators (C2), and especially as a particularly large claim to natural goods, procreation has potentially significant impacts upon the interests of others.[36] As established earlier, the claims associated with procreation will involve the appropriation, use, or destruction of natural goods in ways that may wrong others by infringing upon their fair share of those goods, or harm them by making it more difficult or even impossible to meet their basic needs.

C3: Procreation cannot reasonably be conceived of as a private activity. It is, as established, a fundamentally material practice, reliant upon the appropriation of significant quantities of natural goods. As a material practice, procreation is significantly other-affecting in ways that can wrong or harm morally considerable third parties. As such, and to the extent that they do affect the legitimate interests of others, procreative decisions are reasonably subject to moral censure and even to intervention.

There are likely to be a number of objections to this position, many of which will pertain to specific applications of this general point (i.e., that this or that intervention cannot be justified). Here I wish to address a more general potential objection to the overall point; one that concedes the potential impacts that procreation has (or could have) upon others, but maintains that it is nonetheless a private matter by virtue of the fact that procreation is, or fulfills, a fundamental human interest. As such, the objection goes, we cannot legitimately intervene in the procreative behavior of others, because (as argued in P5 and P14) we have a prima facie negative right to act in ways that promote our fundamental interests. Any normative proposal predicated on ceding the pursuit of our fundamental interests can be reasonably rejected as excessively demanding.

I want to strongly resist this characterization, but in a way that does not deny or downplay the importance of procreation in the lives of a great many people. Procreation is widely held to be one of the activities that give a human life "purpose" or "meaning." Procreation is almost certainly in the interests of many, but the fact that a state of affairs furthers our interests is not sufficient to generate a (negative) right to pursue that state of affairs. We must take care to distinguish between interests as such and fundamental interests, however.

Each of us has an objective, idiosyncratic set of interests—that is, there are states of affairs that would make any given life go objectively better by contributing to our flourishing or improving our well-being in some way or another.[37] Objective interests in this general sense do not generate strong natural rights of the sort discussed previously, or the presumption of non-interference that accompanies such rights. In part this is because we could not possibly achieve or secure all states of affairs in which we potentially have an interest; some will be mutually exclusive or path dependent. More importantly for our purposes, a great many of the states of affairs in which we can be said to have an interest either require the cooperation of other agents (a good to which we have no claim) or conflict with their own interests. My interests might be maximized if I could simply take whatever I wanted or if I could force others to do my bidding, but here of course my interests are trumped (or at least counteracted) by the interests of others. They would be entirely justified in rejecting my attempts to advance my interests in these ways, and in condemning or even restraining my pursuit of them in order to prevent their own interests from being thwarted.

Fundamental interests, on the other hand, are interests the pursuit of which other actors cannot legitimately deny.[38] These are goods that are necessary for a minimally decent life, however this is defined. These will include straightforwardly material goods like adequate food, clean water,

and shelter from the elements, as well as less tangible goods like meaningful human contact or autonomy. The question about procreation is not
whether it constitutes an interest. Clearly it does; for a great many people,
rearing children (and, in particular, their own biological children) is among
the most fulfilling or meaningful activities they will undertake over the
course of their lives. The question is whether the interest many have in
procreating is a *fundamental* sort of interest, which would afford it a distinct normative status from (mere) interest-furthering personal projects.

The argument here is that it is not; procreation (or child rearing) may be
one of the most important activities in the lives of many adults, but they
do not typically lose their ability to function or even to flourish when they
do not or cannot procreate. They may be deeply saddened or disappointed;
they may flourish less than they otherwise would; they may need to find
other goals or projects with which to give their lives meaning, but they are
not obviously or inherently worse off than any other agent with objective
interests that have not been maximized, or strong preferences that have
gone unfulfilled. We can contrast this with the obviously and universally
harmful results of insufficient food, inadequate sanitation, or a lack of
meaningful human contact, for example, any of which can impede or even
preclude having any projects at all.

If procreation were demonstrably and universally necessary to promote
basic flourishing, it might reasonably be argued that it thereby constitutes a
fundamental interest, but this is not the case. Many people lead what appear
to be perfectly adequate lives in spite of—or, in many cases, because of—
the fact that they do not rear offspring. Moreover, it is not necessarily true
that procreation actually or always promotes the interests of procreators. At
least some parents (likely a great many more than would admit it) are worse
off, rather than better off, as a result of their reproductive decisions. Absent
some compelling argument that the voluntarily childless (or regretful parents) are seriously confused or misguided about their interests, there is no
reason to suppose that procreation constitutes a fundamental human interest.[39] As such, there is no reason to suppose that procreation is the sort of
activity with which others cannot reasonably interfere.

But let us grant, for the sake of argument, that the point I have just
made is wrong—that procreation *does* fulfill a fundamental interest. There
are still grounds to reject the notion that it can or should be wholly exempt
from external interference. If our interest in procreation generates a negative right, it is limited in at least two ways.

Firstly, any right to procreate (or, more accurately, any right to nonin-
terference in procreation) will be constrained by the fulfillment of the
interest(s) grounding any such purported right. No matter how strong our

interest in procreation, it is presumably not an unlimited interest. There will be a point at which the good required to fulfill our interest is satisfied, past which continued procreation will be subject to decreasing marginal utility. To the extent that the right protects an interest, rather than an activity, we can identify a point at which the right fails to apply to the activity because the interest has been realized.

By way of an analogy, no one can (*ceteris paribus*) reasonably interfere with my efforts to obtain food in order to avoid starving. They can, on the other hand, reasonably criticize or act in ways that inhibit my efforts to obtain food that I want simply because it is delicious. A fundamental interest in *x* only grounds a negative right to whatever level or amount of *x* is required to achieve a minimally decent life, in other words. It does not ground unlimited access to that good.

If procreation were a fundamental interest, it would still be subject to limits of this sort—that is, there is some amount of procreation that will be sufficient to ensure that the life of the procreator is adequate in that domain. If our individual interests are furthered by engaging in procreation, it is surely by virtue of the contribution that child rearing relationships make to our well-being, rather than the physical act of fertilizing eggs or gestating embryos.[40] To the extent that (interest-promoting) parent-child relationships are predicated upon intimacy, on the thoughtful and deliberate sharing of values and shaping of lives, it seems likely that these goods can be readily satisfied by a relatively small number of children. Moreover, having more children will at some point impede the achievement of those aims rather than promote it.[41] As such, even if we believe (however implausibly) that *every* life would be significantly and objectively improved by procreating, it is almost certainly true that there is a threshold at which fundamental interests are met and further procreative acts become superfluous or even contrary to the interest of procreators, not to mention the interests of others.[42]

Second, and more importantly, the natural world imposes limits upon our procreative claims irrespective of whether they are understood as fundamental interests. In fact, treating procreation as a fundamental interest provides an additional reason to think that the exercise of procreative autonomy must be limited: because there is a point at which unchecked procreation will infringe upon the ability of others to fulfill their interest in procreation. As I have argued here, in a finite world the resource claims associated with acts of procreation will eventually conflict with other resource claims.

A more salient point for those who would defend the notion of a fundamental interest in procreation is that the unlimited exercise of procreative rights will at some point diminish or preclude the ability of others to realize their own purported fundamental interest in procreation. Because procreation is an irreducibly material sort of activity, in a materially limited world there will be a point at which the exercise of procreative rights becomes mutually exclusive—that is, at some point there will not be enough stuff available for all of the offspring we may want to have. We can no more hold an unlimited right to procreation than we can hold an unlimited right to platinum or snow leopards or beachfront real estate—at some point there will not be enough of these to go around, irrespective of how valid we think our claims to them may be. If procreation is a fundamental interest, in short, procreative rights cannot intelligibly be understood as unlimited, because this would interfere with the ability of others to exercise them.

Thus, even if we were to grant that procreation should be treated as a fundamental interest rather than merely as an objective interest, there are still good reasons to believe that it can and in some cases should be subject to limits. If unlimited procreative rights cannot be sustained, there will be a point at which procreative behavior will be legitimately subject to scrutiny or intervention by others.

CONCLUSION

I have made three broad points in this chapter. The first is that in a world in which natural goods are both necessary and finite, individuals cannot reasonably make unlimited claims to natural goods. The second is that insofar as human reproduction inherently involves claims to natural goods, analysis of our ecological impacts cannot legitimately exclude those claims. It is critical to analyze consumption, rather than brute population numbers, but I have argued that procreation must be understood as a consumptive claim to the natural world. Any narrative of consumption (or of overconsumption) that treats procreation as off-limits is fundamentally incomplete and likely to be seriously inaccurate.

The third point is that wrongful, harmful, or excessive claims to the natural world are legitimately subject to condemnation or intervention in order to limit or reverse impacts upon others. There is no credible reason to exclude procreative claims as such, merely because they are procreative. While procreation may significantly further the interests of many procreators, this fact is not necessarily sufficient to outweigh the potential wrongs or harms associated with the creation of new claims. Even if we were to grant for the sake of argument that procreation fulfills a fundamental interest, it does not follow that rights to procreation are or can be unlimited.

None of these points should be especially controversial. Many if not most of the premises here will be difficult to dispute without rejecting the naturalistic understanding of humanity from which they follow. What is striking is the extent to which otherwise rational people reject the conclusions that inexorably seem to follow.

Clearly a great many practical questions remain about when and what kinds of intervention might be warranted. While the discussion here has obvious and potentially significant implications for the real world (particularly given the extent to which we are presently living beyond our ecological means) the development of specific practical prescriptions is outside the scope of this chapter. I will not set out any arguments here about, for example, what the specific boundaries of a reasonable or defensible ecological footprint might be, which agents might be exceeding those boundaries (and through which means), about what number of children it might be appropriate to have in the world we presently inhabit, or about what kinds of preventative or remedial action might be warranted where claims to natural goods (procreative or otherwise) infringe upon the claims of others. These are questions that require a great deal more attention than the available space permits.

The aim of this chapter is to lay conceptual groundwork for practical inquiry by advancing the core principle that we cannot sensibly distinguish between "consumption" and "procreation" in the context of human impacts upon the natural world. The understanding of procreation set out here should inform our thinking about whether limits on procreation might reasonably be set under particular real-world circumstances, what those limits might be, and how they might be advanced or enforced. It suggests that where we think about procreation (and by extension, population), we should do so in a much more nuanced way than some have in the past. If we adhere to the broadly cosmopolitan and egalitarian understanding of entitlement to natural goods on which this chapter is predicated, strictly speaking each new person diminishes the natural goods available to the rest.[43] From the vantage point of likely ecological impact, on the other hand, we should perhaps be more concerned about the two children borne by the average Qatari or Dane or American than we are about the five or six children that the average Afghan or Burundian will likely have.[44]

Admittedly, the arguments made here could, under certain circumstances, potentially lead to some unsettling practical recommendations. We must tread with caution here—though the fact that a conclusion is uncomfortable does not make it false, any intervention should be consistent with the premises by which it is grounded. Potential intervention in procreative behavior is grounded here by appeal to the premises that we ought not inflict undue hardship, harm or deprivation upon others. As such, it remains an open question (at least for the time being) whether and to what extent different forms of interference with procreative autonomy would run contrary to these grounding values.[45] There is a substantial gap between the premise that your procreation infringes upon my legitimate interests and the conclusion that I can forcibly sterilize you, for example. The gap may or may not be bridgeable, but significantly more discussion is required in order to answer questions of this sort.

While a great deal of practical discussion remains, the main point to be taken away here is that—as with all claims to limited natural goods—procreation must be justified and balanced against the interests and claims of morally considerable others. Procreative decisions are among the most ecologically significant decisions we can make, and this means that they cannot reasonably be excluded from thinking about human sustainability or environmental justice. Perhaps as or more importantly in the context of the discussion in this volume, environmental impacts ought not be excluded from our thinking about the morality of procreation.

NOTES

1. Thanks to Sarah Hannan for many valuable discussions on the subject and for her insightful critical feedback on earlier drafts of this chapter.
2. For a recent and much fuller discussion, see Diana Coole, "Too Many Bodies? The Return and Disavowal of the Population Question." *Environmental Politics* 22, Issue 2 (2013): 195–215
3. See e.g., Garrett Hardin, "Living on a Lifeboat," *BioScience* 24, no. 10 (1974): 561–568
4. World Bank Group, ed. *World Development Indicators 2012.* World Bank Publications, 2012; UNFPA. *State of the World Population.* New York: UNFPA, 2012.
5. Ibid. See also Joel E. Cohen et al., "Human Population: The Next Half Century," *Science* 302, no. 5648 (2003): 1172–75.
6. Ibid. See also Wolfgang Lutz, Warren Sanderson, and Sergei Scherbov. "The End of World Population Growth," *Nature* 412, no. 6846 (2001): 543–545.
7. Coole (2013), 204. See also UNFPA (2012), xv.
8. Mathis Wackernagel and William E. Rees. "Our Ecological Footprint: Reducing Human Impact on the Earth." British Columbia: New Society Publishers, 1996; WF, Global Footprint Network, and ESA GFN. "Living Planet Report 2012: Biodiversity, Biocapacity and Better Choices." Switzerland: WWF, 2012.
9. Exceptions are, of course, possible, though unlikely; one could be an extremely wealthy ascetic or hermit, for example. Strictly speaking the connection between wealth and ecological footprint lies not in wealth as such, but in the spending of it.
10. Where I use the term "parents" here I mean it only in the limited, procreative sense except where otherwise specified. That is, I am not referring to

those involved in the rearing of children, only to those involved in their genesis.

11. In what follows, the term "use" will serve as a shorthand for appropriation, exploitation, destruction, transformation, and any other ways in which human beings interact with the natural world in the process of furthering (or attempting to further) their own ends. Also, while I will use "interests" here, this is not necessarily or strictly a welfarist account. Natural goods are as equally necessary for the exercise of autonomy as they are for the meeting of straightforwardly bodily needs.

12. For the sake of argument, I will assume here that a tolerable or "minimally decent" human life includes access to adequate quantity and quality of food, water, and shelter; the absence of disease, pain, or suffering; the ability to exercise some measure of agency or autonomy; meaningful contact with other human beings; and so on.

13. For examples, see Jared Diamond, *Collapse: How Societies Choose to Fail or Succeed*, revised edition (Harmondsworth: Penguin, 2005); Ronald Wright, *A Short History of Progress* (Toronto, ON: Anansi, 2004).

14. I will largely avoid questions here about the claims of non-humans, due more to space constraints than to a belief that non-humans are any less entitled to natural goods than are humans.

15. We might add that "convention" here is nearly always predicated upon the use or the threat of force, whether in the past or on an ongoing basis. This premise should in no way be interpreted as an argument for egalitarianism more broadly; I have no qualms about the unequal distribution of non-natural goods or about individuals selling their fair share of natural goods to others.

16. One key exception to this, as I will discuss, are biological parents. Children have a prima facie positive right against their parents to be provided with the natural goods necessary for a minimally decent life.

17. In cases of overconsumption, it may not even be possible to identify the agent or agents wronged by the excessive claims of another. This does not negate the wrongness of the action, however.

18. Note that I am not claiming that it *is* wrong to violate others' claims—that is, that there are no circumstances under which we can permissibly do so. The claim is merely that they are wronged, even if it may be permissible to do so under some circumstances. For example, taking surplus food to which another has rightful claim in order to avoid starvation wrongs them, but it is also permissible.

19. See also Carol A. Kates, "Reproductive Liberty and Overpopulation," *Environmental Values* 13, no. 1 (2004): 51–79; Thomas Young, "Overconsumption and Procreation: Are They Morally Equivalent?" *Journal of Applied Philosophy* 18, no. 2 (2001): 183–192; Benatar (this volume).

20. That a claim is understood in the abstract does not make it any less material; it simply refrains from speculating about precisely which material goods will be necessary to satisfy the claim.

21. David Benatar, *Better Never to Have Been: The Harm of Coming into Existence* (Oxford: Oxford University Press, 2006).

22. We can of course retroactively endorse having been created, but this is not the same thing.

23. I remain agnostic here about whether parents owe children access to an equal share of natural goods, per P4, or merely to a sufficient supply of natural

goods, per P5. The former is likely to be a great deal more demanding than the latter. For an extended discussion of a fairly similar point, see Peter Vallentyne, "Equality and the Duties of Procreators," in *Children and Political Theory*, eds. David Archard and Colin Macleod (Oxford: Oxford University Press, 2002).

24. It follows that there is a duty to refrain from procreating if it seems likely that one's progeny will be subject to risks or to suffering that could not justifiably by imposed or inflicted upon already-existing people. On this I am firmly in agreement with Benatar, *Better Never to Have Been*. This has interesting and controversial practical implications about the relationship between poverty, affluence, and liberty that I lack the space to take up here.

25. There are interesting questions about the duration of a parental duty to provide offspring with natural goods, as well as about what responsibility individuals should be expected to take with respect to securing their own well-being. I will discuss these briefly in what follows.

26. This is not to suggest that would-be parents are laying claim to anything in an *explicit* sort of way, or even that they have given any consideration to the material consequences of procreation at all. The point is that we can and should ascribe such a claim to them regardless, since the absence of a claim would be morally problematic.

27. Wackernagel and Rees (1996); WWF (2012).

28. See e.g., Andrew Dobson, *Citizenship and the Environment* (Oxford: Oxford University Press, 2003).

29. Cf. Thomas Young, "Overconsumption."

30. To be clear, to attribute ecological impact is not to attribute harm, necessarily. To exist is to have an ecological impact, but this is not itself inherently problematic. The argument here is not that procreation *is* harmful, but rather that it is potentially harmful. What is important is that if and where the impacts associated with existence *become* problematic—for example, when demands upon the natural world outstrip its capacity to meet them—we have an appropriate understanding of who is responsible.

31. Paul A. Murtaugh and Michael G. Schlax, "Reproduction and the Carbon Legacies of Individuals," *Global Environmental Change* 19, no. 1 (2009): 18.

32. Of course, virtually all of our activities "affect others" in some way or another. This discussion must, for the sake of brevity, gloss over an enormously complex concept. For the purposes of this discussion, I will focus narrowly on a wholly negative conception of what makes activities public rather than private—that they expose others (involuntarily) to risk, harm, or other wrongs. This is obviously a crude and colloquial understanding of the public/private distinction, but it will hopefully suffice.

33. For the sake of space, I also leave open here the question of who may legitimately intervene in the behavior of others and under what conditions. I will assume for the sake of argument that a legitimate state may intervene in the behavior of its citizens, setting aside the question of whether any states in fact meet the necessary criteria.

34. There is potential here for endless debate about what constitutes "harm"; particularly if we include (as I think we must) exposure to risk as a kind of harm. Again, for the sake of brevity I must leave this enormously broad question unanswered here. A fuller treatment of the subject would need to address this issue at considerable length.

35. The difficult case is the one in which the interest-fulfilling actions of one agent interfere with the ability of some other agent to fulfill her own interests. Moral theory may have little guidance to offer in such cases.
36. This is not intended to be an exhaustive point about procreation; claims to natural resources are but one of the many ways in which procreative choices can affect others.
37. These are distinct, at least conceptually, from our preferences at any given moment. Ideally our preferences should align with and further our interests but sometimes (perhaps often) they do not—as when the sedentary person lacks a preference for exercise, or the smoker has a preference for cigarettes. Assuming that obesity or emphysema are not compatible with flourishing, we can say in such cases that the holders of such preferences are misguided about what is in their interest.
38. Again, the argument is not that fundamental interests generate positive duties. It is rather (and merely) that they are the sort of goods with which others cannot reasonably interfere. There will also be exceptions, of course, related to the fundamental interests of others. For example, we might reasonably restrict the autonomy of a dangerous psychopath.
39. Some will argue here that even non-procreators have an objective interest in procreation in the abstract (that is, they have an interest in *someone* having children). This may be true if and to the extent that non-procreators are personally invested in the continued existence of a particular society, or of the human species in the abstract. I do not think we can reasonably assume that all (or even most) non-procreators hold these commitments, however. More importantly, there is no compelling reason to believe that anyone *should* be committed to these.
40. See Harry Brighouse and Adam Swift, "Parents' Rights and the Value of the Family," *Ethics* 117, no. 1 (2006): 80–108. There are admittedly other ways in which procreation might further our interests—say, by providing unpaid farm labor—but I take it that these are illegitimate.
41. The question of where this threshold might lie is well beyond the scope of the discussion here—not least because I do not accept the notion of a fundamental interest in procreation. Whether the purported interest requires one child or seven in order to be fulfilled is less important for our purposes than the conceptual point that any such interest does not ground unlimited procreation.
42. Readers may disagree that biological offspring could ever be subject to the sort of diminishing returns noted here. If so, we can substitute the idea of reproductive technology advancing to a point at which it would be feasible for a single individual to create, say, 10,000 children at once. It is hard to imagine a reasonable person arguing that this would further the interests of anyone concerned.
43. To be quite specific, the WWF estimates that the available global biocapacity per person was 3.2 hectares in 1961. By 2008, that amount had been reduced to 1.8 hectares. WWF (2012), 9.
44. World Bank (2012), WWF (2012).
45. The first and best course of action will always be to allow (and encourage) individuals to limit their own fertility, by ensuring easy and unfettered access to the necessary resources to do so. If global population optimists are correct, reliable access to contraception (along with greater gender parity) may be sufficient to bring about a slow and manageable decline in birth rates without any need for additional intervention.

REFERENCES

Benatar, David. *Better Never to Have Been:The Harm of Coming into Existence*. Oxford: Oxford University Press, 2006.

Brighouse, Harry, and Adam Swift. "Parents' Rights and the Value of the Family." *Ethics* 117, no. 1 (2006): 80–108.

Cohen, Joel E., et al., "Human Population: The Next Half Century." Science 302, no. 5648 (2003): 1172–1175.

Coole, Diana, "Too Many Bodies? The Return and Disavowal of the Population Question." *Environmental Politics* 22, no. 2 (2013): 195–215.

Diamond, Jared. *Collapse: How Societies Choose to Fail or Succeed*. Harmondsworth:Penguin, 2005.

Dobson, Andrew. *Citizenship and the Environment*. Oxford: Oxford University Press, 2003.

———. "The Tragedy of the Commons." *Science* 162, no. 3859 (1968): 1243–1248.

Hardin, Garrett, "Living on a Lifeboat." *BioScience* 24, no.10 (1974): 561–568.

Kates, Carol A. "Reproductive Liberty and Overpopulation." *Environmental Values* 13, no. 1 (2004): 51–79.

Lutz, Wolfgang, Warren Sanderson, and Sergei Scherbov. "The End of World Population Growth." *Nature* 412, no. 6846 (2001): 543–545.

Murtaugh, Paul A., and Schlax, Michael G. "Reproduction and the Carbon Legacies of Individuals." *Global Environmental Change* 19, no. 1 (2009): 14–20.

Nozick, Robert. *Anarchy, State, and Utopia*. New York: Basic Books, 1974.

Overall, Christine. *Why Have Children?: The Ethical Debate*. Cambridge, MA: MIT Press, 2012.

UNFPA. 2012. The State of the World Population Report. New York: UNFPA, 2012.

Vallentyne, Peter. "Left-libertarianism: A Primer," in *Left-Libertarianism and Its Critics: The Contemporary Debate*, ed. Peter Vallentyne and Hillel Steiner (New York: Palgrave-Macmillan, 2000), 1–20.

———. "Equality and the Duties of Procreators," in *Children and Political Theory*, ed. David Archard and Colin Macleod (Oxford: Oxford University Press, 2002).

Wackernagel, Mathis, and William E. Rees. *Our Ecological Footprint: Reducing Human Impact on the Earth*. British Columbia: New Society Publishers, 1996.

World Bank Group. World Development Indicators 2012. World Bank Publications, 2012.

World Wildlife Federation, Global Footprint Network, and ESA GFN. "Living Planet Report 2012: Biodiversity, Biocapacity and Better Choices." Switzerland: WWF, 2012.

Wright, Ronald. *A Short History of Progress*. Toronto, ON: House of Anansi, 2004.

Young, Thomas, "Overconsumption and Procreation: Are they Morally Equivalent?" *Journal of Applied Philosophy* 18, no.2 (2001): 183–192.

CHAPTER 5

Creation Theory: Do Genetic Ties Matter?

ELIZABETH BRAKE

INTRODUCTION

Procreation has significant costs of a sort which it is generally wrong to impose on others. For most procreators, procreation will be their single largest effect on the environment, adding another lifetime's pollution and drain on resources. When chosen over adoption, procreation also arguably involves failing in a duty to assist—an indirect cost to those waiting to be adopted. A personal project, even one involving caring relationships, does not justify such use of resources or failure to assist. Without a justification, it appears that procreation is impermissible. A natural thought is that the costs can be justified by the value of the parent-child relationship. But there are compelling arguments that genetic ties are morally irrelevant to the value of such a relationship and so cannot justify procreating when adoption is an option; there is no special genetic basis of parenthood. In this chapter I consider what would have to be said to justify procreation; I argue that procreation can sometimes be justified on the basis of genetic ties.

Procreation requires a justification which distinguishes it from adoption (or fostering, a qualification I'll assume henceforth). There are three salient features distinguishing procreation from adoption (in most cases): genetic ties, gestation, or causal responsibility for the existence of the child. Gestation and responsibility, however, are too weak to justify procreation. In favor of gestation, it might be said that its intimacy and its position as the earliest beginning of the parent-child relationship are reasons in favor of it, for those considering whether to adopt or procreate. But an appeal to the value of gestation would only give women, and women who can themselves gestate, justification for procreation. Further, these reasons for gestating do not seem strong enough to justify the costs imposed, as I will argue. Likewise, an appeal to causal responsibility for the child's existence does not seem a good candidate for justifying creating a child. It may be that procreators wish to be so responsible, that they experience pride in making a child themselves. But again, this self-regarding project does not seem like a good reason to impose costs on others. Further, it would be odd for the justification of an outcome to appeal to causal responsibility for the outcome; what needs to be shown is that there is some good reason for producing that outcome.

With these options excluded, it appears that a justification for procreating rather than adopting must appeal to genetic ties. But justifying procreation by appeal to genetic ties is difficult in light of criticisms of initially plausible reasons for seeking a genetically related child. One initially plausible reason for procreating rather than adopting is the thought that there is a special parental relationship with a genetically related child, benefiting the child, the parent, or both. But there have been compelling objections to claims that parenting a genetically related child, as opposed to an adopted child, has special value. If the initially plausible reasons in favor of procreation are discredited, it is difficult to see how the burden of justification can be met and procreation permitted—unless some other justification is found.

Of course, instrumental reasons for procreation, not having to do with the parent-child relationship or the child's interests, can be given. For example, it is sometimes said that procreation is needed to provide the next generation of workers (and secure the current generation's retirement funds). But such reasons are doubly problematic. First, since other people will procreate anyway and people can immigrate, there is no urgent need to procreate; this reason is at best conditional on underpopulation. Second, this treats the child as a mere means. It should not, at least, be the procreators' primary motivation.

In this chapter I seek to develop a justification for procreation which appeals to genetic ties. The justification will not imply that genetic parenting (so to speak) is better for parent or child than adoptive parenting, nor will this justification be a reason for everyone. My point is certainly not that only biological procreation is permissible (part of my aim is to defend assisted reproductive technologies, or ARTs, against certain objections), nor that procreation is superior to adoption. All I want to show is that it is sometimes justifiable to procreate rather than adopt, that there may be a reason to procreate which is not misguided, vicious, or silly. This is particularly important for those who must take steps other than having sex to procreate—such as same-sex partners and single people.

Another way of understanding the problem is this. Many procreators take themselves to have special reason to procreate with their own gametes. But criticisms of the special value of genetic ties to offspring suggest that such procreators are mistaken, and that procreators have just as much reason to adopt as to use their own gametes. The desire for a genetic child is, on this view, an irrational and morally lightweight preference, akin to a desire for a blonde child. To justify procreation when adoption is an option, what has to be shown is that there is some good reason to procreate with one's own gametes.

Two clarifications. This discussion has no implications for the legal right to procreative autonomy. Forced abortion or contraception violates bodily integrity. But the fact that the choice to procreate should be legally protected does not entail that it is morally justified. Second, terms such as "a child genetically one's own" or "genetic child" need clarification. I am focusing on producing a child genetically linked to oneself—which could be done by using a sibling's gametes as well as one's own. While the focus is on genetics, not gestation, this is not a clean distinction, as a gestational mother contributes mitochondrial DNA to an implanted embryo.

In the second section, I review the problem of negative procreative externalities. In the next section, I review some arguments undermining the initially plausible reasons for procreating. My task in these sections is to show that these arguments, taken together, make it extremely difficult to justify procreation. In the fourth section, I sketch a possible reason to procreate, and in the final section I assess whether this reason can in fact meet the burden of justification.

NEGATIVE EXTERNALITIES OF PROCREATION

The largest impact most people will have on the future of their society, the planet, even the species, is through procreation. While this impact is largely unpredictable, one effect is predictable: there will be a significant environmental cost associated with creating another person. Procreation will be the single largest effect most procreators have on the environment; even an extravagant non-procreator will normally consume far fewer resources than a procreator.

Procreation foreseeably entails costs which are clearly unjustifiable in other contexts. So argues Thomas Young: "Since having even just one child in an affluent household usually produces environmental impacts comparable to what mainstream environmentalists consider to be an intuitively unacceptable level of consumption, resource depletion, and waste, they should also oppose human reproduction."[1] Young compares the childless "Greens" with the otherwise identical "Grays," who have two children: "The average American consumes 4,000 barrels of oil in his or her lifetime (about eighty years), or 50 barrels a year." While the Greens will together consume 8,000 barrels, the Grays will consume 16,000 (not counting consumption by any further descendants). Moreover, "the same logic applies to food intake, sewage waste, CO_2 generation, fossil fuel consumption, mineral use, landfill deposits, and so on."[2]

It might be objected that procreation has positive externalities, such as replenishing the labor force, and so it does not simply waste resources. However, as other people will procreate anyway or immigrate, such reasons cannot justify procreation unless underpopulation threatens. Currently, overpopulation is more of a threat—the U.S. Census Bureau predicts a global population of over 9 billion by 2050, prompting concerns that there will be a global food shortage.[3] I set aside the threat of underpopulation as—currently—unrealistic.

If it is wrong to impose large resource costs without a good reason, procreation is wrong—without a good reason. But why is it wrong to impose such environmental costs? For one thing, citizens of the developed world already use more than their fair share of planetary resources, including the environment's capacity to absorb pollution and carbon dioxide.[4] On these grounds, Christine Overall has argued for a one-child-per-person limit. However, it is not clear how it can be permissible for members of the developed world to have even one child, given that they thereby increase their already-unfair share of resources. Overall defends a reason to have children—the special nature of the parent-child relationship. But such relationships can be pursued through adoption, without adding a significant resource cost.[5]

Someone defending the one-child-per-person rate might respond that there is a difference between procreation and adoption. Such a person might argue that gestation provides a closer, more exclusive, relationship with the child. But even temporarily granting this (until the next section) for the sake of argument, this doesn't seem a strong enough interest to justify the use of significant environmental resources. The relationship in question is valuable mainly to the parent and the child.

An analogy will show that a self-regarding personal project does not justify a large unfair use of resources. Imagine that I could pursue a project important to me, but only at the cost of doubling my use of environmental resources. (And let us stipulate that my share of such resources is already unfairly large, as it undoubtedly is given my typical North American lifestyle.) Perhaps I want to drive a Hummer to the peak of every mountain in North America, or launch a performance art piece involving thousands of small motors which will run in perpetuity, or buy up and burn massive amounts of goods from Wal-Mart. Even if these pursuits produce some aesthetic or hedonic benefits, they are fundamentally projects whose main reward, such as it is, is to me. And it is highly questionable whether my personal fulfillment—given that I can pursue many less costly projects—can justify such costs.

Of course, parenting involves a caring relationship in which virtues are typically developed and exercised. But even such a project can't justify unfair resource use. Consider a modified example:

> *Flying gourmets*: Two friends fly a small plane to all the natural wonders they can, thereby developing and exercising mutual care, resourcefulness, prudence, self-reliance, and trust. During their travels, they consume as many exotic and gourmet foods as possible, developing virtues of openness and appreciation (though perhaps not moderation!). The goal of these expeditions is to develop these virtues within a caring relationship. The journeys double the friends' lifetime use of oil, "food intake, sewage waste, CO_2 generation, fossil fuel consumption, mineral use, landfill deposits, and so on."[6]

Despite its aims of developing virtues within a relationship, the project still seems unjustifiably wasteful. There are many eco-friendly ways the friends could have pursued the same goals—hiking, for example. It could be responded that, while the friends could go hiking instead, a parental relationship can only be established through procreation, and parental virtues can only be developed and exercised through procreation. But it is precisely these points which critiques of geneticism and bionormativity (discussed later) attack: adoptive parents are equally parents. Further, even if parental virtues could only be exercised through procreation, it is still not clear that the pursuit of one's own eudaimonia can justify unfair use of resources.

Let us return to the question of unfair use of environmental resources. It is difficult to know where to set the baseline of fair use: an equal share, or appropriation up to the point at which others are made worse off. One can fill in one's favorite account of fair resource allocation here. But without specifying the baseline, the argument can proceed by analogy. Procreation is like using resources in the flying friends example; to see what is required to justify procreation, we must ask what could justify the use of resources in the example.

It might be thought that there is a second, competing claim of fairness here, that one child per person, Overall's suggested limit, is simply each person's fair procreative share. One shouldn't have to forgo one's fair share simply because other people will procreate thoughtlessly.[7] But why should we think that there must be a fair share of procreating, any more than there is, say, a fair share of sexual activity, or of eating a delicacy like sweetbreads, or of climbing Mt. Everest? There are many things we can do with our bodies, but that does not generate an entitlement to do them. Here the objector might point to the unique goods of procreation. However, if the arguments reviewed in the next section hold, the goods of parenting are not unique to procreation, but can be had through adoption.

Procreation has another kind of cost: producing a new child who absorbs parental resources deprives children waiting to be adopted of potential parents. Of course, it might be objected that procreators do not owe the waiting children anything. But failing to adopt is arguably a failure of the duty to assist those in need: "We can protect parentless children from serious harm at little cost to ourselves by adopting them."[8] While adoption may be costly for those who do not intend to have children, for those who are contemplating parenthood already, it simply shifts resources which the would-be parents plan to spend anyway.

Considerable personal resources are involved in procreation. The estimated cost of rearing a child in the United States is $435,030 to $1.8 million.[9] While small expenditures lie within the realm of moral discretion, such large outlays seem to require moral justification. Return to the flying friends analogy, stipulating that their expenditures are equivalent to what it costs to raise a child. This use of funds seems open to moral criticism. The flying friends could have pursued their goals less expensively—buying hiking boots instead of small planes—and used the surplus hundreds of thousands of dollars to assist others. If adoptive parenting and genetic parenting are on a par, opting for the latter requires some justification.

There are numerous objections to a duty to adopt. Not everyone has the skills or resources or the willingness to parent. Given this, the duty to assist those waiting to be adopted falls upon those who do have those skills, resources, and willingness to rear a child. There is also the question of feasibility. Adoption may be difficult, especially for single people or same-sex partners. If someone can't adopt, they do not do wrong in not adopting. But Daniel Friedrich responds that the difficulty of adoption entails a duty to improve the system rather than dissolving the duty. Friedrich points out that there are many more "adoptable" children outside the adoption system than children within the system.[10] However, asking someone to forgo parenting entirely while they work to create institutions of adoption is too steep a cost. (Some very stringent views might still hold that the parenting project should be sacrificed in order to aid as many children as possible, but this seems to demand too much.) The duty to adopt is conditional on feasibility. But while the duty to assist should not be so stringent as to make all personal projects impossible, if a personal project can be pursued in a way which fulfills the duty, it should be, unless there is good reason not to.

These two cost-based reasons against procreation cannot be answered in the absence of a *pro tanto* justification for procreating. This must be more than a mere preference, since a mere preference to use an extra 4,000 barrels of oil or spend $1 million on a project would not morally justify doing so. If there is no such justification, then the costs to the environment and to existing children waiting for adoption give strong moral reason against procreation.

It might be thought that the value of producing one's own genetic child justifies the costs. But the value of genetic ties is controversial. Some ethicists, for instance, have criticized seeking a genetic child through ART. But if the value of having a genetic child can't justify ART, it can't justify procreation without ART either. The costs of ART are only a small fraction of the overall costs of procreation.

REJECTING BIONORMATIVITY

Criticism of the value of genetic ties arises in several ethical debates. One is the question of who is a child's moral parent. Many bioethicists have argued compellingly against geneticism, or the view that genetic ties are necessary or sufficient for moral parenthood. A second debate is over whether adopted children are worse off, or adoptive parenting less valuable, for lack of a genetic tie. A third concerns ART. Critics of ARTs have argued that seeking a genetic child is a vanity project, and a scientifically misguided one at that. These arguments make it difficult to justify procreation. If genetic parenting has no special value, no relation to moral parental status, and does not benefit the child, then what could justify procreation?

In rejecting geneticism, Michael Austin, for example, writes that the "mere genetic connection is neither necessary nor sufficient for parenthood."[11] Austin allows some significance to the biological tie, because "we" value it: "Biological or genetic connections may be important to us because they constitute an important part of begetting and rearing a child, but the most important components of parenthood are its social, moral, and relational aspects."[12] But moral parenthood—possession of moral parental rights and obligations—does not require a genetic tie (adoptive parents are moral parents), nor does a genetic tie entail moral parenthood (gamete donors are not moral parents).

What other moral significance might genetic ties have? Perhaps it is that genetic ties forge a special connection between genetic parent and child. On Barbara Hall's view, the moral basis of parental rights is self-ownership: parents "provide the constitutive genetic material."[13] Charitably interpreting this, Kolers and Bayne speculate that someone might think that "genetic relations are (metaphysically) deeper than mere material ones. . . . This point is surely behind many geneticist intuitions, but it is not convincing." Identical twins, who share a genome, differ in many ways: "Individuation is not solely a genetic phenomenon: neither genes nor environment act independently in development or individuation; rather, they interact. There is no genetic development without environmental contribution, and no material development without genetic contribution."[14] An adopted child sharing my environment is as much mine, in the sense of a shared identity, as a child sharing my genes. Similarly, Sally Haslanger rejects David Velleman's view that it is wrong to create a child who will not know its biological parent because genetic ties are crucial to identity. Haslanger points out that we can forge identity in many ways.

If genetic ties are irrelevant to moral parental status or to the parent-child connection, what reason is there not to adopt instead? Rejecting geneticism seems to imply that procreation cannot be justified when adoption is an option.[15] Even worse, criticisms of geneticism and bionormativity suggest that procreation may be downright vicious. They point out that there is no guarantee that a child genetically one's own will have the desired characteristics. Moreover, they allege that seeking to reproduce one's own traits involves motives antithetical to parental virtues.

Attacking "bionormativity," Haslanger "resist[s] new ideologies that entrench and naturalize the value of biological ties."[16] She suggests that valuing genetic ties for the similarities they produce is often deluded: "Judgments of similarity should be viewed with caution. In the case of racial or ethnic identity, the belief in shared 'blood' provides a myth of commonality. Myths of commonality run rampant in families. And such myths of commonality trace politically significant contours."[17] Not only are perceptions of similarity often projections, they are informed by problematic assumptions about racial and gender traits. While Haslanger explicitly states that she does not mean to criticize the nuclear family itself, but rather the bionormative judgment that it is "universal, necessary, and good,"[18] her reasoning implies that another potential justification for procreation—reproducing family similarities—is grounded in delusion and stereotyping. Overall also argues that procreating to pass on a genetic link, hoping to create a child like oneself, reflects misconceptions about genetics. She writes: "There is no guarantee that offspring will inherit their parents' abilities or that, even having inherited them, they will decide to act upon them."

Moreover, Overall suggests that such a desire may be vain: "Is anyone's biological composition so valuable that it must be perpetuated?"[19] Indeed, "the assumption itself that one's genetic inheritance is inherently good and worth preserving no matter what is conceived."[20] Austin rejects a defense of the special value of genetic parenthood for similar reasons. According to Edgar Page, "A biological connection between the parent and child . . . is crucial to the value parenthood has for us."[21] Adoption, Page writes, "is bound to be second best to natural parenthood."[22] On Page's view, "the biological connection that exists between natural parents and their child" is significant because "parents . . . create a whole person in their own likeness, in which they see a part of themselves."[23] But Austin rejects this: "if our valuing of biological parenthood is grounded in a desire to create someone in our own likeness, then that valuing is morally problematic . . . The desire to create a child in our own likeness is overly narcissistic."[24]

Overall also raises the concern that a parent who expects a child to fit a certain template may fail to respect the child's individuality; expecting the child to have specific traits is, Overall suggests, likely to result in bad parenting. Similar concerns arise in the literature on genetic engineering and human reproductive cloning: for example, The President's Council on Bioethics warns of the dangers of parental attempts to "control" their offspring genetically.[25] Similarly, Page's defense of "natural" parenthood suggests that parents should be open and accepting, not fixated on certain traits. He argues that adoption is a choice, and so inferior in this respect, whereas procreation involves accepting inescapable genetic destiny. One does not choose one's genetic child conditionally, but accepts it just as it comes. Thus "natural parenthood" involves an openness or acceptance which adoption does not. However, as Austin points out, both kinds of child rearing are chosen, and one can be as accepting of and committed to an adopted child as to a genetic child. (Skeptics might read Henry James' *What Maisie Knew*, in which Maisie's step-parents are more committed to her than her genetic parents.)

Charges that parental hopes of passing on family traits are misguided, conceived, or politically problematic are overstated. First, while genetic outcomes are unpredictable (at least until conception has occurred, and with current technology), this does not mean there is no basis for reasonable expectation of a family resemblance. Procreation tends to produce similarities based on genetics. Families may mistake—and thereby mythologize—such likenesses, mistaking nurture for nature or seeing likenesses which do not exist; but this does not mean that genetics are altogether irrelevant. Empirically, genetics matter. Genes make it more likely a child will have certain traits or family resemblances. Of course, they do not guarantee that the child will have these traits, and genetically unrelated children may have the desired traits. But a genetically related child is likely to have some traits linking them to ancestors—an aunt's hair, or a grandfather's nose, or a brother's stride. (Consider the way we speak—when a child's hair resembles his aunt's we say he has "his aunt's hair." Is it that the color is just like his aunt's rare and distinctive shade? Or is it that we imagine, somehow, the hair has travelled via the gene from aunt to child?)

Not only do genes influence physiological traits, they underpin behavior and personality traits. In a recent twin study in behavioral genetics, researchers investigated links between genetics and eudaimonia (citing Aristotle, no less!) and found that "psychological well-being is underpinned by a general genetic factor influencing self-control, and four underlying biological mechanisms enabling the psychological capabilities of purpose, agency, growth, and positive social relations." For the traits in question, the "effects of shared environment were weak and nonsignificant."[26] It is reasonable, in the light of genetics, for parents to assume a likelihood of passing on some traits, including behavioral traits, on a "family resemblance" basis. Such an empirically based assumption need not entail that parents will reject a child lacking such resemblance.

The objection assumes that procreators seeking to pass on a genetic tie expect to pass on specific traits such as mathematical aptitude. But this is uncharitable to the expectations of prospective parents. Presumably many procreators do want a genetic tie. Presumably many who could adopt choose to procreate because they want a genetic child, and this likely has something to do with expectations regarding genetically heritable traits. (In some cases, of course, it may be due to the difficulty of adoption, but I suspect many procreators do simply want a child with a genetic tie.) But it seems implausible that such procreators are either scientifically naïve or hubristic enough to expect a "mini-me" or that they expect a child to inherit any specific trait, such as mathematical aptitude.

Presumably, prospective parents do not expect their children to inherit specific traits so much as some set of traits linking them to the parent, procreative partner, and extended family. Most prospective biological pro-creators probably assume that a child will have some traits they recognize, in new combinations. This is after all how Wittgenstein derives the con-cept of "family resemblance": "We see a complicated network of similari-ties overlapping and criss-crossing: similarities in the large and in the small. I can think of no better expression to describe these similarities than 'family resemblances'; for the various resemblances between mem-bers of a family – build, features, colour of eyes, gait, temperament, and so on and so forth – overlap and criss-cross in the same way."[27] So long as procreators understand the possible variations—perhaps considering the variety in their own genetic families—their expectations may be reasona-ble and not harmfully rigid.

The claim that procreating to pass on genetic traits must rely on a mis-understanding of genetics should be rejected. I turn now to the normative claim that seeking to reproduce one's own or family traits is either con-ceited or politically problematic. The desire to have a child like oneself may be narcissistic, as Austin and Overall suggest, although even this seems too fast. An introvert could hope for a similar child because they would understand each other better; one could want a child like oneself to im-prove the parent-child relationship. Such desires are not inherently nar-cissistic. They are just unrealistic, as the relevant traits may not emerge. But the procreator may also wish to reproduce her ancestors' or partner's genes, or those of a friend who donates gametes. Vanity or conceit need not be involved at all.

Haslanger's worry is that perceptions of family traits reflect assump-tions about racial characteristics. A perception of one's ancestors as hard-working, for example, may be shaped by cultural representations of mem-bers of one's ethnicity. Moreover, traits themselves shaped by culture may be mistaken as genetic; the assumption that feminine traits are genetic is faulty to the extent that femininity is shaped by culture. But these worries are not decisive. First, even procreation for racial or ethnic reasons need not be racist (though it may be racialist), if motivated by the belief that one's own group is threatened by dominant racism. Second, desiring to reproduce family traits is not inherently racialist. While we may be influ-enced by racialist stereotypes, we may also accurately perceive personal resemblances. (To the extent that all of our perceptions are informed by racialism, there is a much bigger problem which I bracket here.)

We can now clarify what a procreative justification must involve. So far, I have argued that a justification must appeal to genetic ties to dis-tinguish procreation from adoption. In this section, we have seen many candidates for the moral relevance of genetic ties rejected: a special link with parenthood or identity, the value of the parent-child relationship, or reproducing specific traits. The best candidate for the moral relevance of genetic ties is likely something to do with genetically heritable traits. It is reasonable to assume that some "family resemblance" is likely but unreasonable to expect any specific traits (excepting dominant ones), so the genetic tie can only reasonably figure as making family resemblance likely.

A critic might object that, given the possibility no family resemblance will emerge, this expectation is too weak to serve as a reason. But this sets too high a standard for decision-making. We often make decisions with far less likelihood of a specific outcome and far greater indeterminacy. Life's great ventures are usually like this. For example, we can predict how a prospective spouse might behave in the future, but people change; we make medical decisions based on statistical likelihoods, not certainties; and so on. From a deontological standpoint, a reasonable expectation of bringing about some good may be enough to serve as a justification.

Of course, even if the motive of reproducing a family resemblance is reasonable and not vicious, it still needs to provide a justification. What is the good to be brought about? How could reproducing a family resemblance justify the costs of procreation? In the next section, I argue that the genetic tie, together with the very same fact that generates the moral problem with procreation—its great impact on the future—can also generate *pro tanto* justification for procreation. (By *pro tanto*, I mean that it provides justification to some extent. But at the same time, it may ultimately be outweighed by other considerations.)

PROCREATION AS WORLD CREATION

What can be said in favor of procreation, other than preference, instinct, or a desire to continue the family line? Such relatively trivial reasons look unlikely to justify it in the face of its costs. Here I sketch a good reason which is also likely reasonably faithful to the intentions of many procreators. Let me be clear: the justification does not entail that procreation is superior to adoption, only that there is a reason which in some cases serves as a *pro tanto* justification. This reason does not hold for everyone, but only in some cases where people want to procreate. Hence it is not pro-natalist, urging procreation on everyone. This justification could still be defeated if the costs became great enough—for example, during environmental crisis.

A procreative justification needs to extend beyond the personal project of parenting. No matter how good the parent-child relationship is, it is difficult to see how a personal project affecting a few people justifies using resources unfairly and failing in a duty to assist (this is also why the experience of gestation is not a good justification). But one morally striking feature of procreation is precisely its impact on others: it is the largest impact most procreators will have on the future. Could this impact include benefits which justify the costs?

Procreation shapes the future by populating it. It is a direct contribution to the gene pool and to the future agents who will make decisions changing the world. Once again, this could be taken to give instrumental reason to procreate, such as replenishing the labor force. But, as we saw, these instrumental reasons (currently) seem empirically far-fetched, and they do not discriminate between procreating and saving lives. Further, such reasons treat the child as a means to an end; the primary reason for procreating should not be instrumental. Does creating the future population have any justificatory force which does not rely on treating the child as a mere means?

The natural thought is that producing ethical and environmentally conscious children will have good effects as they go on to shape the future, and, as virtuous agents, they are valuable in themselves. This faces the objection that parents cannot predict what their children will value and how they will act. This objection may overstate the case: one can at least ensure children are informed and develop good habits. But there is another problem with this line of thought: it does not justify procreating as opposed to adopting or contributing to environmental awareness campaigns.

To justify procreation, the reason must involve reproducing a family resemblance, or aspects of one's family mixed with aspects of one's loved ones. This is how many philosophers have approached procreation.[28] The couple sees themselves blended in their offspring, their union made actual. Such a view has lent itself to problematic claims for the superiority of biological procreation, as in new natural law theory. However, setting aside the wilder claims made on behalf of procreation, is there any good reason for the aim of reproducing a family resemblance?

The objection might arise immediately that seeking a family resemblance is inherently problematic because it may lead to treating the child as a mere means, a vessel conveying traits. This seems to be the heart of worries such as Overall's—someone aiming to reproduce traits will value the child only for those traits, and only if it has the desired ones. But a child can be accepted and valued in itself as a unique individual with family traits. By analogy, we can value a David Hockney painting as typical of Hockney while still valuing it in itself as a unique work. We could commission a new work by Hockney, assuming we will value it for the reasons we value his other work, while realizing that this painting may radically diverge from his previous work. Our connection of the new, unique work to other Hockneys can enhance our appreciation of it and sense of its value, while we also admire what is new in it. Valuing inherited traits in a new and distinct individual is not at odds with accepting his or her individuality.

Still, what value beyond personal satisfaction might there be in reproducing genetic traits of loved ones in a new being? Let us return to the analogy with artistic creation. One might commission a painting for many reasons—as an investment, to enhance one's reputation as a connoisseur, simple delight. But one might also hope that the painting will add something of value to the world, that an additional Hockney will be of value to posterity. And we may hope that this valuable work will have further good effects, training future eyes to see Hockney better, allowing one more minor museum to display a Hockney. This is an aesthetic justification. Can we say anything comparable in the case of creating a person—that doing so adds something of value to the world?

Of course, on most moral theories all humans are of value, in some sense. So creating a human is, inherently, creating something of value. But this is too coarse-grained a reason to justify procreating with one's own genetic materials as opposed to saving already-existing valuable lives. Let's consider a more fine-grained justification. Procreators, who are populating the future, might contribute to a good future by passing on their genes. One way they might do so is by creating future people who will make good choices and be virtuous agents, prudent environmental stewards, peaceful, courageous, and so on—today's procreators might produce agents who will make the future world better. In addition to having good side effects through the agency of offspring, procreation might also make the world better directly, by creating individuals who bear qualities good in themselves, which they in turn may pass on to further descendants. The offspring are, like the Hockney, doubly valuable—valuable for their effects, and in themselves.

The thought that some human traits are valuable in themselves, in a morally relevant way, needs development. This thought is compatible with asserting moral equality. By analogy, the Hockney might share in the generic value (whatever that is) of being a great work of art while also embodying specific values of distinctively Hockneyesque light and color and composition. So too the offspring might share in the value humans have simply as humans, but also embody specific valuable traits such as an aunt's temperament or a brother's fortitude. Some genetic traits do not seem likely to justify procreation—for example, aesthetic preference for blond hair and blue eyes seems morally lightweight, a taste, not a justification. But there are many different genetic traits—qualities of temperament, for instance—which are plausibly valuable in their relation to moral character and to societal benefit. Consider the study claiming to show that the bases of eudaimonia are genetic; psychological well-being and self-control are surely valuable, for the agent and in social relations.[29] Some traits might be admirable in themselves; others valuable for the pleasure they give others, the good they might produce in the world, or their support of moral agency. There are many bases of value here, the promotion of which could be enjoined (for instance) by a Kantian imperfect duty to promote the good of humanity.

Intending to pass on such valuable traits on a family resemblance basis is at least relevant as a justification for procreation. The general motive of creating a good future through parenting can of course be shared by adoptive parents or procreators using anonymous gamete donors—it does not uniquely apply to procreation. Procreators could share such a motive, believing that reproducing their genes will benefit the world, without conceit or narcissism. In reflecting on which traits are valuable, people might well be drawn to the traits of loved ones—family, their partner, a friend who donates gametes. Their specific imagination of goodness, of virtuous and prudent agents, might draw on such familiar traits. And so they may seek to pass on these traits, through genes or through upbringing.

Assuming there is a large plurality of valuable human traits, different procreators will be sensitive to the value of different traits. Not everyone will appreciate the same traits in the same way; people will appreciate different traits due to their ancestral familiarity or presence in a friend or partner. Thus, the fact that different procreators value different traits is compatible with there being a large plurality of valuable traits. People are attuned by experience to different sub-sets.

Once again, the objection arises that qualities of loved ones can equally be cultivated in adopted children. To justify procreation, the expected traits must be genetic—temperament, aptitudes, behavior. But one cannot know which traits one's genetic offspring will have. Rather than sweet Aunt Ruby, the child might take after curmudgeonly Uncle Oscar. To be subjectively justified, the procreator must have reason to be optimistic about how traits will appear and recombine in the new person. This limits the possible scope of the justification—potential procreators whose family mainly possesses vicious, unredeemable qualities would lack this justification. (Genetic technology may help here: while the justification does not require genetic enhancement in all cases—it does not require maximizing valuable traits, just that they be good enough—perhaps enhancement could provide justification for those uncertain about passing on valuable traits.)

It is possible that a procreator may be mistaken in her belief that her choice is justified. Procreators may be wrong in these attributions of value (as Overall and Haslanger suggest). They may overvalue their family. Overall calls the belief that one's own genes are worth passing on "conceited"; while valuing loved ones' traits is not conceited, it may be deluded. In that case, procreators would be subjectively but not objectively justified. A pressing question in any instance is whether procreators are objectively correct in their belief that their genetic inheritance is likely to produce valuable qualities.

A further worry arises here. Talk of genetic traits worth passing on suggests a vicious eugenics.[30] But on my account, justification can be had by all procreators who might pass on valuable family traits—justification is not limited to any group, and there is no reason to think valuable traits would fall along racial or ethnic lines. But the deeper worry concerning eugenics is that any talk of objective justification, any suggestion that some genes are objectively worth passing on, lends itself to invidious rankings of genes. Given the history of eugenics, concern is merited; but conceptually, we can hold that certain genetically heritable traits are valuable without linking those traits to race or ethnicity and with no implications for wrongful eugenic methods (and we can vigorously oppose such methods and such racial or ethnic claims). While this point overlaps with debates over disability which I cannot do justice to here, my position is that valuing a trait such as mental health is compatible with the claim that those lacking such a trait are morally equal, and even with valuing mentally unhealthy traits in different respects (such as a connection to creativity). The pluralism I envision comprehends attributing value to (for example) traits of children with Down's syndrome, or deaf children, or children with other heritable impairments. Passing on these traits might be a way to enrich the future with different perspectives and strengths.

Valuing ancestral traits need not involve a vicious ranking of ancestors, or even of traits. Choosing the good is not a matter of consulting a catalogue, selecting from and ranking a varied random assortment of goods; rather, we think back to what we have known that is good. Different families provide different windows into the plurality of valuable human traits. We can believe that a child resembling our family will have qualities that are good in themselves, without thereby assigning lower rankings to other good qualities. (Is this valuing the child only for its qualities? No more than valuing the Hockney for its Hockneyesque color and brushwork does—these qualities constitute it.) The thought that some genes are worth passing on need not involve a ranking of valuable traits, but a pluralistic theory of value.

So far, we can say that procreation might be subjectively justified if procreators reasonably believe the genetic outcome is likely good enough to justify the costs, and objectively justified if their belief is accurate. But could the outcome ever justify the costs?

CAN WE EVER JUSTIFY PROCREATION?

If humans are not facing extinction or underpopulation, but instead overpopulation, how could creating valuable lives justify the costs to the environment and to children waiting for adoption? While procreation affects the future, one could have a much greater effect by saving many lives. According to Peter Singer's website, "The Life You Can Save," $1865 can save one life from malaria;[31] $1 million could create one valuable person (if that is what it costs to rear a child) or save 500 valuable people from malaria. It would be hubris to claim the one life is more valuable than the 500. Given these figures, combined with the harms consequent on the environmental costs, it will be near-impossible for a consequentialist to defend procreation (unless the costs are reduced, or the situation changes greatly; of course, there will be environmental harms from saving many lives, but these likely won't outweigh the expected utility of the extra lives—leading us into repugnant conclusion territory). Can a nonconsequentialist fare better in justifying procreation?

The answer depends on what can justify failing to assist and using resources unfairly. To justify procreation, the expectation of future good from one's personal project must be able to justify failing to assist. Let's return to the flying friends example and imagine that the friends intend to make the world better through their flights—perhaps by raising consciousness for Amnesty International. They reasonably believe that some good will come from their endeavors. But they could instead have saved 500 lives from malaria. Are these friends failing in their duty to assist? The duty to assist is an imperfect duty, allowing latitude. In my view, moral perfection would require donating the funds to malaria prevention rather than pursuing the uncertain awareness-raising project, but we are not required to be morally perfect. Likewise, moral perfection might require adoption, but the procreator has justification for pursuing his project so long as he reasonably expects some good to come of it. This does not get him off the hook entirely: he must still assist in some other way with his remaining resources.

What about the environmental costs? We have moral reason to limit unfair use of resources. Environmental fairness surely requires limiting numbers of children. But perhaps producing valuable persons who will likely have good effects can justify some unfair use of resources. By analogy, driving further to a farmers' market uses more fuel but may be justified because it supports change in farming practices. Whether producing valuable citizens can justify the costs will depend on how grave the predictable harms of the resource use are, whether we can "pay back" what we have taken from the general store, and whether we have wrought irreparable damage. We might be required, for example, to purchase carbon offsets for each child. And procreators might be required to decrease their use of resources to offset the costs of procreation—taking the child on short trips near home rather than flying long distances, becoming vegetarian, and so forth. Whatever environmental efforts are required already by fairness, procreators might be required to do even more.

The *pro tanto* justification for procreation which I have sketched is the reproduction of valuable genetic traits in the future population. There are many problems with it: the uncomfortable implication that those who will not pass on valuable traits have no justification to procreate, the need for a theory of which genetically heritable traits are valuable, the uncertainty of family resemblances. But, despite these problems, here's the thing: given the costs of procreation, there must be some good justification for it, a purpose that can't be pursued through adoption, a reason that justifies creating a person. What could such a reason be if not grounded in the traits such a person might have and the thought that those traits might produce goods justifying the costs? As far as I can see, the account of justification sketched here is the most plausible one available.[32]

NOTES

1. Thomas Young, "Overconsumption and Procreation: Are They Morally Equivalent?," *Journal of Applied Philosophy* 18, no. 2 (2001): 183. See also Corey MacIver, "Procreation as Appropriation," and David Benatar, "The Misanthropic Argument for Anti-natalism," in this volume.
2. Young, "Overconsumption," 190.
3. See U.S. Census Bureau data at: http://www.census.gov/population/international/data/worldpop/graph_population.php. On food security, see the UN factsheet: http://www.un.org/waterforlifedecade/food_security.shtml
4. The environmental effects of such resource consumption are also harmful. By contributing to climate change, increasing landfills, polluting, and using water,

we foreseeably make small contributions to harming others. See John Broome, *Climate Matters: Ethics in a Warming World* (New York: Norton, 2012). Here I focus on constraints of fairness.

5. Christine Overall, *Why Have Children?: The Ethical Debate* (Cambridge, MA: MIT Press, 2012), 180–184, 212–217.
6. Young, "Overconsumption," 190.
7. Thanks to Cheshire Calhoun for this objection.
8. Daniel Friedrich, "A Duty to Adopt?" *Journal of Applied Philosophy* 30, no. 1 (2013): 25.
9. See http://bucks.blogs.nytimes.com/2012/11/13/the-cost-in-dollars-of-raising-a-child/. The lower number is the U.S. government estimate, the higher that of the *New York Times* journalist.
10. Friedrich, "A Duty to Adopt?" 34.
11. Michael Austin, "The Failure of Biological Accounts of Parenthood," *Journal of Value Inquiry* 38, no. 4 (2004): 499; for other examples see Elizabeth Brake, "Fatherhood and Child Support: Do Men Have a Right to Choose?" *Journal of Applied Philosophy* 22 no. 1 (2005); Giulianna Fuscaldo, "Genetic Ties: Are They Morally Binding?" *Bioethics* 20 no. 2 (2006), J. L. Hill, "What Does it Mean to be a 'Parent'?"; and Avery Kolers and Tim Bayne, "'Are You My Mommy?' On the Genetic Basis of Parenthood," *Journal of Applied Philosophy* 18 no. 3 (2001).
12. Austin, "Biological Accounts," 507.
13. Kolers and Bayne, "Are You my Mommy," 276, citing Barbara Hall, "The Origin of Parental Rights," *Public Affairs Quarterly* 13, no. 1 (1999): 74–78.
14. Kolers and Bayne, "Are You my Mommy," 277.
15. It also appears to undermine widely held assumptions about parental rights. As Anca Gheaus asks: "If parenthood and parenthood-related rights are justified by appeal to children's interests [rather than genetic ties], why not allocate babies, at birth, to those who would be the 'best' parents?" Anca Gheaus, "The Right to Parent One's Biological Baby," *Journal of Political Philosophy* 20 no. 4 (2012): 434.
16. Sally Haslanger, "Family, Ancestry and Self: What is the Moral Significance of Biological Ties?," *Adoption & Culture* 2, no. 1 (2009): 4, accessed November 1, 2013, http://dspace.mit.edu/handle/1721.1/64650.
17. Haslanger, "Family, Ancestry and Self," 16.
18. Ibid., 30.
19. Overall, *Why Have Children?*, 61.
20. Ibid., 62.
21. Edgar Page, "Donation, Surrogacy, and Adoption," *Journal of Applied Philosophy* 2, no.2 (1985): 171. Cited in Austin, "Biological Accounts," 509.
22. Ibid., 171.
23. Austin, "Biological Accounts," 508.
24. Ibid., 509.
25. The President's Council on Bioethics, *Human Cloning and Human Dignity: An Ethical Inquiry* (Washington, D.C., 2002), accessed November 1, 2013, http://bioethics.georgetown.edu/pcbe/reports/cloningreport/, Chapter 5, 75–116.
26. Despina Archontaki, Gary Lewis, and Timothy Bates, "Genetic Influences on Psychological Well-Being: A Nationally Representative Twin Study," *Journal of Personality* 81, no. 2 (2012): 221.
27. Ludwig Wittgenstein, *Philosophical Investigations*, trans. G. E. M. Anscombe, P. M. S. Hacker, and Joachim Schulte (Oxford: Blackwell, 2009), 36.

28. There is a long philosophical tradition, contemporary representatives being new natural lawyers (such as John Finnis) and Edgar Page, "Parental Rights," *Journal of Applied Philosophy* 1, no. 2 (1984).

29. Archontaki, Lewis and Bates, "Genetic Influences."

30. See Overall, *Why Have Children?*, 62. Feminists criticize pro-natalist pressure on women to conceive and bear children pointing, for example, to the "self-blame" it can produce. See Carolyn McLeod and Julie Ponesse, "Infertility and Moral Luck: The Politics of Women Blaming Themselves for Infertility," *International Journal of Feminist Approaches to Bioethics* 1, no. 1 (2008): 126–144.

31. http://www.thelifeyoucansave.org/WheretoDonate.aspx

32. Many thanks to the fellow contributors to this volume and the editors for their insightful and constructive comments.

REFERENCES

Archontaki, Despina, Gary Lewis, and Timothy Bates. "Genetic Influences on Psychological Well-Being: A Nationally Representative Twin Study," *Journal of Personality* 81, no: 2 (2012): 221–230.

Austin, Michael. "The Failure of Biological Accounts of Parenthood," *The Journal of Value Inquiry* 38, no. 4 (2004): 499–510.

Benatar, David. *Better Never to Have Been*. Oxford: Clarendon, 2006.

Brake, Elizabeth. "Fatherhood and Child Support: Do Men Have a Right to Choose?" *Journal of Applied Philosophy* 22, no.1 (2005): 55–73.

Brighouse, Harry, and Adam Swift. "Parents' Rights and the Value of the Family," *Ethics* 117, no. 1 (2006): 80–108.

Broome, John. *Climate Matters: Ethics in a Warming World*. New York: Norton, 2012.

Friedrich, Daniel. "A Duty to Adopt?" *Journal of Applied Philosophy* 30, no. 1 (2013): 25–39.

Fuscaldo, Giulianna. "Genetic Ties: Are they Morally Binding?" *Bioethics* 20, no.2 (2006): 64–76.

Gheaus, Anca. "The Right to Parent One's Biological Baby," *Journal of Political Philosophy* 20, no. 4 (2012): 432–455.

Hall, Barbara. "The Origin of Parental Rights." *Public Affairs Quarterly* 13, no. 1 (1999): 73–82.

Haslanger, Sally. "Family, Ancestry and Self: What is the Moral Significance of Biological Ties?" *Adoption & Culture* 2, no. 1 (2009). Accessed November 1, 2013, http://dspace.mit.edu/handle/1721.1/64650.

Hill, J. L. "What Does it Mean to Be a 'Parent'? The Claims of Biology as a Basis for Parental Rights," *New York University Law Review* 66, no. 3 (1991): 353–420.

Kolers, Avery, and Tim Bayne. "'Are You My Mommy?' On the Genetic Basis of Parenthood," *Journal of Applied Philosophy* 18, no. 3 (2001): 273–285.

McLeod, Carolyn, and Julie Ponesse. "Infertility and Moral Luck: The Politics of Women Blaming Themselves for Infertility," *International Journal of Feminist Approaches to Bioethics* 1, no.1 (2008): 126–144.

Overall, Christine. *Why Have Children?: The Ethical Debate*. Cambridge, MA: MIT Press, 2012.

Page, Edgar. "Parental Rights," *Journal of Applied Philosophy* 1 no. 2 (1984): 187–203.

Page, Edgar. "Donation, Surrogacy, and Adoption," *Journal of Applied Philosophy* 2 no. 2 (1985): 161–172.

The President's Council on Bioethics. *Human Cloning and Human Dignity: An Ethical Inquiry.* Washington, D.C., 2002. Accessed November 1, 2013. http://bioethics. georgetown.edu/pcbe/reports/cloningreport/.

Wittgenstein, Ludwig. *Philosophical Investigations.* Translated by G. E. M. Anscombe, P. M. S. Hacker, and Joachim Schulte. Oxford: Blackwell, 2009.

Young, Thomas. "Overconsumption and Procreation: Are They Morally Equivalent?" *Journal of Applied Philosophy*, 18 no. 2 (2001): 183–192.

CHAPTER 6

Do Motives Matter?

On the Political Relevance of Procreative Reasons

STEVEN LECCE AND ERIK MAGNUSSON

INTRODUCTION

Are there good and bad reasons for having children and, if so, how should they influence the moral appraisal of our procreative conduct? A growing body of literature focuses on the moral relevance of procreative reasons, or the extent to which *why* we have children might matter for assessing the permissibility of our procreative acts.[1] At the center of this discussion is the "reasons-relevance thesis,"[2] which holds that ". . . parents' reasons often play a critical role in determining the acceptability of their procreative conduct."[3] On this view, what matters for assessing procreative permissibility is not necessarily the consequences of the procreative act, but rather the motives[4] with which it is undertaken. The reasons-relevance thesis thus challenges much contemporary thinking about procreative ethics where the *effects* of a procreative act—on the resultant child, as well as third parties—are considered central to its moral evaluation.[5]

The idea that our motives play a part in determining the moral character of our actions is an influential one[6] and, when applied to procreation, seems to reflect a widely held intuition. We tend to cast aspersion on people who undertake procreation haphazardly, and one explanation is that an act as momentous as bringing a person into existence should be undertaken for the right kinds of reasons. It seems to make a moral difference whether a child is created to be the object of a loving relationship, to serve as an old-age pension plan, or to be a trophy to his father's virility. Not surprisingly, then, much of the current literature has thus focused on assessing *what* constitutes good and bad reasons for procreating,[7] and *on what grounds* those reasons should factor into the appraisal of our procreative conduct.[8]

Our focus in this chapter is different. While the current literature assesses the *moral* relevance of procreative reasons, we ask instead a distinctively *political* question: from the state's perspective, for the purposes of determining family law and public policy, to what extent, and on what grounds, does it matter *why* people have children? This political question raises a unique set of issues that has not yet been adequately understood and addressed. Of primary interest to us is the issue of reasonable disagreement about ethics, and the ways in which it complicates an extension of the reasons-relevance thesis into the political domain. In pluralistic societies, people disagree sincerely and vehemently about *why* we should have children. Some believe that we should have children "for their own sakes," and that our childbearing practices should be motivated by selfless devotion; others have religious reasons for having children, such as an injunction from god to "go forth and multiply"; others have more transparently selfish motives for having children, such as achieving a certain social status or saving a dying relationship; and the list goes on and on. Given such pervasive and reasonable disagreement about *why* we should have children, on what grounds could the state take a stand on permissible versus impermissible procreative motives?

One possibility, of course, is on perfectionist[9] grounds: perhaps some people are simply mistaken about why we should have children, and the state has a duty to promote the right reasons through law and public policy. However, if we accept that ethical disagreement is *reasonable*, then those laws and policies will simply express a lack of respect to citizens who disagree with their underlying reasons. They may also place those citizens at a marked disadvantage in pursuing their childbearing projects, not because their projects are unjust, but because they are motivated by what the state deems to be the "wrong" kinds of reasons. Such effects would seem to violate an attractive principle of equal citizenship, according to which each citizen's right to pursue their own justice-respecting projects matters, and matters equally.

On an alternative view of political morality—the one we endorse in this chapter—law and public policy should be justified to citizens independent of the comprehensive ethical doctrines that divide them.[10] The state should not be in the business of promoting controversial ethical ideals, but should instead be concerned solely with promoting justice: with facilitating a ". . . just distribution of freedom, resources and other advantages between citizens, [and] ensuring that each is given a fair chance to formulate and pursue his or her own conception of the good life."[11] We argue that this view of political morality—political liberalism—leads us to the following conclusion about the political relevance of procreative reasons: if procreative reasons matter politically, it is only because, and insofar as, those reasons impact on the justice-based entitlements of other people, including resultant children and third parties. In the absence of these impacts, procreative reasons are not politically relevant, and the state should abstain from taking any ethical stand on *why* people should have children.

This finding generates two important conclusions for *political* procreative justice: first, the state *must* tolerate otherwise morally suspect procreative motives, so long as when acted upon, these do not impinge on the justice-based entitlements of other people. This requirement will exclude some morally suspect motives, but not for contested ethical reasons; rather, they will be excluded for reasons concerning justice, reasons which can be justified to citizens independent of the ethical doctrines that divide them. Second, the state *cannot* tolerate procreative acts that compromise the justice-based entitlements of other people, *even if* they are motivated by good intentions. In sum, good motives do not vindicate unjust acts and, to this extent, our argument coheres with the large segment of procreative ethics that focuses on outcomes as centrally relevant to the determination of procreative permissibility.

Our chapter develops these arguments to construct a distinctly political view of procreative motivation. We do not offer a comprehensive account of politically permissible and impermissible procreative reasons but instead offer an account of the *grounds* on which such reasons may be relevant, and thus a *means* by which the permissible/impermissible distinction can be drawn. We proceed in three steps. The first part evaluates the reasons-relevance thesis by distinguishing three grounds on which procreative reasons might be relevant: by their predictiveness of procreative outcomes; by their justificatory role in procreative decision-making; and, finally, by the attitudes and judgments they express to the moral community. The second part explains the idea of reasonable disagreement about procreative motives; it contrasts epistemic versus moral conceptions of reasonableness, and also direct versus indirect applications of public reason to procreation. The final part outlines the central political implication of our view, the Principle of (presumptive) Procreative Motivational Irrelevance (PPMI), which admits of two possible interpretations. On the Weak Version, the liberal state must abstain from pronouncing upon the presumed adequacy or inadequacy of people's procreative motives, provided that, when acted upon, such motives do not predictably and reliably adversely impact on the justice-based entitlements of other people. On the Strong Version, the proviso is expanded—not only rights violations but also the subversion of fundamental liberal *values* triggers political regulation and, possibly, restraint. Under either version, PPMI means that the state may *not* take into account the expressiveness or justificatory role of procreative reasons when determining law and public policy, but this still leaves more (Strong Version) or less (Weak Version) space for the state to consider certain aspects of their predictiveness.

WHY DO MOTIVES MATTER?

Imagine the following scenario. Alan and Brenda have a young son, Charlie, who is dying of leukemia. The doctors say that Charlie will need a bone marrow transplant in order to survive, and may also require a kidney transplant in the further future. Because a compatible donor cannot be found, Alan and Brenda decide to create one by having an additional child, using in vitro fertilization and preimplantation genetic diagnosis to ensure a healthy match. If the procedure succeeds, Brenda will give birth to a compatible donor child, and Charlie's life will be saved. Should they go through with the procedure and thereby create a donor sibling?

This is tricky. While we may sympathize with Alan and Brenda's desire to save their existing child, many of us may also have moral reservations about creating a child for the express purpose of providing compatible organs or body tissue for an imperiled brother or sister. One explanation for these reservations is the thought that it matters *why* we have children: there are good and bad reasons for having children, and it is not clear that Alan and Brenda's reasons are good enough. But even if this is the case, we need an explanation for *why* that is so. We need a basis for distinguishing between good and bad procreative reasons before we can designate Alan and Brenda's reasons as bad ones (if they are bad ones). So why might it matter *why* we have children?

Predictiveness

Perhaps our reasons for having children matter because they tell us something both important and reliable about the likely consequences of our procreative acts—in particular, because they tell us something about likely welfare outcomes for resultant children.[12] For instance, on the basis of Alan and Brenda's reasons, we may be able to predict that the child they produce will be destined to undergo, without its consent, one or more invasive surgeries unnecessary for its own health, some of which may be painful and pose long-term health risks.[13] If we think that these outcomes are morally impermissible in light of some independent standard—say, one indicated by the rights of the child who results—we might on that basis designate Alan and Brenda's procreative reasons as bad ones.[14]

Several features of the *predictive* account are noteworthy. First, it does not attribute any intrinsic relevance to procreative reasons, but sees them only as derivatively relevant by revealing something about the likely consequences of the procreative act. In this sense, Alan and Brenda's reasons for having children *are* relevant for assessing the morality of their procreative conduct, but only because they supply information about its likely consequences, which are the real subject of moral evaluation. The predictive account thus coheres with much contemporary thinking about procreative ethics, which sees outcomes, rather than motives, as the dominant factor in determining procreative permissibility.

Second, the predictive account depends upon an independently derived moral standard by which we can evaluate different procreative outcomes. In particular, it assumes that we have a relatively settled and determinate view about what appropriate welfare outcomes for children are, and that we can measure possible procreative outcomes against that standard. For argument's sake, assume that such a standard is set by the United Nations Convention on the Rights of the Child (1989) (CRC), such that appropriate welfare outcomes are those that are consistent with a child's enjoyment of their CRC rights.[15] Morally good procreative reasons would then be all those reasons that, when acted upon, predictably yield outcomes that are consistent with a child's enjoyment of their CRC rights.

Finally, the predictive account attributes moral relevance to procreative reasons *only* to the extent that they are actually predictive of procreative outcomes, and is thus constrained by a number of epistemic considerations. While we may be able to glean a certain amount of information about the likely consequences of a procreative act on the basis of the reasons for which it is being undertaken, we must note that this information will not be complete, and that its reliability will vary significantly from case to case. For instance, on the basis of Alan and Brenda's reasons, we are able to predict with a reasonable degree of certainty a number of likely welfare outcomes for the resultant child, which we can then evaluate according to their consistency with the child's enjoyment of their CRC rights. But this will not be true in all cases: other procreative reasons may reveal less information about the likely consequences of acting on them, and the reasons themselves may even change between the time of conception and birth. These kinds of epistemic considerations may cast a shadow over the predictive account, leading critics like Mianna Lotz to claim that ". . . we are not entitled to infer very much at all from procreative reasons to [procreative outcomes]."[16]

Justification

Even if epistemic considerations sometimes limit the predictiveness of procreative reasons, we still know a few things about the likely consequences of *any* procreative act, regardless of the reasons for which it is undertaken. For instance, we know that by bringing a child into the world, we are inevitably exposing it to a host of unconsented to burdens (and benefits),[17] including the ". . . pain, suffering, difficulty, significant disappointment, distress, and significant loss that occur within a typical life."[18] According to some commentators, whether or not we view these consequences as permissible turns crucially on *why* we have children in the first place. In other words, our procreative reasons may serve an important *justificatory* role.

Christine Overall appears to endorse this view, that human procreation should not be seen as a presumptively permissible endeavor, but something that requires moral justification. But the high stakes involved in procreative decision-making mean that procreation cannot be justified with reference to our apparent right to do so, nor can it be justified on the basis of abstract deontological or consequentialist considerations.[19] Rather, procreation must be justified on the basis of reasons that concern the good of the child who is brought into being, namely, ". . . the creation of the mutually enriching, mutually enhancing love that is the parent-child relationship."[20] Only reasons of this nature may offset the significant moral hazards associated with procreative decision-making.[21]

David Wasserman makes a similar point. He agrees that human life always contains an array of significant hardships, and that by creating a child, we thereby expose it to those hardships without its consent. Whether or not the child has a legitimate moral complaint against us, then, depends on our reasons for creating it, and whether or not those reasons embody a concern for its own good. On this view, parents "must be able to justify the decision to subject their children to those hardships, and they can do so only if part of their reason for having those children is to give them lives good and rich enough to offset or outweigh those hardships."[22] It follows, then, that parents' reasons for having children "play a critical role in determining the acceptability of their [procreative] decision and the plausibility of any complaint from the child they create."[23]

On the justificatory account of why procreative reasons matter, it is not clear whether or not Alan and Brenda's reasons are morally sufficient. On the one hand, in principle, there may be nothing incompatible with creating a child for the purpose of organ or tissue donation, while simultaneously wanting that child for its own sake. John Robertson makes this point by noting that "In most instances [of conceiving children to obtain tissue] the child so conceived will be welcomed into the family and loved regardless of tissue status and success of the transplant."[24] On the other hand, however, Alan and Brenda's reasons may be seen in an important way as failing the justificatory threshold. Assuming that they did not originally intend on having additional children, their decision to have the child is inextricably tied to the medical needs of Charlie, rather than to a prior desire to create a new relationship. This fact may diminish the extent to which their procreative reasons can serve their purported justificatory role.

Expressiveness

Finally, our reasons for having children might matter because of the attitudes or judgments they express to the moral community.[25] Disability advocates have often objected to reproductive technologies aimed at correcting, ameliorating, or preventing disabilities on so-called "expressivist" grounds. The idea is that the development and use of such technologies expresses negative judgments about the value of people living with disabilities, and that such judgments themselves constitute an injury and an injustice to those people.[26] A similar point can be made in relation to procreative reasons. Our reasons for having children inevitably express certain attitudes and judgments, to ourselves and to onlookers, about the sanctity of human life and the value of the parent-child relationship, among other things. One of the ways in which our reasons might matter, then, is in light of the "meaning or message"[27] that those reasons convey, and whether or not we consider them to be palatable from a moral point of view.

The expressiveness account may provide a possible objection to Alan and Brenda's reasons for having an additional child. By some accounts, Alan and Brenda's decision might express the allegedly negative judgment that it is permissible to use a child instrumentally as a means toward another child's ends. Such a judgment may be condemned in one of two ways. First, it may be condemned on consequentialist grounds by the possible implications of that judgment being generally accepted.[28] The worry here is that if we permit the judgment in Alan and Brenda's case, we may be led to permit it in other cases as well, which may put other children at risk of harm or injustice. However, it is important to note that the expressivist objection does not depend on these consequentialist considerations. Rather, the judgment may also be condemned on deontological grounds, by failing to respect the personhood or independent moral status of the child who is purportedly used. In this sense, even if Alan and Brenda's child will be born into conditions that are consistent with its enjoyment of its CRC rights, their procreative act may still be condemned on expressivist grounds by failing to respect the personhood or moral status of that child (or for some other expressive reason).

PROCREATIVE MOTIVES AND REASONABLE DISAGREEMENT

Assume that one or more of these accounts is correct, such that it matters morally *why* we have children. Should states take this into account when determining family law and public policy? Most theorists have avoided this question, preferring to restrict their analysis of procreative motivation to the moral domain. Thus, while Overall argues that we can distinguish between morally good and bad procreative reasons, she also urges that this "... says nothing about what the state should or should not do to curtail procreation."[29] However, of the theorists who *have* considered the question, virtually all deny that procreative reasons are politically relevant. Two lines of argument are typically deployed in favor of this claim. The first is that considerations of procreative freedom prevent states from discriminating among citizens' procreative motives.[30] The idea is that if we recognize a general right to control the use of one's reproductive capacities, then we may also recognize a right to control one's reproductive capacities for *whatever* reason one sees fit, including those that are morally suboptimal. In this sense, procreative freedom might be understood as a "right to do wrong," or a right to act in ways that diverge from what morality requires or recommends.[31] Laws or public policies that prohibited or discouraged certain procreative acts on the basis of their motives alone might run afoul of this right, and be deemed undesirable or illegitimate on that basis.

However, in addition to considerations of procreative freedom, there may also be a number of epistemic problems that make it difficult or impossible for states to consider procreative motives when determining law and public policy. One is that it is a very difficult question just how, and to what extent, procreative motives factor into the morality of procreative conduct, and by some accounts, this difficulty ". . . weighs against any attempt to condition the state's provision of reproductive assistance on parental reasons or motives."[32] A deeper epistemic worry, however, is that parents' *own* procreative reasons are often unknown, inarticulate, multifaceted, or subject to change. This (undoubtedly prevalent) uncertainty may pose problems for lawmakers wishing to take into account procreative motivation when determining law and public policy. As Wasserman claims, "If parents themselves are often uncertain, confused, or self-deceived about their reasons for such critical decisions, how can the institutions that attempt to regulate their conduct hope to achieve a tolerable degree of certainty? These difficulties make it clear that the state lacks both the knowledge and the moral authority to regulate [procreative behavior] on the basis of parental motivation."[33]

We do not necessarily disagree that considerations surrounding procreative freedom or epistemic uncertainty might limit the political relevance of procreative reasons, though the extent to which they do may be overstated. While it is certainly plausible that procreative freedom protects the ability of citizens to formulate and act on a wide range of procreative motives, it is less plausible that it protects their ability to act on *any* procreative motive they see fit, particularly if it risks harm or injustice to the resultant child or third parties.[34] Similarly, while there may often be difficult epistemic hurdles to identifying and evaluating citizens' procreative reasons, this is not always the case. As the example of Alan and Brenda makes clear, there *are* cases in which parents' procreative motives are both accessible and articulate, and these kinds of cases surely matter both morally and politically.

However, another largely overlooked set of considerations that bears upon the political relevance of procreative reasons concerns the inherently *contested* nature of good and bad procreative reasons. A democracy provides its citizens with a wide range of civil and political liberties, which both reflect and shape a public culture marked by a heightened degree of moral, religious, and ethical pluralism. In such a setting, it is not surprising that people usually disagree about the nature of human well-being and flourishing: under the permissive conditions of the liberal democratic state, people will often endorse competing "conceptions of the good life." While contestation, disagreement, and pluralism all figure prominently in contemporary theories of justice—especially in political liberalism—they have had less influence on thinking about the ethics of procreation and parenthood. Notice, however, that procreative reasons are themselves typically embedded in conceptions of the good life, so that we cannot contrast good versus bad reasons for having (or not having) children without invoking some background theory about what is ultimately valuable in life, one that explains the significance of, say, cultural continuity among genetically related people, child-parent intimacy, and so on. In this sense, just as democratic societies are characterized by a reasonable plurality of opposing and irreconcilable conceptions of the good life, so too are they characterized by a reasonable plurality of procreative motivations.

To get a sense of how deeply such disagreement runs, consider the following non-exhaustive list of some of the divergent and even conflicting reasons that parents may give for having children: (1) to fulfill a biologically driven urge; (2) to experience the wonders of gestation and childbirth; (3) to pass on one's genes and establish genetic connections with future generations; (4) to initiate a parent-child relationship and the unique brand of intimacy it makes possible; (5) to ensure the survival and/or proliferation of a religious, cultural, or national group; (6) to adhere to religious doctrine, such as an injunction from God to "go forth and multiply"; (7) to satisfy others' desires, such as a child's desire for a sibling or a parent's desire for a grandchild; or (8) to conform to the expectations of a pronatalist culture.

Each of these reasons stems from distinct conceptions of the good life, and reflects drastically different ideas about the purpose and value of procreation. This is not problematic in a strictly moral domain, where our goal is to simply evaluate or rank them according to the metric provided by a particular ethical theory (say, the promotion of aggregate utility or respect for others' personhood). However, it poses a significant problem in a political context marked by deep disagreement about ethics itself. States may have a legitimate interest in taking into account procreative motivation when determining family law and public policy, particularly in areas such as the regulation and provision of assisted reproductive technologies (ARTs). But in the absence of ethical consensus about the value of procreation, on what basis could the state take a stand on good versus bad procreative motives? And how could they do so without arbitrarily privileging the procreative projects of one segment of the community over the differently motivated projects of another?

Ethical disagreement is *the* political problem for liberal theorists who want to reconcile equal freedom with subjection to state power. If that power is to be legitimated, so the argument goes, everyone must consent to it, but how is this possible in light of the very disagreement that motivates this contractual ideal of political legitimacy in the first place? There are two solutions that will *not* work, given this framing of the problem, and stating why helps reinforce our preferred alternative: on the one hand, perfectionism, because it requires what we do not have—an uncontested criterion of ethical truth; on the other hand, a modus vivendi of actually held procreative views, because, to be frank, some of them are morally unacceptable, even crazy. Some people may want children because, say, the Aryan race must one day overpower blacks, Jews, homosexuals, and other "vermin," and having more kids is their primary contribution to advancing the Aryan cause. This brief survey of different procreative reasons does not imply that we need a political morality that is maximally sensitive to actually held (including crazy) procreative motives. Given liberalism's commitment to equal freedom against the backdrop of ethical disagreement, we have to find a way to *constrain* that pluralism and generate mutually acceptable conclusions about procreative rights and responsibilities in a way that does *not* presuppose the truth or rightness of the competing accounts on offer. Surely we need the state to discriminate between acceptable and unacceptable procreative reasons— no sane view of political morality will endorse, say, having children in order to produce slave labor—but how can it do this without taking ethical sides?

The solution is to be found in the now-familiar doctrine of liberal neutrality. In this chapter, we (largely) presuppose rather than argue for the soundness of that doctrine. Our goal, instead, is to motivate the basic idea and sketch our preferred interpretation of it. This paves the way for our discussion in the third section, which highlights the consequences of that interpretation for the political relevance of various procreative reasons.

State neutrality between competing ethical ideals is a defining feature of what political theorists now call *political*, as opposed to comprehensive liberalism. Whereas comprehensive, that is to say perfectionist, liberalism articulates political principles on the basis of a distinctively liberal conception of the good life—one rooted in, say, personal autonomy—political liberalism does so instead on the basis of a deliberately restricted set of *political* goods and values—for example, freedom, equality, a fair distribution of resources and opportunities, mutual security, and the rule of law. The first component of liberal neutrality, then, is a restriction on the kinds of goods and values that might be appealed to in the justification of law and public policy. The idea, which is at least as old as Locke's *Letter Concerning Toleration*, is breathtakingly simple. If subjection to political authority is to be consistent with equal freedom, somehow, that authority must be based upon everyone's consent. However, given ethical disagreement, political principles that presuppose the validity of contested ethical beliefs will fail the contractual ideal of legitimacy because people holding different beliefs will reject them. The solution is to justify state action upon the basis of the interests and ideals that we *share* as democratic citizens, rather than upon the comprehensive doctrines that divide us. Locke calls these "civil interests"; Rawls calls them "primary goods."

The second component of liberal neutrality follows from the first. As we just saw, in a setting of pervasive disagreement, a consensual basis for the justification of law and public policy requires an anti-perfectionist state, one that does *not* take ethical sides, as it were. But the public conception of justice that emerges from this contractual framework is only a necessary, not sufficient, condition of political legitimacy. A shared commitment to justificatory neutrality will not rule out further disputes concerning the meaning, scope, and practical implications of neutral justice. For example, while distributive fairness *is* an eminently political value (amenable to neutral justification), surely there will still be disagreement about what counts as fair, and so we also need to know what kind of evidence or argumentation may be legitimately offered in support of, or against, alternative conceptions of this, and all other, political values. Unless anti-perfectionist principles, that is, are supplemented with a "companion agreement"[35] on the kinds of reasons, information, knowledge, and evidence that are appropriate to settling political questions, the equal freedom of democratic citizens will be violated at a second, interpretive level. Absent this companion agreement, the ground rules of political life that largely determine everyone's opportunities and life chances will be based upon idiosyncratic values and defended by appeal to mutually inaccessible thought processes. A theory of liberal neutrality is distinguishable from its rivals, then, in terms of the substantive principles it endorses and the particular constraints that embody its account of public reason. We reason *publicly* by appealing to political values and also by limiting our arguments for and against alternative interpretations of our shared interests to those that could be accepted by free and equal members of a democratic society.

So the relevant justificatory constituency is made up of all *reasonable* citizens, not citizens per se, and this means that political legitimacy requires the state to remain neutral between all *reasonable* conceptions of the good life. In sum, we satisfy the contractual ideal of a society that can secure everyone's consent, despite deep pluralism, by adopting a normative consensus that abstracts from contested ethical values—that is the point of the neutrality constraint.

Given these premises, we think that public reason must apply to procreative motives, such that the state is forbidden from acting upon their supposed ethical truth or falsity. Later, we explain what this application yields in connection with the expressive, justificatory, and predictive versions of the "reasons-relevance" thesis. For now, two things are worth clarifying. First, we endorse an *indirect* rather than a direct application of public reason to procreative motives. Direct application would have procreators specifically motivated by *political* values. There are several reasons for thinking that this is unattractive.[36] Indirect application, by contrast, means that prospective procreators do *not* have to base their reproductive choices upon quintessentially political values; they may procreate for any reason they wish subject to the proviso that, when acted upon, those reasons do not undermine the basic rights and freedoms of democratic citizens. For us, procreators must comply with, not be motivated by, politically liberal values.

Second, we interpret "reasonableness" in moral rather than epistemic terms. A commitment to liberal neutrality and its attendant (indirect) application of public reason to procreation implies that the state cannot discriminate between all *reasonable* procreative motives. The state may (and, in fact, must) discriminate between reasonable and unreasonable procreative motives. What could it mean, then, to say that a procreative motive is unreasonable and therefore beyond the ambit of liberal toleration? Within the context of an *epistemic* theory of public reason, an unreasonable procreative motive would be one that failed to satisfy relevant criteria of justified belief because, say, it ignored countervailing evidence, it was adopted under duress, it was based upon seriously mistaken beliefs about reproductive science, and so on. We think that epistemic theories of justified belief are too restrictive as bases for toleration in a democratic society. There is no reason to think that people who believe things for the wrong (or no) reasons will be antecedently more likely to violate other people's rights.[37] Additionally, liberal neutrality justified on the basis of an epistemic conception of public reason runs the risk of self-defeat. Supposedly, the state must remain neutral between competing conceptions of the good life because people can reasonably disagree about them. But people also disagree about the neutrality requirement itself, so what's so special about political liberalism such that its principles, alone, are vindicated by the right epistemic view?

For us, reasonable pluralism means that there is a multiplicity of conceptions of the familial (and therefore the procreative) good that are compatible with liberal principles of justice, because those principles do *not* depend upon those conceptions for their derivation. Being politically unreasonable, then, means endorsing familial/procreative conceptions outside of this relatively permissive range, and in a way that has illiberal or intolerant implications. Saying that a procreative motive is politically reasonable, and therefore publicly justified, amounts to claiming that symmetrically situated and ideally rational agents constrained in a variety of ways would agree to a principle authorizing its performance. Unreasonable persons are those who reject such principles, or are willing to act on other ones that cannot be justified in this way. Clearly, epistemology also plays a role within the context of this contractual argumentative framework, but not foundationally, and only to model what are quintessential *political* ideas about democratic equality and reciprocity.

PRINCIPLE OF (PRESUMPTIVE) MOTIVATIONAL IRRELEVANCE

What happens to the reasons-relevance thesis when it is extended beyond the moral and into the political domain, such that it must be indirectly constrained by liberal neutrality?

To begin answering this question, let's return to an amended version of the Alan and Brenda case. Recall, the couple wants to create a compatible donor child for their sick son Charlie and, as before, they must use in-vitro fertilization and preimplantation genetic diagnosis to ensure a healthy match. However, this time, because of both the risks associated with the complicated medical procedures in question and the socialized costs (they are Canadians), Alan and Brenda must submit an application to their public health board to be approved for the procedure. It turns out that several board members are uncomfortable with the idea of creating a child (partly) in order to save another. Given the view of political morality endorsed here, on what basis might the board deny Alan and Brenda's application?

They *cannot* appeal to the expressiveness of the procreative act, because people reasonably disagree about what the act actually expresses, and about whether or not that expression is, all things considered, morally palatable. Even if board members *are* tempted by the thought that there is a genuine collective interest in procreation being undertaken "with a serious intent that reflects and expresses a concern and regard for the moral community itself,"[38] that interest will *not* yield determinate and publicly justified reproductive conclusions because, as we have seen, in a context of ethical disagreement, people are divided over precisely which procreative reasons either support or subvert the moral community in question. The same set of procreative motivations that transgress the ideals of one segment of the community will usually cohere with those of another.

Children are inevitably born in a wide range of cultural, familial, technological, economic, and political settings. In some ways, then, we start out life in a radically dissimilar fashion. In other ways, however, despite these obvious contrasts, human existence is also a great leveler: *all of us* will, at one point or another—sometimes throughout life—experience pain, hardship, and disappointment. So endemic and serious are these difficulties that they lead some critics to conclude that procreation is *never* morally permissible. But even if we confidently reject that finding as overdrawn, we might still think that the permissibility of subjecting prospective people to the burdens of existence at least partly depends upon *why* we have children.

Procreative motives cannot play this alleged justificatory role, however, because, as we saw earlier, they are embedded within conceptions of the good with which reasonable people disagree. Since the liberal state must remain neutral between such conceptions, it cannot privilege any particular procreative reasons to generate a threshold that establishes if and when such reasons are good *enough* to ground procreative rights. Some parents want children in order to share a particularly close and loving relationship with biological relatives; others want them so that there will be another generation to carry on their religious, cultural, or national identities; still others want them in order to leave a genetic legacy and forge connections with future generations. Suppose each couple is in Alan and Brenda's position—they are applying to a local health board for ART. On the assumption that public resources are scarce so that some selection criterion is required, it should *not* be based upon an official ranking of the supposed justificatory adequacy (or deficiency) of people's procreative motives.

Law and public policy, then, may only appeal to the predictiveness of procreative reasons. Possible procreative outcomes can be evaluated by reference to children's, or third-parties', justice-based entitlements, and this standard (we suppose) does not have to depend upon contested ethical assumptions. Therefore, procreative reasons *may* matter politically, but only in cases where they are identifiable, articulate, and reliably predictive. On our view of the matter, the indirect application of public reason to procreative motives generates the following version of that claim:

> The Principle of (presumptive) Procreative Motivational Irrelevance (PPMI):
> *The state must abstain from pronouncing upon the presumed adequacy or inadequacy of people's procreative motives PROVIDED that, when acted upon, such motives do not predictably and reliably subvert liberal justice.*

In general, this means two things: first, that otherwise ethically suspect procreative motives are politically tolerable provided that, when acted upon, they do not undermine the publicly justified rights and responsibilities of democratic citizens; and second, ethically pure or unimpeachable procreative motives do nothing to vindicate breaches of those rights and responsibilities.

The PPMI's Proviso might be interpreted more or less stringently, with very different implications for reproductive law and policy. Under the Weak Version, the Proviso is overridden only in cases of rights violations. Here, Alan and Brenda's savior-sibling project is relevant. Presumably, the prospective "savior" has—or *will have*—rights to, among other things, bodily integrity and freedom from assault. To the extent that the couple wants another child *in order to benefit their existing one*, and that benefit can only be extracted from the benefactor non-consensually, their procreative motive will predictably result in violating that benefactor's rights (depending, perhaps, on the nature of the procedure). Prima facie, the state might have grounds for limiting, insofar as it can, the conception of savior siblings. A less draconian measure would be to forbid the medical procedures in question and make that ban publicly and antecedently known. In doing so, it would supply prospective parents with a legal baseline, as it were, that allows them to reform and, if necessary, altogether abandon their procreative projects.

Under the Strong Version, the Proviso is overridden not only in cases such as the one just mentioned where predictable rights violations trigger state involvement, but *also* in cases where the prediction is about the subversion of fundamental liberal *values*. A key example here would be sex-selective abortion. Politically, one might think that it should not matter *why* people choose to have children, as long as the basic interests and, therefore, rights of those children who *do* come into existence are secured. Of course, this is precisely what the Weak Version of PPMI says. When that version is deployed in a context that both denies fetuses legal personhood (so that they cannot be rights-bearers) and also, as liberal democracies try to, affords great normative weight to women's equality and personal autonomy, it leads to a very permissive set of abortion rights. Such is the status quo in contemporary Canada, for example. But it seems reasonable to think (as we do) that women's equality and autonomy are *also* subverted by whatever background attitudes and practices—cultural, religious, economic—make sex-selective abortion putatively rational or desirable for some people in the first place. Because gender equality *is* a fundamental liberal value, then, there is a prima facie reason for the state to ban sex-selective abortions. Of course, that reason could be defeated if reproductive autonomy always trumped *all* other liberal values, gender equality included, but we should be skeptical about this kind of lexical priority. Is choice really the most important value? Always? Liberalism is committed to personal freedom, but that freedom is often constrained both for the sake of other people's freedom, and also for the sake of other values. So while the Weak Version of PPMI might not diverge fundamentally in its practical implications from those yielded by arguments based upon, say, reproductive freedom or epistemic uncertainty about procreative motivation, the Strong Version *does*—it implies that *some* procreative motives, such as wanting *only* a boy, are politically intolerable, because they violate the indirect application of public reason to reproductive behavior. If restricting access to abortion for some reasons is unacceptably authoritarian and therefore illiberal, or if it wrongly adds the insult of sacrificing the reproductive autonomy of some women to the injury of already oppressive and unjust background conditions, then, in the least, the state should find subtler ways of bolstering fundamental liberal commitments. Perhaps, in appealing to the Strong Version of PPMI, the state might consider *denying* reproductive assistance when, given people's procreative motives, it will be predictably misused.

A lingering worry with our argument might be that, under either version, the PPMI is actually a form of liberal expressivism in disguise. As we presented it, the PPMI is an implication of the indirect application of public reason to the wide range of familial conceptions of the good likely to persist under democratic institutions. The idea is for the state *not* to judge the intrinsic ethical merits of those conceptions, except to the extent that procreative motives embedded within them are likely to violate independently defensible political values. However, if those political values tacitly *do* rest on contested ethical ideals—say, a form of Kantian personal autonomy, or Millian individuality—then the PPMI's avowed neutrality is a sham.

There is no way adequately to respond to this worry here. In fact, this is *the* objection to political liberalism as a whole, so it's unsurprising that it might recur in connection with the application of that view to procreative motivation. However, the distinction between moral and epistemic conceptions of reasonableness hinted at earlier tells us something important about what shape a plausible response will take. In this chapter, we have assumed a particular idea of democratic equality, one that links the protection of certain vital interests to recognizing people as having equal standing as citizens in a self-governing polity. A full defense of that idea would explain how democratic equality alone is sufficient to generate the procedural constraints— including public reason—that yield the PPMI and why, absent their predictiveness, state regulation of procreative motives is impermissible. One can then reject the PPMI, either by claiming that inequality is a better premise for reasoning about political justice, or by showing that the particular form of public reason we adopt does not properly model democratic citizenship. For us, it is perfectionists who shoulder a more daunting argumentative burden; they must explain why, in the absence of rights violations or the undermining of fundamental liberal values, some people's ethical beliefs should be forcibly imposed upon others who reject them, and in a legislative area as important as procreation.

CONCLUSION

This chapter has principally tried to establish *how*, not what, to think about procreative motivation from a political point of view. In a democracy, reasonable people will disagree about why procreation matters and therefore also about good versus bad reasons for having children. Taking equal freedom seriously in such a context leads to an account of political legitimacy according to which state action must be *publicly* justified. According to the reasons-relevance thesis, procreative motives often play a critical role in the overall moral permissibility of human reproduction. However, when we adopt a political perspective and thus indirectly apply public reason to procreative motives, we are led to the Principle of (presumptive) Procreative Motivational Irrelevance (PPMI), which rules out both expressive and justificatory versions of the reasons-relevance thesis. As a consequence, only predictiveness can ground law and public policy that takes into account procreative motives. If our reasons for having children matter politically, this is only because of how they predict either the support or subversion of liberal justice.

NOTES

1. See Susanne Gibson, "Reasons for Having Children: Ends, Means, and Family Values," *Journal of Applied Philosophy* 12, no. 3 (1995): 231–240; Mianna Lotz, "Procreative Reasons-Relevance: On the Moral Significance of *Why* We Have Children," *Bioethics* 23, no. 5 (2009): 291–299, and "Rethinking Procreation: Why it Matters *Why* We Have Children," *Journal of Applied Philosophy* 28, no. 2 (2011): 105–121; Claudia Mills, "Are There Morally Problematic Reasons for Having Children?" *Philosophy and Public Policy Quarterly* 25, no. 4 (2005): 2–9; Christine Overall, *Why Have Children?* (Cambridge, MA: MIT Press, 2012); and David Wasserman, "Having One Child to Save Another: A Tale of Two Families," *Philosophy and Public Policy Quarterly* 23, no. 1/2 (2003): 21–27, and "The Nonidentity Problem, Disability, and the Role Morality of Prospective Parents," *Ethics* 116, no. 1 (2005): 132–152.
2. This term is Mianna Lotz's. See Lotz, "Procreative Reasons."

3. Wasserman, "Having One Child," 152.

4. While we acknowledge important distinctions in other contexts, for the purposes of our discussion the terms "reasons," "motives" and "intentions" are used interchangeably.

5. See, for example, David Benatar, *Better Never to Have Been* (Oxford: Oxford University Press, 2006); Allen Buchanan, Dan W. Brock, Norman Daniels, and Dan Wikler, *From Chance to Choice: Genetics and Justice* (Cambridge: Cambridge University Press, 2000); John A. Robertson. *Children of Choice* (Princeton, NJ: Princeton University Press, 1994), and Seana Valentine Shiffrin, "Wrongful Life, Procreative Responsibility, and the Significance of Harm," *Legal Theory* 5, no. 2 (1999): 117–148.

6. This is, of course, a central theme in Kant's moral philosophy. See Immanuel Kant, *Groundwork on the Metaphysics of Morals*, trans. James W. Ellington (Indianapolis, IN: Hackett, 1983). It also presents itself in the literature surrounding the "Doctrine of Double Effect." See, for example, Scanlon, T. M. *Moral Dimensions: Permissibility, Meaning, Blame* (Cambridge, MA: Belknap Press, 2008); and Judith Jarvis Thomson, "Self Defense," *Philosophy and Public Affairs* 20, no. 4 (1991): 283–310.

7. See Lotz, "Procreative Reasons"; Mills, "Are There Morally Problematic Reasons"; Overall, *Why Have Children?* especially chapters 4, 5, and 10; and Wasserman, "Having One Child."

8. Lotz provides a brief but helpful typology of potential grounds in *Procreative Reasons*, 294–299.

9. Perfectionism is a view of political morality that grants the state the authority to enforce controversial views of the good life. For defenses of the perfectionist state, see: Joseph Raz, *The Morality of Freedom* (Oxford: Clarendon Press, 1986); George Sher, *Beyond Neutrality: Perfectionism and Politics* (Cambridge: Cambridge University Press, 1997); Stephen Wall, *Liberalism, Perfectionism and Restraint* (Cambridge: Cambridge University Press, 1998).

10. See John Rawls, *Political Liberalism* (New York: Columbia University Press, 1993); Charles Larmore, *The Morals of Modernity* (Cambridge: Cambridge University Press, 1996); Steven Lecce, *Against Perfectionism: Defending Liberal Neutrality* (Toronto: University of Toronto Press, 2008); Jonathan Quong, *Liberalism without Perfection* (Oxford: Oxford University Press, 2011).

11. Quong, *Liberalism*, 1.

12. See Lotz, *Procreative Reasons*, 294–296.

13. Overall provides a useful overview of some of these risks in her discussion of savior siblings; see Overall, *Why Have Children?*, 81–93.

14. Throughout this discussion, we ignore any potential problems that might arise on account of the nonidentity problem. We agree with Claudia Mills that our objection, or lack of objection, to certain procreative motives should not turn on "philosophical puzzles about the ontological status of not-yet-conceived persons," but should rather turn on a consideration of the justice-based entitlements of other people. This sentiment is brought to the fore by changing a few facts of the case. Suppose that rather than creating a compatible donor child, Alan and Brenda decide to adopt one from a developing country. Here the predictive objection can still be made in response to their reasons for adoption, suggesting that the ontological status of the prospective child is not really what we care about. For a useful discussion of this point, see Mills, "Are There Morally Problematic Reasons," 4.

15. David Archard argues for such a standard in "Wrongful Life," *Philosophy* 79, no. 3 (2004): 403–420.
16. Lotz, *Procreative Reasons*, 295. Lotz's point was about the relationship between procreative reasons and parental capacity specifically, though her point generalizes to other kinds of welfare outcomes as well.
17. We assume, against philosophers like David Heyd, that existence can be a benefit and/or a harm to the person who is brought into being. For a defense of this view, see Nils Holtung, "On the Value of Coming into Existence," *Journal of Ethics* 5, no. 4 (2001): 361–384. For a critical perspective, see David Heyd, *Genethics* (Berkeley: University of California Press, 1992).
18. Seana V. Shiffrin. "Wrongful Life, Procreative Responsibility, and the Significance of Harm," *Legal Theory* 5, no. 1 (1999): 137.
19. See Overall, *Why Have Children?*, chapters 2, 4, and 5, respectively.
20. Ibid., 217.
21. Susanne Gibson espouses a similar view. According to her, ". . . reasons for having children may be judged morally desirable or undesirable according to the extent to which they enhance or detract from the possibility of forming a particular kind of relationship with that child." See Gibson, *Reasons*, 238.
22. Wasserman, "Having One Child," 135–136.
23. Ibid., 136.
24. Robertson, *Children of Choice*, 217.
25. Lotz, "Procreative Reasons," 297–299; see also Lotz, "Rethinking Procreation."
26. See Allen Buchanan, "Choosing Children Who Will Be Disabled: Intervention and the Morality of Inclusion," *Social Philosophy and Policy* 13, no. 2 (1996): 28.
27. Lotz, "Procreative Reasons," 297.
28. Buchanan, "Choosing Children," 28.
29. Overall, *Why Have Children?*, 118.
30. John Robertson, for example, believes that ". . . procreative liberty should include the right to have children for any motive . . ." See Robertson (1994), 217.
31. See Jeremy Waldron, "A Right to Do Wrong," *Ethics* 92 no. 1 (1981): 21–39.
32. Wasserman, "Having One Child," 21.
33. Ibid., 27. Wasserman's point is about the regulation of assisted reproductive technology specifically, but in the context of our discussion, his point generalizes to other kinds of procreative behavior as well.
34. Archard (2004) argues that the right to procreate is "internally constrained" by the interests of the resultant child. For similar views, see Hugh Lafollette, "Licensing Parents," *Philosophy and Public Affairs* 9, no. 2 (1980): 182–197; Onora O'Neill, "Begetting, Bearing, and Rearing," in *Having Children: Philosophical and Legal Reflections on Parenthood*, ed. Onora O'Neill and William Ruddick (New York: Oxford University Press, 1979); and Bonnie Steinbock and Ron McClamrock, "When is Birth Unfair to the Child?" *Hastings Centre Report* 24, no. 6 (1994): 15–21.
35. John Rawls, *Justice as Fairness: A Restatement* (Cambridge, MA: Harvard University Press, 2001), 89.
36. For an exploration of those reasons, see Steven Lecce, "How Political is the Personal? Justice in Upbringing," *Theory and Research in Education* 6, no. 1 (2008): 21–45.
37. See Lecce, *Against Perfectionism*, Chapter 8.
38. Lotz, "Procreative Reasons," 112.

CHAPTER 7

We Can Make Rational Decisions to Have a Child: On the Grounds for Rejecting L.A. Paul's Arguments

MEENA KRISHNAMURTHY

INTRODUCTION

L.A. Paul wrote what is now an infamous paper on the question of whether an individual can make a rational decision to have a child.[1]

The Scenario

You have no children. However, you have reached a point in your life when you are personally, financially, and physically able to have a child. You sit down and think about whether you want to have a child of your very own. You discuss it with your partner, and contemplate the choice, carefully reflecting on the choice by assessing what it would be like for you to have a child of your very own and comparing this to what it would be like to remain childless.[2]

The Options

HC: Have a child

~HC: Not have a child

Paul's Conclusion

You cannot make a rational decision to either HC or ~HC.

Her argument for this conclusion relies on <u>the standard model of rationality</u>:

1. To determine which of two actions is a rational choice, you must calculate the expected value (EV) of these two actions.
2. To determine the EV of two actions, you must determine, in relation to each action, (1) the value of the outcomes that will result from the action, and (2) the probability of these outcomes occurring. The EV of an action is the product of (1) and (2).[3]
3. The action with the highest EV is the rational choice.

Paul focuses on the standard model because she believes that it is implicit in how we typically make what we consider to be rational decisions.

The Argument for Paul's Conclusion

Claim1: To make a rational decision about whether you ought to HC or ~HC, you must determine the expected value (EV) of HC and ~HC. The one with the highest EV is the rational choice.

Claim2: To determine the EV of HC and ~HC, you must determine (1) the value of the outcomes of HC and ~HC; and (2) the probability of those outcomes occurring.

Claim3: You can determine the value of the outcomes of HC and ~HC only by knowing what it is like (WIL) for you to HC and ~HC.

Claim4: You can only know WIL for you to HC by being in a state where you HC.

Claim5: Since, as of yet, you are not in a state where you HC, you cannot know WIL for you to HC.

Claim6: Since you cannot know WIL to HC, you cannot determine the EV of HC.[4]

Claim7: Since you cannot determine the EV of HC, you cannot make a rational decision to HC or ~HC.

Conclusion: Therefore, you cannot make a rational decision to either HC or ~HC.[5]

The main example that Paul uses to make her case is that of <u>Mary and seeing the color red</u>:

> Mary is confined to a black-and-white room, is educated through black-and-white books and through lectures related on black-and-white television. In this way she learns everything there is to know about the physical nature of the world . . . It seems, however, that Mary does not know all there is to know. For when she is let out of the black-and-white room or given color television, she will learn what it is like to see something red.[6]

> When Mary leaves her cell, she has a radically new experience: she experiences redness for the first time, and from this experience, and this experience alone, she knows what it is like to see red.[7]

What is most important about this example is that Mary, because of her exclusively black-and-white experiences, is unable to "project forward to get a sense of what it will be like for her to see red."[8] Her knowledge about her other experiences (reading about red, for example) cannot serve as a basis for knowing what it is like to see a color such as red.

Now imagine that Mary is deciding whether she ought to step outside of the black-and-white room to see red. Paul claims that, according to the standard model, Mary will be unable to make a rational decision about whether to choose to see red or not. On the standard model, in order to make a rational decision about whether she ought to see red, Mary must determine the expected value of not seeing red and of seeing red. To do this, she must determine the value that the outcomes of seeing red and of not seeing red will have for her and the probability of these outcomes occurring. On the standard model, the action with the highest EV is the rational one. Paul argues that Mary cannot know the value of seeing red for her and, in turn, that she cannot determine whether seeing red or not seeing red will have a higher expected value for her.[9] This means that Mary cannot make a rational choice to see red or not to see red.

Why is Mary unable to determine the value of seeing red for her? Paul argues that Mary is in an epistemically impoverished position in relation to seeing red. She does not know what it is like to see red. Since she does not know what it is like to see red, she does not know what emotions, beliefs, desires, and dispositions will be caused by her experience of seeing red.[10] Maybe she will feel excited or maybe she will feel frightened. Moreover, she does not know what it will be like to have any of the emotions, beliefs, desires, and dispositions that result specifically from her experience of seeing red. Even if she does know that she will find redness fun, exciting, or frightening, she does not know what it will be like to find "red," in particular, fun, exciting, or frightening. "These are all ways of saying that . . . she cannot know the value of what it'll be like for her to see red."[11]

Paul argues that the individual who is choosing to have a child, before actually having that child, is in a situation that is similar to Mary's. On Paul's view, having a child, like seeing red for the first time, is a unique and transformative experience. It is unlike any experience you have had before. So, before having a child, you do not and cannot know what it is like to HC. Without knowing what it is like to HC, you do not and cannot know what having a child will feel like. You also do not and cannot know what emotions, beliefs, desires and dispositions you will have as a result of what it is like to HC. May be you will feel joy or may be you will feel fear. Furthermore, even if you do know that you will find having a child joyful or frightening, you do not and cannot know what it is like to find having that child, in particular, joyful or frightening.[12] All of this means that you are unable to determine the value of what it will be like for you to HC. In turn, you cannot determine the EV of HC. You are unable to make a rational decision about whether to choose to HC or ~HC.

Paul's paper has rightfully received a significant amount of attention. Paul skillfully brings together issues in philosophy of mind, epistemology, decision theory, and normative ethics to raise a strong challenge to the common-sense conclusion that we can make rational decisions to HC. The strength of her argument lies in the fact that it relies on and vividly captures something that many of us who have had children believe to be true—namely, that there is something uniquely transformative about the experience of having a child. Few arguments in the philosophical literature on rationality, moral knowledge, or having children have so clearly made a case for the importance of experience in making rational decisions about the value of having a child.

Despite the obvious merits of her argument, I have grounds for questioning its soundness. In what follows, I show that, ultimately, her arguments do not plausibly demonstrate that the standard model of rationality precludes rational decisions to HC. I argue that there are phenomenal and nonphenomenal values that can be used to determine the value that HC will have for us and, in turn, that can be used to make rational decisions to HC or ~HC. I also argue that we can have an approximate idea of what it is like for us to have a child, even before we actually have a child and that, on the standard model, this is sufficient to make rational decisions to HC or ~HC.

There are at least three grounds for rejecting Paul's argument against the rationality of choosing HC.

#1: *Grounds for Rejecting Claim3* (You can determine the value of the outcomes of HC only by knowing WIL for you to HC)

Paul argues that the value of the outcomes of HC is determined by "what it is like for you to have your child, including what it is like to have the beliefs, desires, emotions and dispositions that result, directly and indirectly, from having your own child."[13] She refers to these sorts of values as "phenomenal values." Since HC is something that happens to you specifically, the phenomenal value (the value of "what is like for you") is the most important and is likely the sole important factor in determining whether it is rational for you to HC.[14]

This argument moves too quickly. First, there are phenomenal values that can play an important role in determining the value of the outcomes of HC for you, even if you do not know what it will like be for you to HC. For example, many individuals place positive value on transformative experiences themselves. They place positive value on experiencing things that are new and that cannot be known on the basis of past experiences. For example, imagine that a friend of mine tells me that she tried Indian food and that she enjoyed her experience of it. As a result, I become curious about Indian food. However, imagine that, having never tried Indian food before, I have no idea what it will be like to eat Indian food. It seems that, even in this case, it could be rational for me to try some Indian food. If I place positive value on having new experiences, then I can know, beforehand, that I will place positive value on the experience of eating new food such as Indian food, even if I do not ultimately enjoy eating the Indian food itself (i.e., I can be glad I tried Indian food, even if I do not end up liking the food itself). Similar factors likely explain why so many people choose to travel to countries that they have never been to and that are very different from those that they have already travelled to or lived in. Many individuals simply place value on experiencing what it is like to undergo a transformative experience. Similar factors can also apply in the case of choosing to HC. If you value having transformative experiences and having a child is transformative in the way that Paul suggests and you know this to be the case (say, after reading Paul's paper), it will follow that you can know that having a child will have a positive value for you and, in turn, that you can make a rational decision to HC.

Second, there are many nonphenomenal values that can play an important role in determining the value of the outcomes of HC. For example, if you are a member of a dying (or minority) culture that has only two members left (say, you are the last of two Mohicans) and you see yourself as having an obligation to support the persistence of this culture, then you might determine that the outcomes of HC will have positive value for you for nonphenomenal reasons. Alternatively, if you see yourself as having a moral obligation to help the destitute, then you might determine that adopting a child (and thus choosing HC) will have positive nonphenomenal value for you.

Paul explicitly states that, in her argument, she ignores "external nonphenomenal factors" that an individual might take into account when deciding whether to HC or ~HC. She suggests that, even if external values are considered, her argument remains plausible. This is because, on her view, even if such external nonphenomenal factors are taken into account, they are unlikely to "swamp any personal phenomenal effects."[15]

This assumption is false. As is the case in the two examples cited, the nonphenomenal value of HC may very well outweigh any of the personal phenomenal values you might associate with HC and you can determine (through introspection) that this is the case. Indeed, because of the weight you place on your nonphenomenal values, you might even be entirely neutral with respect to the phenomenal values associated with choosing to HC (i.e., "it doesn't matter what it is like for me. I must meet my obligations to my culture/to the poor").

In an e-rejoinder, Paul acknowledges that "if you're really not basing your decision at all on what being a parent is going to be like for you then you can make a rational decision. But relying only on criteria like that is not the usual way to decide to have kids."[16] Her contention is that this is not the way that we usually conceive of rationality. This response is not convincing, however. First, at least some of the time, this is the way that people typically make decisions to HC. People choose to HC for nonphenomenal (moral) reasons. Second, even if it is not the way that people typically choose to HC, this fact does not in and of itself make it an irrational way to decide to choose to HC. Moral values can determine the value that choosing to HC (or ~HC) will have for us. So, Paul must acknowledge that, even if they constitute only a small number of the decisions that are actually made, it can be rational to choose to HC.

Recall that Paul's original conclusion was that, on the standard model, we cannot make rational decisions to HC or ~HC. This discussion illustrates that, when properly understood, her arguments support a much weaker conclusion (assuming we accept the rest of her arguments), namely, that we cannot make rational decisions to HC *on the basis of what it is like to HC*, which still leaves open the possibility of making rational decisions to HC or ~HC on the basis of certain *phenomenal values*, such as those relating to the value we place on transformative experiences themselves, and *nonphenomenal values*, such as those relating to our moral values.[17] Understood in this way, the conclusion of Paul's argument is much less controversial than it first appeared. It does not challenge the possibility of making rational decisions to have a child. It just narrows the grounds for such decisions to the sorts of phenomenal and nonphenomenal considerations that I discuss.[18]

#2: *Grounds for Rejecting Claim4* (You can only know WIL for you to HC by being in a state where you HC)

Although Paul does not always tackle this issue directly, her view is that there are no other bases for determining what it is like to HC than actually having a child. You cannot know what it is like to HC from your experiences with other people's children, for example.[19] On Paul's view, having a child (of your own) is a transformative and unique experience.[20] Upon becoming a parent, you will experience things you have never experienced before. Among other things, you will experience what is like to see, touch, care for, and attend to your newborn child. Before having these experiences, you do not and cannot know what it is like to have such experiences.

The problem with Paul's argument is that it conceives of the experience of what it is like to HC as one unified and distinct experience—namely, the what it is like experience of having a child. However, alternatively, one can conceive of the experience of what it is like to HC as being made up of distinct what it is like experiences; for example, of what it is like to care for, what it is like to meet the needs of, and what it is like to play and spend leisure time with, and laugh with and be angry at.[21] While we do not and cannot have experiences of these types in relation to the child we are considering having before having her, we can and have had them with other individuals.[22] From these types of experiences, we can and do know something about what it will be like to have experience of these types, even if we do not know what it will be like to have these types of experiences with our own child specifically.[23]

To make the point more vivid, return to the case of Mary. As Paul suggests, seeing red will be transformative for Mary. This transformation occurs because Mary, having only experienced black and white, has no experience of what it is like to see color and, as a result, cannot project from her past experiences to know what it will be like to see red. This is why, before seeing red, she cannot know what it will be like to see red. However, things are different if Mary is in a pink room and is considering seeing red. If she is in a pink room she can, on the basis of her experiences of seeing pink, know something about what it will be like to see red, since pink is not only a color but is also a red-like color and she knows this to be the case. So, she can know what feelings, beliefs, desires, and dispositions will be caused by her experience of seeing a red-like color. She can know, for example, that she enjoys seeing red-like colours, finds it exciting and that she desires to see more. Moreover, to the extent that pink is a red-like color, she can know something about what it will be like for her to find "red-like colors," in particular, joyful and exciting.[24] In short, having experiences of a closely related type such as seeing pink, a red-like color, can serve as basis for knowing what it is like to see red.

Unless they have never been around children, the situation of most people deciding whether to HC is more analogous to Mary in the pink room than it is to Mary in the black-and-white room. We can have experiences of a variety of types that are relevantly similar to the sorts of experiences that we will have when we have a child of our own. For example, we can know what it is like to touch and to see a newborn. We can know what it is like to care for and to attend to a newborn (after spending significant time with one). In this way, we can know something about what it will be like to have the types of experiences that we will have when we have a child of our own.[25]

Paul's arguments suggest the following response. The experiences of what it is like to love and to care for a newborn that is not your own are phenomenally very different from what it is like to love and to care for a newborn that is *your own*. There is just something phenomenally unique about having these types of experiences with *your own* child.[26] So, we cannot know what having a child of our own will be like on the basis of our experiences with other people's children. Similarly, even if Mary has had experiences of pink, Paul could argue, Mary still cannot know what it will be like to see red. What it is like to see red is very different from what is like to see pink, even though pink is a red-like colour. Seeing red, specifically, is a unique and transformative experience.

The problem with this response is that it will make many, if not most, of our everyday experiences unknowable, since something similar could be said of each experience that we have. In some sense, each experience that we have is both transformative and unique. Each experience that we have changes us in some way and is unlike any other experience we have had before it. While I may have seen red before, I have not seen it on this day, in this particular light, and so on. While I may have eaten chocolate ice cream before, I have not done it on this day, in this weather, in this mood, and so on. So, my experience of seeing red or eating chocolate ice cream, or whatever is, in a sense, unique and transformative. In turn, it would follow, I cannot project from my past experiences of seeing red or eating chocolate to know what it will be like, respectively, to see red or to eat chocolate ice cream on this day, at this time, and in this way. So, if we take this rebuttal seriously, it would work to rule out projection in most cases.

There are two problems with this response. The first problem is that most of us do not find each new experience of eating chocolate ice cream transformative in the way suggested. It does seem that we can project from our past experiences of seeing red or eating chocolate ice cream to know what it will be like, respectively, to see red or to eat chocolate ice cream on this day, at this time, and in this way. To the extent that Paul's arguments suggest otherwise, they go against common sense.

The second problem is that if Paul's arguments rule out projection in most cases, then her arguments prove too much. Paul claims that her arguments are meant to show that the standard model fails in relation to life transforming decisions, not all decisions.[27] If, however, we accept Paul's claim4, that you can only know WIL for you to HC by being in a state where you HC, and the response that seems to follow from accepting this claim (as I outlined above), then her argument proves too much because they rule out projection in most cases. If projection is ruled out in most cases, and we cannot know what it is like to eat ice cream or to see red on this day, in this weather, in this mood and so on, and knowledge of what it is like is necessary to make a rational decision, then it follows that we cannot make rational decisions in most cases. It will not only be irrational, on the standard model, to choose to have a child. It will also be irrational to choose to see red, to eat chocolate ice cream, to drive your car, to brush your teeth, and so on. This sort of rebuttal pushes too far and takes us beyond Paul's stated aims of merely showing that the standard model fails only in the case of life transforming decisions. It also makes Paul's argument as a whole less plausible, since, as Paul seems to acknowledge, the standard model does lead to rational choices in the case of most non-life transforming decisions.

#3: *Grounds for Rejecting Claim3* (You can determine the value of the outcomes of HC and ~HC solely by knowing what it is like [WIL] for you to HC and ~HC)

This discussion raises perhaps the most important grounds for questioning claim3. It concerns Paul's emphasis on the importance of *knowing* what it is like to have a child of your own. On the standard model, in order to determine the EV of HC, you must determine the value of the outcomes of HC and the probability of these outcomes occurring. On Paul's view, the value of the outcomes of HC is determined only by *knowing* what it is like to HC. But why think that we have to "know" what it is like to HC in order to determine the value of the outcomes associated with HC? On the standard model, rationality requires that we determine the value that we estimate will be associated with the outcomes of HC, not the *known* value of the outcomes of HC. Something less than full knowledge of what it is like to HC is sufficient to determine the EV of the outcomes of HC and, in turn, to make a rational choice to HC. So, even if we allow Paul's claim (claim4) that we can only know what it is like to HC by being in a state where we actually HC, not on the basis of similar types of experiences, we can, on the basis of related experiences, at least *estimate* what value the outcomes of HC will have for us. This is sufficient to make a rational decision about whether to HC. In turn, claim3 is false. We do not need to *know* what it is like to HC to determine the value of the outcomes of HC.[28]

In response, Paul could claim something stronger: we cannot form even an approximate idea of what it is like to HC before actually having a child of our own. In turn, we cannot form even an estimation of the value of the outcomes of choosing to HC. This is a difficult claim to accept. On the basis of closely related experiences, it does seem that we can have at least an approximate idea of what is like to have a child and, in turn, that we can at least estimate the value of the outcomes of HC. Given that most of us accept this view and, on the face of it, it seems plausible, the onus is on Paul to show that this view is false.

CONCLUSION

I have tried to show that there are three main grounds for rejecting Paul's arguments. First, Paul's claim3, that we can only determine the value of the outcomes of choosing HC by knowing what it is like to HC, is false. We can determine the value of the outcomes of choosing to HC on the basis of certain *phenomenal values*, such as those relating to the value we place on having transformative experiences themselves, and *nonphenomenal values*, such as the moral value we place on preventing the demise of our cultural or ethnic group.

Second, in relation to claim3, I suggested that *knowledge* of what it is like to HC is not needed to determine the value of the outcomes of choosing to HC. Something less demanding, such as having an estimate of the value of these outcomes, which can be based on an approximate idea of what it is like to HC, is sufficient.

Third, her claim4, that you can only know what is like to have a child by actually being in a state where you have a child, is false. We can on the basis of experiences of similar types know what it is like to have a child. Just as Mary can, on the basis of the experience of seeing a red-like color such as pink, know what is like to see red, we can, on the basis of our experiences with other children, know what is like to have a child. Denying this claim would mean that many of our daily decisions are irrational, something which runs strongly against our common sense and Paul's own views.

In short, contrary to what Paul suggests, we can, on the standard model, make rational decisions to have a child.[29]

NOTES

1. "What Mary Can't Expect When She's Expecting," *Res Philosophica* 92, no. 2 (2015): 1–23.
2. Paul, "What Mary Can't Expect," 1.
3. In other words, where EV = Expected Value, V = Value, and O = the set of resulting outcomes, and Ø = the action, EVØ = VO(Ø) × P(Ø)
4. It is unclear whether Paul thinks a similar argument can be made in relation to ~HC. It does seem that before choosing to have a child, you are already in a state of ~HC. So, you have experienced what it is like to ~HC and, in turn, you can know the EV of ~HC. This would explain why she focuses on HC and our lack of WIL experiences of HC before choosing to HC. Her argument seems to be that, even if we can determine the EV of ~HC, not being able to determine the EV of HC leaves us unable to make rational decisions about whether to HC or ~HC. If she is correct about not being able to determine the EV of HC, this would be sufficient to show that you cannot make rational decisions about whether to HC or ~HC, since you need to know the EV of both HC and ~HC in order to determine which is the rational choice.

    However, one could argue, along the lines of Paul, that the WIL experience of actually choosing ~HC will be phenomenally different for you than the WIL experience of ~HC before ~HC is actually chosen. The experience of WIL to choose to remain childless is potentially different from the experience of WIL to currently be childless. So, perhaps her arguments support the conclusion that we cannot know WIL to experience ~HC before we choose ~HC. For my purposes, I will focus on her arguments relating to HC, since this is her focus. However, much of what I say here about HC should apply in relation to ~HC as well.
5. That is, you cannot make a rational decision to HC or ~HC on the "standard model" of what this requires.
6. Frank Jackson, "What Mary Didn't Know," *The Journal of Philosophy* LXXXIII, no. 5 (1986), 291, quoted in Paul, "What Mary Can't Expect," 6.
7. Paul, "What Mary Can't Expect," 6.

8. Paul, "What Mary Can't Expect," 6.
9. In other words, she cannot know $V(\emptyset)$.
10. Paul, "What Mary Can't Expect," 7.
11. Paul, "What Mary Can't Expect," 7.
12. Notice that this argument applies to those who are deciding to have their second and not only their first child. You are epistemically impoverished in the same way in both instances. You lack knowledge of what it is like to have a particular child before you have that particular child (even if that child is your second child).
13. Paul, "What Mary Can't Expect," 5.
14. According to Paul, "The value of what it is like for the agent plays the central, if not the only, role in the decision to procreate." (Paul, "What Mary Can't Expect," 5).
15. Paul, "What Mary Can't Expect," n. 4, 2.
16. L.A. Paul and Kieran Healy, "What You Can't Expect When You are Expecting," accessed September 23, 2013, http://crookedtimber.org/2013/02/27/what-you-cant-expect-when-youre-expecting/
17. Paul suggests that "In the past, external facts and circumstances played a much larger role in the causal processes leading up to parenthood. Before contraceptive devices were widely available, you didn't choose to have a child based on what you thought it would be like . . . to the extent that you actively tried to choose to have children, often it was because you needed an heir, or needed more hands to work the farm, or whatever" (p. 28). She does not explicitly state that these constitute more rational bases for making decisions to have children, but her arguments support this conclusion.
18. In general, Paul's focus on phenomenal knowledge as a prerequisite for being able to determine the value of the outcomes of HC is not well founded. There is nothing in the standard model that states that we can only determine the value of the outcomes of X when we know what it is like to X. This is Paul's addition and she seems to derive this requirement from a notion of common-sense rationality. She suggests that this is implicit in how we typically come to make what we think are rational decisions. Paul claims that we typically make decisions that we believe are rational on the basis of what we think a particular action will be like for us. The standard model does not claim to be and certainly does not need to be understood as representing common-sense rationality. So, even if Paul is right, proponents of the standard model can accept her claims that we cannot determine the phenomenal value of HC before having a child of our own. They can just emphasize that there are other nonphenomenal values that can and ought to be the basis of rational decisions.
19. On Paul's view, you also cannot know what it is like to HC on the basis of conversations with other people about their experiences of WIL to HC.
20. Note that Paul thinks this is true in cases where the child that you have is your biological child and where the child is adopted.
21. In "Big Decisions, Opting, Converting, and Drifting," *Royal Institute of Philosophy Supplement*, 58 (2006), 157–172, Edna Ullman-Margalit suggests that big or life-changing decisions are often made up of smaller and less significant decisions. Similarly, the choice to HC can be described as being made up of less significant or smaller choices. It involves deciding to stop using birth control, to take prenatal vitamins, to start seeing an OB/GYN, and a number of other small choices. Though I will not pursue this concern here, it may be that the

standard model can be used to make such smaller decisions and, in turn, can ultimately provide a basis for making rational choices to HC.

22. There may also be other ways of gaining phenomenal or "what it is like" knowledge through related types of experiences caused by imagination, empathy, and art. Art and film, through stimulation of empathy and imagination, may be the basis for phenomenal knowledge, since they may cause what it is like to feel, believe, desire, and to be disposed to do something. For example, artistic works about parenthood, giving birth to and rearing and raising children may cause experiences of what it is like to have a child of one's own, without causing the person to actually have a child. Eric Schliesser also suggests that a rich vocabulary can help us to gain phenomenal knowledge. He argues, for example, "we can know what it is like to see purple rain without ever seeing purple rain" (http://www.newappsblog.com/2013/02/weekly-philo-of-economics-the-uncertainty-of-parenthood.html). Perhaps similar things can be said about language relating to having a child. If this is right, then literature, fiction, and nonfiction may also give us grounds for knowing what it is like to have a child.

23. Another useful way to think about this worry may be in terms of the distinction between "type" and "token". In other words, I am suggesting that Paul fails to make the distinction between type and token. It may be true that you lack knowledge of the specific token, "a child of your own," but you do have knowledge of the type of experiences that are part of having a child of your own such as "caring for" and "loving."

24. These are all ways of saying that she can know the value of what it will be like for her to see red-like colours such as red.

25. It has been suggested to me that perhaps one thing we cannot know what it is like before doing it is bearing and giving birth to a child. These are experiences that are unlike any others that a person can have before actually bearing and giving birth to a child. There are no relevantly related types of experiences. This is something that I am not convinced of. In other cultures, where people are more involved in pregnancy and delivery, people can know something about what is like to have a child. Art and film may also cause related types of experiences. Moreover, even if it is true that we cannot know what it is like to bear and to give birth to a child before actually doing so, these are only some of the what it is like experiences that result from choosing to HC. Choosing to HC will involve much more than bearing and giving birth to a child, and we can know something about what it is like to have those types of experiences. This knowledge can be the basis for making rational decisions to HC.

26. This argument can be understood as claiming that there is something uniquely transformative about this particular token of the type.

27. Paul, "What Mary Can't Expect," 1.

28. Paul suggests that we cannot determine the phenomenal value of the outcomes of HC on the basis of what other people report about their experiences of what it is like to HC. Paul's conflation of knowledge with rationality may explain this claim. It may be true that we lack knowledge of what the value of the outcomes of HC is, even after talking with other people. Yet, it does seem true that we can gain an approximate idea of what it will be like for us to HC and, in turn, that we can gain an approximate idea of what value the outcomes of HC will have for us. This is particularly true if we collect reports from people we deem to be relevantly similar to ourselves.

29. Thanks to Esa Diaz-Leon, Joe Oppenheimer, Tim Meijer, Andreas Albertsen, Christy Mag Uidhir, and participants in the Permissible Progeny conference at the University of Western Ontario for very helpful comments on an earlier draft. Special thanks go to L.A. Paul for writing such a stimulating paper and for providing comments on an earlier draft.

REFERENCES

Jackson, Frank. "What Mary Didn't Know." *The Journal of Philosophy* 83, no. 5 (1986), pp. 291–295.

Paul, L.A. "What Mary Can't Expect When She's Expecting," *Res Philosophica* 92, no. 2 (2015): 1–23.

Paul, L.A., and Kieran Healy. "What You Can't Expect When You Are Expecting." Accessed September 23, 2013, http://crookedtimber.org/2013/02/27/what-you-cant-expect-when-youre-expecting/.

Ullman-Margalit, Edna, "Big Decisions, Opting, Converting, and Drifting," *Royal Institute of Philosophy Supplement* 58 (2006): 157–172.

CHAPTER 8

Can a Right to Reproduce Justify the Status Quo on Parental Licensing?

ANDREW BOTTERELL AND CAROLYN MCLEOD

INTRODUCTION

What is the normative status of the current system of licensing parents, according to which adoptive parents, and adoptive parents alone, are subject to parental licensing requirements?[1] Consider the following argument in favor of this system: people have a right to reproduce, and so licensing people who want to reproduce (with or without assistance from others) is not morally justified, but because prospective adoptive parents do not exercise this right when they have children, licensing them is morally justified. This chapter focuses on this argument and demonstrates that it fails, primarily because the right to reproduce does not allow one to draw the distinctions that must be drawn if the current system of licensing parents is to be justified. We conclude that arguments based on the right to reproduce cannot support this system. Having demonstrated in an earlier paper[2] that arguments based on other purported differences between adoptive and non-adoptive parenting do not support this system either, we conclude more generally that the system is morally unjustified.

We spend a good deal of time in this chapter discussing the nature and content of the right to reproduce. Although frequent appeals to this right are made in discussions concerning parental rights, children's rights, and other rights and obligations that have to do with the creation and parenting of children, it remains unclear what the right to reproduce amounts to. Is it equivalent to the right to pass on one's genetic material? Is it distinct from the right to become a parent? Does appeal to the right to reproduce add anything to appeals to the right to bodily autonomy? These questions require answers because the nature and content of the right to reproduce have important implications for how we assess the morality of begetting, bearing, and rearing children—in Onora O'Neill's evocative phrase—as well as for whether parental licensing is morally justified.[3]

BACKGROUND

When we refer to parental licensing, we have in mind, at a minimum, restrictions on the freedom to parent a child imposed by the state on people who may never have mistreated children.[4] The state requires that these people show some competency in being a parent before they become one in a social sense. The relevant restrictions are *prospective* in this sense (although they could be retrospective in the same sense). Adoptive parents tend not to receive an actual *license* to parent (similar to a driver's license); still, what they undergo is parental licensing. They are prevented from becoming parents unless or until they complete a home study, which consists of background checks on the financial, medical, and family histories of individuals; an evaluation of how child-friendly their home is, and so on. Some prospective adoptive parents also attend mandatory parenting classes and must promise to submit periodic reports to governmental and/or private adoption agencies after they have adopted a child.

To be sure, the state sometimes interferes with the ability of non-adoptive parents to care for their children, though normally it does so retrospectively and not in a way that involves licensing. The state seeks to determine in such cases whether parents *are* mistreating their children, not whether they *will* mistreat them and should not be parents for this reason. Moreover, the state usually intervenes in this way only when there is evidence of severe parental incompetence, whereas prospective adoptive parents have to show a relatively high level of competence before they can become parents.

In summary, individuals wishing to become adoptive parents face licensing requirements that typically involve extensive (and often expensive) background checks and sometimes include mandatory educational programs. Moreover, these requirements tend to be unique to adoptive parents. Individuals who become parents by the traditional route or with the use of assisted reproductive technologies (ARTs) are not normally subject to the same—or indeed any—restrictions. The question with which we were concerned in our previous paper on parental licensing was this: Is the status quo with respect to parental licensing morally justified?[5] Our answer to this question was "no."

We arrived at this negative conclusion via a negative route. We considered a number of arguments—the best that we could find in the literature and the best that we could develop on our own—in support of the status quo on parental licensing. And we endeavored to show that none of these arguments is any good.[6] Our contention was not that parental licensing is morally justified or unjustified,[7] but merely that the status quo on licensing could not be morally justified. Our goal was to highlight what we took to be a fundamentally unfair situation in which adoptive parents are treated very differently than other parents.

THE RIGHT TO REPRODUCE ARGUMENT

In discussing the status quo on parental licensing, however, there was one objection to which we paid insufficient attention. According to this objection, the reason why non-adoptive parents should be free of any licensing is two-fold: first, because such parents (or prospective parents) have a right to reproduce; and second, because licensing requirements would unjustifiably interfere with that right. Support for this general argument can be found in the work of Christine Overall. Overall observes that as a matter of fact "individuals who do not seek [medical] reproductive services are not subjected to any test or qualification for parenting" and then notes that "if there is no screening system for prospective parents who do not need reproductive services, it seems unjust to subject to screening those who have the misfortune of needing medical help [to conceive]."[8] The reason why such screening would be unjust is, according to Overall, that "such a system would be a severe imposition on people's bodily freedom and autonomy."[9] Since, for her, there is an important relationship between people's (especially women's) bodily freedom and autonomy and their right to reproduce—the former helps to ground the latter—her more general point is that licensing requirements for individuals wishing to conceive using ARTs would unjustifiably interfere with their reproductive rights.

Opposition to this argument can be found in the work of Hugh LaFollette.[10] LaFollette rejects the idea that a right to reproduce—or, as he calls it, a "right to have children"—could justify licensing only adoptive parents.[11] Such a right does not preclude the licensing of biological parents, according to LaFollette, because having the right is conditional on being the sort of person who would not abuse or neglect children. In other words, for LaFollette, no one has a right to have children that they will abuse or neglect.[12] We will return to the question of how to interpret a right to reproduce. Suffice it to say that LaFollette does not believe that such a right supports the status quo on parental licensing. However, while we agree with LaFollette's conclusion, our reasoning differs from his. Compared to him, we also delve more deeply into what might ground a right to reproduce.

To recap: the argument based on the right to reproduce in favor of the status quo on parental licensing—what we will call the *Right to Reproduce Argument*—is composed of two claims. The first is that there is a right to reproduce. The second is that while licensing biological parents is inconsistent with that right, licensing adoptive parents is not inconsistent with it. These two claims will structure the discussion that follows. Our general argument takes the form of dilemma: either the right to reproduce is groundless and so of dubious coherence, or it cannot draw the needed distinction between adoptive and non-adoptive parents. We therefore conclude that a right to reproduce cannot justify the status quo on parental licensing.

THE FUNCTION OF RIGHTS: INTERESTS AND CHOICES

Before we can assess the Right to Reproduce Argument, we need to say more about what the right to reproduce amounts to. This will involve saying something about what rights are; about how rights can be grounded or justified; and in particular, about what the right to reproduce includes and excludes.

At a minimum, to have a right is to have an entitlement. If I have a right then I am entitled to demand that others do or refrain from doing certain things. So, for example, if I own a piece of property, then I am entitled to prevent others from coming onto it, and that entitlement stems from my ownership rights. Similarly, my right to bodily autonomy entails that I get to determine the ends to which my body may be put, and so others may not touch me without my consent. It is tempting to conclude that rights must therefore serve a function, that they must *do* something for those who hold them. But what function might rights serve? Two answers have traditionally been given to this question.

On the one hand, some theorists claim that rights function to protect certain important *interests*; Joseph Raz is perhaps the most prominent modern exponent of this view. According to Raz, an interest is an aspect of a person's objective well-being, and in order to ground a right, an interest must be "a sufficient reason for holding some other person(s) to be under a duty."[13] This view of rights has become known as the interest theory. In defense of it, Harry Brighouse and Adam Swift say that rights should be "moral constructs designed to protect interests, [because interests] are the truly fundamental moral considerations."[14]

On the other hand, some theorists claim that rights function to give an individual *control* over what other individuals can do. According to H. L. A. Hart, rights make an individual a "small-scale sovereign."[15] On this view, rights-holders have the ability to require others to act in various ways; in exercising a right they also exercise authority, and can command obedience in others. This theory has become known as the *choice* or *will theory*, since according to it rights function to protect *choices* that flow from the exercise of one's *will*.

The interest and the choice theory both have their strengths. The choice theory, for example, is ideally structured to make sense of the normative link between having a right and being in a position to exercise control: to have a right is to have the authority to demand that others do or refrain from doing certain things. And the interest theory gives effect to the plausible idea that there is a connection between having a right and being better off as a result of having that right. For if rights protect interests, and if interests are the truly fundamental moral considerations, then having a right to φ ought to be preferable to not having a right to φ, at least with respect to the content or object of that right.

But as Leif Wenar[16] points out, both the choice theory and the interest theory run into problems when viewed as general accounts of the nature of rights. We will briefly highlight two such problems. First, the choice theory has trouble accounting for the fact that some rights are innate and cannot be waived. Recall that on the choice theory, to have a right is to exercise authority or control over what someone else can do. The fact that I own my bicycle authorizes me to prevent others from using it. But by the same token, because I am the owner of the bicycle I can waive such rights of exclusion and allow others to use it, or even give it away to somebody else. In short, according to the choice theory it ought always to be possible to release others from duties that flow from one's rights. But some rights— such as the right not to sell oneself into slavery—appear to be inalienable, and that makes trouble for the choice theory.

Turning to the interest theory, it too is problematic because it cannot make sense of us having strong interests in things without having a right to those things, nor can it make sense of us having a right to something without having any interest in that thing. With respect to the first sort of case, while a man might have a very strong interest in having the Ontario Lottery and Gaming Corporation pay his spouse for her winning lottery ticket, *he* has no right against the lottery that it perform that action. Only his spouse, who is the bearer of the winning ticket, has that right. This is an example of an interest without a right. With respect to the second sort of case, judges have the right to pronounce verdicts of guilt and impose punishment on individuals who have committed criminal offenses. But in doing so, they are required to act in a disinterested and impartial manner. Thus, if a judge did have a strong interest in the outcome of a particular case, we would be inclined to say that she *lacks* a right to decide it. This is an example of a right without an interest. In sum, it would appear that the links between rights and interests, and between rights and choices, are more complicated than interest and choice theorists make them out to be.[17]

Similar sorts of considerations, both pro and con, also arise in the reproductive context. For example, there are reasons to think that the right to reproduce serves to protect interests. As Christine Overall argues, both the right to reproduce and the right not to reproduce are "grounded in general human interests; people need protection from compulsory procreation as much as (or perhaps even more than) they need protection from denied procreation."[18] One might also argue that even if, as a matter of fact, rights sometimes protect choices, the choices that people make in reproductive contexts deserve protection only if those choices reflect some more fundamental interest. On the other hand, an interest theory also faces challenges when applied to a right to reproduce. Thus, in discussing the relationship between the right to reproduce and the interest in rearing a child, Muireann Quigley argues that this interest cannot ground the right to reproduce given that the interest in rearing a child can vary over time, and between people.[19] For can it really be said that only at times when X has a strong interest in rearing a child does she have a right to reproduce, or that if X has this interest but Y lacks it then Y, unlike X, has no right to reproduce? The strangeness of these results suggests that an interest in rearing a child, or any interest for that matter, cannot be what grounds the right to reproduce. At the very least, it suggests that the relationship between interests and the right to reproduce is less straightforward than an interest theory makes it out to be.

Parallel considerations arise when we consider the claim that the right to reproduce ought to be grounded in choices. In support of this idea, it might be noted that people very often choose to reproduce regardless of whether they have an objective interest in reproducing; perhaps, all things considered, their lives will go less well should they reproduce. Still, they might have a right to reproduce. In addition, one might insist that the right to reproduce is justified, in part at least, by people's bodily autonomy—that is, their ability to *choose* autonomously what they want to have happen to their bodies—which is violated when they are subject, for example, to forced abortion or forced sterilization. On the other hand, one might worry that if the right to reproduce is essentially a *reproductive* right, and if a right to bodily autonomy has no necessary connection to reproduction (a person can exercise this right in non-reproductive contexts), then the latter cannot, without more, ground the right to reproduce.

In short, while there are reasons to take both an interest theory and a choice theory of rights seriously when thinking about the right to reproduce, other considerations pull in the opposite direction. What is clear, however, is that—at least in the context of the Right to Reproduce Argument—the right to reproduce is a negative right. On this understanding, the right does not entitle its bearer to any particular means or outcome, but amounts to an entitlement not to be interfered with in procreation. According to the Right to Reproduce Argument, in other words, licensing non-adoptive parents is inconsistent with the right to reproduce because licensing interferes with one's ability to reproduce.

GROUNDING A RIGHT TO REPRODUCE

In summary, there are two dominant theories about the functions of rights, the choice theory and the interest theory. And there is the particular right with which we are presently concerned, namely the right to reproduce understood negatively as a right not to be interfered with in matters intimately connected with procreation. If there is such a right, it follows that—unless the right is sui generis—it must be grounded either in a fundamental interest or in a right to autonomy. Finally, recall that the reason we are interested in the right to reproduce is because it forms a core part of an argument in favor of the status quo on parental licensing, a state of affairs that we believe is fundamentally unfair.

Now let us explain why the Right to Reproduce Argument fails. First, we will consider whether the right to reproduce can be grounded in a fundamental interest in genetic or biological reproduction, or in child rearing. Next, we will discuss whether this right can be explained in terms of a general right to bodily autonomy or in a particular right to procreative autonomy. We will argue that either the right to reproduce cannot be grounded in these interests or choices; or if it can, that it is incapable of underwriting a distinction between adoptive and non-adoptive parents that would support the status quo on parental licensing.

Grounding the Right to Reproduce in Interests

There are two broad categories of interests that could plausibly be said to ground a right to reproduce: interests having to do with creating children to which one is genetically or biologically related, and interests having to do with rearing children—that is, with becoming a parent.

The Interest in Genetic or Biological Reproduction

Presumably, many people value having offspring to which they are genetically related or, in the case of women, to which they are biologically related through gestation and possibly also through genetics. In other words, many people have an interest in being "begetters" or "bearers" of children. However, as various authors including O'Neill have argued, a *mere* interest in genetic or biological reproduction cannot ground a right to reproduce.[20] For no one has a right to create a child without taking any responsibility for the rearing of it. Reproduction is valuable largely because of the opportunity it gives people to parent a child (i.e., to be "rearers"). A desire *simply* to reproduce is not sufficient to ground a right because, contrary to what John Robertson suggests, whether one reproduces or not could not be central to one's "dignity, and the meaning of one's life."[21] Surely we would not agree, for example, that what *truly* afforded a man dignity and imbued his life with meaning was the passing on of his genetic material. Hence, we would not accept a man's "claim to a right to the unfettered distribution of his sperm."[22] Similarly, we would reject a woman's assertion that she has a right *simply* to experience pregnancy and childbirth given the consequences that typically, and as a matter of fact, follow such experiences. In short, while genetic reproduction or gestation is important when conjoined with the possibility of becoming a parent, an interest in doing either or both on their own is not significant enough to ground a right to reproduce.[23]

But regardless of whether the right to reproduce is just a right to have genetic or biological offspring, the fact is that some non-adoptive parents have no genetic or biological connection to their children, which means the right to reproduce thus understood could not justify the status quo on parental licensing. For example, if a couple uses a gamete donor to conceive, the resulting child will bear no genetic relation to one of the parents and so the right to reproduce would not prohibit imposing on such couples—or at least on the non-genetic parent—licensing requirements. However, with the status quo, there is no licensing for these couples or individuals (at least so long as they are heterosexual).[24] Similarly, there is no licensing in most jurisdictions for couples who use gamete donors and a contract pregnant woman to have a child, even though the resulting child will bear no biological connection to either parent, and so the right to reproduce understood as a right to have genetic or biological offspring could not protect either of them from licensing. In summary, the Right to Reproduce Argument fails on the above interpretation of a right to reproduce.

The Interest in Rearing Children or in Parenting

Another interest that could ground a right to reproduce is an interest in child rearing or parenting. As previously noted, some argue that the right to reproduce should be understood in terms of the value of becoming a parent.

According to Overall, an interest in having children, which is vital to many people, helps (along with women's "bodily freedom and autonomy"[25]) to explain a right to reproduce,[26] although what makes having children worthwhile is the parent-child relationship.[27] Thus, in her view, the interest that contributes to the justification of a right to reproduce is indeed an interest in parenting. In describing the parent-child relationship and its value, Overall refers to the "mutually enriching, mutually enhancing love that is [this] relationship,"[28] the asymmetrical nature of this relationship,[29] the opportunity it brings "for the growth of experience, the expansion of knowledge" or more generally for "self-transformation."[30] In some ways, her discussion is reminiscent of Harry Brighouse and Adam Swift's argument in support of the idea that people have a right to parent (which, as we will see, is different from a right to reproduce).[31]

Parenting can be very valuable, to be sure; however, grounding a right to reproduce in an interest in parenting is problematic because the satisfaction of this interest does not always require reproduction. The reason, of course, is that people can become parents and experience the unique value of parenting by, for example, adopting a child. Consequently, it is not clear that people have a right to reproduce simply in virtue of their interest in parenting.[32] In other words, their right to parent does not necessarily amount to a right to reproduce. What grounds a right to parent—experiencing the challenges and joys of a parent-child relationship—cannot ground a right to reproduce when those experiences can be had without reproducing.

Explaining the right to reproduce in terms of an interest in parenting is also problematic in this context because, so understood, the right cannot justify the status quo on parental licensing. It does not allow us to draw the required distinction between adoptive and non-adoptive parents. For on this interpretation, the right to reproduce is really no different than a right to parent, which is a right that prospective adoptive parents have as much as other prospective parents do. In sum, if the right to reproduce is to support the status quo on parental licensing, then it needs a different moral basis.

Another interpretation of the right to reproduce based on an interest in parenting is possible, however. According to this view, the right to reproduce protects an interest not in parenting a child, but rather in parenting "one's own child," as many people put it; that is, one's biological child. Such a view is worth taking seriously for obvious reasons. If the right to reproduce is based in an interest in parenting one's biological child, then, given that the right, so understood, is not exercised by adoptive parents—their children, while their own,[33] are not biologically related to them—it presumably *could* distinguish non-adoptive parents from adoptive parents and in turn justify the status quo on parental licensing.

But *can* the right to reproduce understood in terms of an interest in parenting one's "own"—that is, one's biological—child do the work we need it to do? We think that it cannot. First, given that there is a straightforward sense in which adoptive parents can legitimately say of their adopted children that they are "their children," the concept of a child of one's own is too thin to ground a right the absence of which is supposed to permit the state to interfere with the fundamental interests of adoptive parents in becoming parents.

Second, the reasons that have been offered in support of the idea that people have a vital interest in having a genetic or biological connection to their children simply could not ground a right to reproduce. For instance, the reasons people tend to give for why they need to be genetically related to their children are either implausible, reflecting a naïve understanding of genetics, or are too weak to support a right to reproduce.[34] A reason that is commonly given is family resemblance: that is, wanting children with whom one shares various characteristics, which one might feel is important for bonding with one's children. However, underlying assumptions here about bonding and family resemblance are contentious. First, studies indicate that mother-child attachment is normally as strong with adoption as it is with biological reproduction.[35] Second, family resemblances are not as genetic as, and tend to be significantly more social than, people usually assume they are.[36] These resemblances are also normative, because they stem from a normative genetic conception of family, according to which *family* resemblances need to be genetic.[37] The connection between family resemblance and this conception of family may help to explain the social pressure adopted siblings can feel to reveal this fact when people comment on how much they look alike as siblings.[38]

Similarly, reasons people might give in support of parenting their "own child," understood simply as a child they have given birth to, are unpersuasive. The idea that one needs to gestate and give birth to one's child, or participate in those experiences as someone's partner, in order to satisfy one's interest in parenting strikes us as prima facie wrong. What could support this view other than a commitment to the idea that parents who are biologically connected with their children are more naturally parents or are better parents than those who do not share such a biological connection? In response, one might argue that the act of gestation makes one more likely to parent well, at least in the absence of mandatory counseling or licensing. In particular, one might, like Anca Gheaus, believe that "[i]n spite of, and sometimes in virtue of, its tribulations, pregnancy . . . helps prepare people for the dramatic change brought about by parenthood."[39] This point could support not only the right that Gheaus defends—namely the right to "parent one's biological baby"—but also a right to reproduce.[40] For if pregnancy prepares one for parenthood, and if one has an interest in parenting and parenting well, then that interest might ground a right to become pregnant and to gestate—that is, a right to reproduce.

However, even assuming that Gheaus's claim about pregnancy is true, it does not show that pregnancy is uniquely preparatory in the way in which the Right to Reproduce Argument would require. For all that Gheaus argues the preparation involved in adopting a child could be just as beneficial as that of pregnancy, even if there were no mandatory counseling or licensing for adoption. Gheaus says it very well may be that "[b]earing parents have an advantage over adoptive parents" in terms of how ready they are for parenthood, and that the status quo on parental licensing is legitimate for this reason (although not this reason alone[41]). But this analysis ignores the tribulations that adoptive parents often experience that do not concern licensing.[42] Examples include financial burdens, emotional burdens brought about by the fear that the adoption will never be complete or that one will lose a child to which one was matched, and the social burden associated with people questioning one's decision to adopt a child (because their friend did so and it was a disaster) or to pursue a particular kind (international vs. domestic, public vs. private) of adoption. Persisting with adoption in spite of, and even perhaps in virtue of, these difficulties arguably prepares people well for becoming an adoptive parent. Gheaus needs to show otherwise for her argument to succeed.

To summarize, in our view the right to reproduce cannot be grounded in an interest in parenting "one's own," that is, one's biological child; and only in circumstances where adoption is not an option (or perhaps not a good option) can the right to reproduce be explained simply in terms of an interest in parenting. Again, one needs a different interpretation of a right to reproduce to make the Right to Reproduce Argument work.

Other Interests

Are there other interests that could be appealed to in an attempt to ground the right to reproduce? There are, though many of them are not plausible candidates, such as an interest in giving "the gift of life," fulfilling duties to family, or conforming to bionormative and pro-natalist social ideals.[43] However, there is one candidate that might seem promising: the interest people may have in avoiding some of the tribulations of adoption that are unique to it (or that seem to be, at any rate). These difficulties can include explaining to one's child why he is different from other children in not coming from his mommy's tummy, or why his birth parent(s) or family relinquished him for adoption; having to convince one's child that one is her "real" mom or dad; making tricky decisions about the birth family and one's child's present or future relationship with it; dealing with behavioral problems in one's child that stem from him being institutionalized for long periods of time or perhaps simply from being adopted; and navigating a racist society as a white parent of a child of a minority race.

While we in no way believe that the above challenges are trivial, we do want to say the following about them: (1) biological parents can face similar difficulties (that arise, e.g., because of divorce or behavioral problems in children that are not the result of either adoption or divorce); (2) the behavioral problems of adopted children tend to be exaggerated; in point of fact, "[t]he vast majority of children who are adopted are well within the normal range of well-being and show behavioral patterns that are similar to their non-adopted peers"[44]; (3) tackling some of the unique challenges of adoption, especially those that exist because of racism or the bionormative ideal of the family,[45] is worthwhile and can be rewarding;[46] and (4) there is value for parents in adopting children that goes beyond fighting prejudice and includes, most of all, enhancing a child's life prospects.[47] In short, the idea that people have, in effect, an interest in *avoiding* adoption is questionable. And if that is true, then such an interest cannot ground a right to create a child rather than have one via adoption.

Grounding the Right to Reproduce in the Right to Autonomy

If the interest theory is incapable of grounding a right to reproduce that draws the sort of distinction that would support the status quo on parental licensing, then perhaps the choice theory can do what the interest theory cannot. We turn now to this possibility, and analyze two categories of autonomous choice that seem relevant here. The first is bodily autonomy; the second is procreative autonomy.

Grounding the Right to Reproduce in Bodily Autonomy

It is tempting to argue that the right to reproduce is simply a manifestation of the right to bodily autonomy, where bodily autonomy is interpreted as being "self-determining . . . with respect to one's body" (and not simply as having the capacity for such self-determination, which is Overall's view[48]). The right to bodily autonomy has been used most often to undergird women's right *not* to reproduce. As Overall argues, without the right to bodily autonomy, women are "little more than procreative slaves," because they will be made to reproduce against their will.[49] But the right to bodily autonomy has also been invoked to support some women's and others' right *to* reproduce, and more specifically, not to be subject to such practices as forced abortion, forced sterilization, and forced contraception.

We take it as given that with a right to bodily autonomy comes an entitlement not to be subject to the sort of practices just mentioned. Whether one needs to refer to a *special* right to reproduce to acknowledge this entitlement is questionable, however. For what is wrong with these practices insofar as they infringe on people's bodily autonomy is simply that they involve unwanted touching or violations of the body, not that they prevent people from reproducing. As noted above, the right to bodily autonomy has no necessary connection to reproduction, and that is true even when the right is invoked to oppose such horrors as forced sterilization.

But one might object that while there is no necessary connection between bodily autonomy and the right to reproduce, there is all the same a deeply intimate connection between a right to bodily autonomy and reproduction, particularly for groups of people that have been targeted by eugenics programs (e.g., people with disabilities and minority racial or ethnic groups). The state needs to acknowledge that such individuals have a right to reproduce, grounded in their right to bodily autonomy, if only for the political purpose of thwarting efforts to prevent them from reproducing in the future. However, we believe that in claiming that these people have a right to reproduce, one is insisting not simply that they should be self-determining with respect to their bodies, but also that their interest in reproducing or their choice to reproduce is as legitimate as anyone else's. This is to say that their right to reproduce is grounded in something *more than* a right to bodily autonomy. All the same, the right to reproduce so understood remains very narrow, amounting either to a negative right not to be subject to eugenics programs in the first place, or to a right exercisable by members of a group that has been the target of eugenics programs to engage in reproductive activities, free from state interference. Consequently, even if a right to reproduce is recognized in the context of eugenics programs, such a right remains restricted to such contexts; it cannot be appealed to more generally in support of the Right to Reproduce Argument.

In summary, without downplaying the obvious importance of a right to bodily autonomy, we are skeptical that it alone could ground a right to reproduce. But we also question whether the Right to Reproduce Argument in favor of the status quo on parental licensing would succeed even if the right to reproduce were understood in this way. Recall that according to this argument, the right to reproduce protects people from licensing who engage in assisted, not just unassisted, reproduction. But could the right serve this purpose if it amounted to nothing over and above a right to bodily autonomy? It would have to guarantee not only that one should not be subject to unwanted touching by others (and thus not be subject to forced abortions and the like), but, in addition, that one should be subject to *wanted* touching by others (and thus to medical interventions to cure or bypass infertility). However, we find this interpretation of the right to bodily autonomy implausible. We are reminded here of Judith Thomson's discussion of a right to life.[50] Recall that according to Thomson, even if one needs Henry Fonda's cool hand on one's fevered brow in order to live, one does not have a right to it despite having a right to life. Similarly, a right to bodily autonomy does not entitle one to everything that one needs in order to exercise it, and so refusals by others to help one be self-determining with respect to one's body by engaging in assisted reproduction might be legitimate. In addition, some actions of others that inhibit such self-determination—including imposing licensing requirements—might be appropriate.

In short, although the right to reproduce understood in terms of a right to bodily autonomy would bar the state from having a licensing program that relies on measures such as forced abortion, it would not prevent the state from licensing all people who become parents via reproduction. In particular, it would not prevent it from licensing people who can only reproduce with assistance from others.

If a general right to bodily autonomy cannot ground the right to reproduce, then perhaps a more narrowly tailored right can. So consider the idea of explaining the right to reproduce in terms of the specific right to procreative autonomy. According to this view, certain choices—such as voluntarily becoming pregnant, or carrying a fetus to term, or giving birth—are essentially procreative in nature. Although in making such choices individuals may exercise other, non-procreative abilities, the choices are nonetheless inextricably linked to procreation. Yet because they are linked to procreation—that is, to begetting and bearing children—and because adoptive parents do not exercise procreative autonomy when forming a family via adoption, a right to reproduce grounded in procreative autonomy can support the status quo on parental licensing. For this right distinguishes some choices—namely those of people who become parents via the exercise of procreative autonomy—from others—those of people who become parents via the exercise of non-procreative autonomy—and so justifies the differential treatment of these two groups with respect to parental licensing.

Unsurprisingly, we are of the view that the right to reproduce understood in this way cannot justify the status quo. First, it is not clear why procreative choices *should* be accorded the normative weight that this understanding gives them. Second, even if the right to reproduce served to protect procreative autonomy, not everyone's choice to become a non-adoptive parent is, in fact, an exercise of procreative autonomy, and so the Right to Reproduce Argument would fail on this interpretation of the right. To see why, consider in particular the case of individuals who become parents using both donor gametes and contract pregnancy. It is very hard to view such individuals as exercising procreative autonomy since *they* are not procreating. To be sure, without their contributions and input a new life would not be created. But that cannot be sufficient for the exercise of procreative autonomy. For without the skill and help of the staff at an IVF clinic many couples would also be incapable of becoming parents. And it does not follow that the right of the staff to do what they do is grounded in, or is a manifestation of, their procreative autonomy. There is therefore a gap between playing an essential role in the process or act of procreation and exercising a right to procreative autonomy. There is also no clear difference between adoptive and non-adoptive parents in terms of whether the exercise of this right is what supports their choice to become parents. Consequently, the right cannot validate the Right to Reproduce Argument.

These observations lead to another possibility—that the right to procreative autonomy is at bottom the right to bring new people into existence. For whatever right adoptive parents exercise when they choose to become adoptive parents, it surely does not involve the bringing into existence of new children; rather, it involves assuming responsibility for children who already exist. So could it be that, in the end, the right to reproduce is the right to, quite simply, create life? And could that right be sufficient to justify the conclusion of the Right to Reproduce Argument? We think it could not, because it is by no means obvious that there is a right to create life, or that the right to reproduce is such a right. As we noted in connection with an interest in genetic or biological reproduction, it is doubtful that a woman who gives birth to a child and then promptly abandons it can be said to be exercising a right to reproduce, even though she is bringing a new person into existence.

But perhaps more importantly, it is simply not obvious that a right to reproduce understood as a right to bring new people into existence could justify the status quo on parental licensing. The reason is sometimes couples decide together to create a new life, even though one member of that couple must, in order to become a parent of the life thereby created, adopt the child. We have in mind here lesbian and gay couples.[51] Their case makes trouble for the claim that the exercise of a right to create new life is what distinguishes adoptive parents from non-adoptive parents. For if what is at issue is the exercise of a choice to create new life, and if that choice is exercised jointly by a couple, one member of whom must adopt the resulting child in order to become its legal parent, then it follows that in becoming parents, *adoptive* parents sometimes exercise the right to bring new life into existence—assuming, again, that such a right even exists.

Grounding the Right to Reproduce in a Right to Beget Equally?

Let us consider one final application of the choice theory of rights. According to Muireann Quigley, in a liberal democratic society such as ours the right to reproduce is best viewed as being grounded in an equality of liberty. Reflecting on John Rawls's claim that we are each entitled to an equal right to liberty and on Ronald Dworkin's view that we are each owed "equal concern and respect," Quigley argues for what she calls the *right to beget equally*, understood as "the equal right of individuals to attempt to reproduce in a manner pursuant to their values."[52] Her discussion of Rawls and Dworkin leads her to conclude that so long as individuals "choose to have children," each individual "ought to have an equal right to 'concern and respect' in the political decisions about the 'goods and opportunities' that a society has to offer regarding [having children]."[53]

In many ways, Quigley's idea is attractive: that in thinking about what individuals are entitled to as a matter of reproductive justice their concerns ought to be given equal weight. Still, we doubt that equality of liberty could, alone, ground the right to reproduce. Moreover, the problem with appealing to equality of liberty in the present context should be obvious: the status quo on parental licensing is a clear example of an institutional arrangement in which the liberty of some—non-adoptive parents— is given more weight than the liberty of others—adoptive parents. To impose on some prospective parents onerous licensing requirements while exempting other prospective parents from those same conditions does not show "equal concern and respect in the political decisions that govern" access to various mechanisms by which individuals become parents. To the contrary, the right to reproduce understood as a right to beget equally surely entails that the status quo on parental licensing is unjustified.

CONCLUSION

We set out in this chapter to expand on our earlier critique of the status quo on parental licensing by revealing the flaws in a particular argument in favor of it, an argument that we have called the "Right to Reproduce Argument." In doing so, however, we have leveled a critique against the very notion of a right to reproduce. Although we are open to there being a narrowly tailored right to reproduce that protects groups of people from being targeted by eugenics programs, we have argued that there is no general right to reproduce. Our reasoning was that none of the various interests or choices that in our opinion could ground such a right seems to be able to do the job. The options we considered included an interest in reproducing genetically or biologically; an interest in parenting simpliciter or in parenting one's biological child; a right to autonomy; a right to procreative autonomy; and a right to beget equally. The strongest among these candidates, in our view, is the interest simply in parenting. However, as we indicated, this interest can be satisfied through adoptive parenting and will only justify a right to reproduce when there are no children available for adoption. Thus, we conclude that the first horn of the dilemma that we aimed to prove at the outset—either there is no free-standing right to reproduce or, if there is, it cannot support the status quo on parental licensing—may very well be true, with the possible exception, again, of a narrow right to reproduce that concerns a resistance to eugenics. Regardless of whether one accepts this conclusion, however, one ought to conclude that the second horn of the dilemma is true. The upshot is that one ought to reject not only the Right to Reproduce Argument, but also regard with suspicion all arguments that rely on a general right to reproduce.

NOTES

1. "Parents" here refers to legal parents. Foster parents are also licensed. Much of what we say in this chapter about adoptive parents applies equally to foster parents.
2. See Carolyn McLeod and Andrew Botterell, "Not For the Faint of Heart: Assessing the Status Quo on Adoption and Parental Licensing," in *Family-Making: Contemporary Ethical Challenges*, ed. Françoise Baylis and Carolyn McLeod (Oxford: Oxford University Press, 2014).
3. Onora O'Neill, "Begetting, Bearing, and Rearing," in *Having Children: Philosophical and Legal Reflections on Parenthood*, ed. Onora O'Neill and William Ruddick (New York: Oxford University Press, 1979).
4. As Hugh LaFollette notes, parental licensing, like all licensing, involves "prior restraint": as he puts it, "A parental licensing program would deny licenses to applicants judged to be incompetent even though they had never maltreated children." (Hugh LaFollette, "Licensing Parents," *Philosophy and Public Affairs* 9, no. 2 [1980]: 188.) Similarly, we deny licenses to drive cars to people who have never caused an accident. One has to show some competency in the area before being licensed.
5. To be clear, not every form of adoption involves parental licensing; rather, the status quo singles out a certain kind of adoption—non-family-member adoption—for such licensing. In this chapter, we ignore this complexity, along with other complexities with the status quo; for discussion, see McLeod and Botterell, "Not For the Faint of Heart: Assessing the Status Quo on Adoption and Parental Licensing."
6. For discussion, see the section, "The Arguments in Favour of Licensing Adoptive Parents" in McLeod and Botterell, "Not For the Faint of Heart: Assessing the Status Quo on Adoption and Parental Licensing."
7. For discussion of whether parental licensing is morally justified, see in particular LaFollette, "Licensing Parents"; and the papers collected in Peggy Tittle, ed., *Should Parents Be Licensed?* (Amherst, MA: Prometheus Press, 2004).
8. Christine Overall, *Why Have Children?* (Cambridge, MA: MIT Press, 2012), 23.
9. Ibid.
10. See Hugh LaFollette, "Licensing Parents" and "Licensing Parents Revisited," *Journal of Applied Philosophy* 27, no. 4: 327. In "Licensing Parents," LaFollette gives a general argument in favor of parental licensing that goes as follows: we are justified in licensing individuals who engage in an activity A if (1) A is potentially harmful to others, (2) the performance of A requires a certain competence, and (3) we have a moderately reliable procedure for determining the presence or absence of such competence in relation to A. This argument applies to activities such as driving a car, and also to many professions—such as being a doctor, lawyer, or airline pilot—all of which require that individuals receive a

license before they are entitled to engage in these professions. But interestingly, according to LaFollette, the argument also applies to parents, because parenting a child meets conditions 1, 2, and 3.

11. LaFollette, "Licensing Parents," 186.
12. Ibid., 187–188.
13. Joseph Raz, "On the Nature of Rights," *Mind* 93 (1984): 195.
14. Harry Brighouse and Adam Swift, "Parents' Rights and the Value of the Family," *Ethics* 117, no. 1 (2006): 87, ftn. 13.
15. H. L. A. Hart, *Essays on Bentham: Studies in Jurisprudence and Political Theory* (Oxford: Clarendon Press, 1982), 183.
16. Leif Wenar, "Rights," in *The Stanford Encyclopedia of Philosophy* (Fall 2011 edition), ed. Edward Zalta, http://plato.stanford.edu/archives/fall2011/entries/rights/ (accessed December 31, 2013).
17. Although we are for the purpose of this discussion treating interest theories and choice theories as distinct and exclusive accounts of the functions of rights, it should be acknowledged that hybrid theories are possible, according to which rights are grounded in both interests and choices. Samantha Brennan defends such a theory when she argues that, with respect to children, "children move gradually from having their rights primarily protect their interests to having their rights primarily protect their choices." (Samantha Brennan, "Children's Choices or Children's Interests: Which Do their Rights Protect?" in *The Moral and Political Status of Children*, ed. David Archard and Colin Macleod [Oxford: Oxford University Press, 2002], 63.) She calls this a gradualist account of rights. For discussion, see again Brennan "Children's Choices or Children's Interests: Which Do their Rights Protect?"; Samantha Brennan, "The Good of Childhood and Children's Rights," in *Family-Making: Contemporary Ethical Challenges*, ed. Françoise Baylis and Carolyn McLeod (Oxford: Oxford University Press, 2014); and Peter Vallentyne, "The Rights and Duties of Childrearing," *William and Mary Bill of Rights Journal* 11, no. 3 (2003): 991.

  Likewise, within a choice theory it is possible to distinguish between different kinds of choices, as Hugh LaFollette does when he distinguishes descriptive autonomy—the volitional and intellectual abilities that render an individual capable of making autonomous choices—from normative autonomy—roughly, those considerations that entitle an individual to make certain choices for him- or herself. See Hugh LaFollette, "Circumscribed Autonomy," in *Having and Raising Children*, ed. Julia Bartkowiack and Uma Narayan (State College, PA: Penn State University Press, 1998). Applied to the case of children, LaFollette argues that even if children are not descriptively autonomous, they should nonetheless be granted (circumscribed) normative autonomy, from which it follows that various rights possessed by children can be grounded in this kind of choice.
18. Overall, *Why Have Children?*, 32.
19. Muireann Quigley, "A Right to Reproduce?" *Bioethics* 24, no. 8 (2010): 403.
20. See O'Neill, "Begetting, Bearing, and Rearing." See also Quigley, "A Right to Reproduce?"; Bonnie Steinbock, "A Philosopher Looks at Assisted Reproduction," *Journal of Assisted Reproductive Genetics* 12, no. 8 (1995): 543; Yvette Pearson, "Storks, Cabbage Patches, and the Right to Procreate," *Bioethical Inquiry* 4, no. 2 (2007): 105; and Tina Rulli, "Preferring a Genetically-Related Child," *Journal of Moral Philosophy*, online (2015): doi 10.1163/17455243-4681062.
21. John Robertson, *Children of Choice* (Princeton, NJ: Princeton University Press, 1994), 24.

22. Quigley, "A Right to Reproduce?," 406.
23. For more on the alleged value of passing on one's genes, see Neil Levy and Mianna Lotz, "Reproductive Cloning and a (Kind of) Genetic Fallacy," *Bioethics* 19, no. 3 (2005): 232; Overall, *Why Have Children?*; and Rulli, "Preferring a Genetically-Related Child." On the value of experiencing pregnancy and child-birth, see Overall, *Why Have Children?*; and Rulli, "Preferring a Genetically-Related Child." To be clear, we do not deny that pregnancy and childbirth can be valuable; we simply reject the view that an interest in having these experiences alone could ground a right to reproduce.
24. We noted that in this chapter we would disregard certain complexities with the status quo on parental licensing. One of them is the licensing of the homosexual partner who is not genetically related to a child that the couple produces using ARTs. In some jurisdictions (e.g., many states in the United States), this individual has to adopt the child as a non-family member. For discussion, see Julie Crawford, "On Non-Biological Maternity, or 'My Daughter is Going to be a Father!'" in *Family-Making: Contemporary Ethical Challenges*, ed. Françoise Baylis and Carolyn McLeod (Oxford: Oxford University Press, 2014).
25. We discuss the right to bodily autonomy below.
26. Overall, *Why Have Children?*, 20–21.
27. Ibid., 212.
28. Ibid., 217.
29. Ibid., 215.
30. Ibid., 219.
31. Brighouse and Swift, "Parents' Rights and the Value of the Family." Brighouse and Swift argue that many people have a fundamental interest in intimate relationships of a certain kind, and that only the relationship that obtains between a parent and his or her child can satisfy this interest. The reason lies in the unique characteristics of the parent-child relationship, which (1) is structurally unequal, given children's intrinsic vulnerability; (2) is structured in a way that prevents children from exiting the relationship; (3) is shaped by the particular ways in which children express their love for their parents, viz., spontaneously, unconditionally, and unreflectively; and (4) puts parents in charge of their children's well-being and development.
32. See Jurgen De Wispelaere and Daniel Weinstock, "State Regulation and Assisted Reproduction: Balancing the Interests of Parents and Children," in *Family-Making: Contemporary Ethical Challenges*, ed. Françoise Baylis and Carolyn McLeod (Oxford: Oxford University Press, 2014). Granted, the opportunity to adopt a child can be limited or even nonexistent. The availability of children for adoption, both domestically and internationally, can be quite low. However, the low numbers and long waiting lists are, as Tina Rulli argues, an "artifact of adoption opposition" (Tina Rulli, "The Unique Value of Adoption," in *Family-Making: Contemporary Ethical Challenges*, ed. Françoise Baylis and Carolyn McLeod [Oxford: Oxford University Press, 2014]). In our view, they are an artifact more specifically of the fact that society places greater value on people's right to reproduce than on the right of children to have families. Taking the latter right seriously along with people's right to parent should silence some opposition to adoption and free up for adoption more children who do not have parents.
33. Rulli, "The Unique Value of Adoption"; and Christine Overall, "What is the Value of Procreation?" in *Family-Making: Contemporary Ethical Challenges*, ed. Françoise Baylis and Carolyn McLeod (Oxford: Oxford University Press, 2014).

34. Various authors defend this claim and we will not restate all of their arguments here. However, see Levy and Lotz, "Reproductive Cloning and a (Kind of) Genetic Fallacy"; Overall, "What is the Value of Procreation?"; and Rulli, "Preferring a Genetically-Related Child."

35. L. Singer and others, "Mother-infant Attachment in Adoptive Families," *Child Development* 56, no. 6 (1985): 1543; and Koepke and others, "Becoming Parents: Feelings of Adoptive Mothers," *Pediatric Nursing* 17, no. 4 (1991): 333. (Thanks to Tina Rulli for these references.) See also Holly Fontenot, "Transition and Adaptation to Adoptive Motherhood," *Journal of Obstetric, Gynecologic, and Neonatal Nursing* 36, no. 2 (2007): 175.

36. Levy and Lotz, "Reproductive Cloning and a (Kind of) Genetic Fallacy."

37. See Rulli, "Preferring a Genetically-Related Child"; Charlotte Witt, "Family Resemblances: Adoption, Personal Identity, and Genetic Essentialism," in *Adoption Matters: Philosophical and Feminist Essays*, ed. Sally Haslanger and Charlotte Witt (Ithaca, NY: Cornell University Press, 2005), 135; and Sally Haslanger, "You Mixed? Racial Identity without Racial Biology," in *Adoption Matters: Philosophical and Feminist Essays*, ed. Sally Haslanger and Charlotte Witt (Ithaca, NY: Cornell University Press, 2005), 265.

38. Thanks to Joe Heath for this example.

39. Anca Gheaus, "The Right to Parent One's Biological Baby," *Journal of Political Philosophy* 20, no. 4 (2012): 432.

40. The two rights are different: the right to parent one's biological baby, as Gheaus understands it, allows people to "keep the babies that result from their own pregnancies," but not to endeavor to conceive those babies in the first place.

41. She gives one further reason: "[I]f there is already a relationship between babies and bearing parents when babies are born, and this relationship is constitutive of adequate parenting, then there is less reason, other things being equal, to scrutinise both the parental entitlement and the parental adequacy of bearing parents than that of adoptive parents." (Gheaus, "The Right to Parent One's Biological Baby," 22) To respond, one would only be inclined to say that gestating and giving birth to a child is constitutive of adequate parenting if one already believed that biological parents have an entitlement to parent that adoptive parents lack. But given that that is precisely what is at issue, it cannot be assumed from the outset.

42. To be clear, the tribulations brought on by licensing are not relevant here because whether adoptive parents should be licensed is what is at issue.

43. On which, see Overall, "What is the Value of Procreation?"

44. Lucy Blake and others, "The Families of Assisted Reproduction and Adoption," in *Family-Making: Contemporary Ethical Challenges*, ed. Françoise Baylis and Carolyn McLeod (Oxford: Oxford University Press, 2014), citing Ann Brand and Paul Brinich, "Behaviour Problems and Mental Health Contacts in Adopted, Foster, and Nonadopted Children," *Journal of Child Psychology and Psychiatry* 40, no. 4 (1999): 1221.

45. See Charlotte Witt, "A Critique of the Bionormative Concept of the Family," in *Family-Making: Contemporary Ethical Challenges*, ed. Françoise Baylis and Carolyn McLeod (Oxford: Oxford University Press, 2014).

46. Rulli, "The Unique Value of Adoption"; and Sally Haslanger, "Family, Ancestry, and the Self: What is the Moral Significance of Biological Ties?," *Adoption and Culture* 2, no. 1 (2009): 91.

47. See Blake and others, "The Families of Assisted Reproduction and Adoption";
and Rulli, "The Unique Value of Adoption."
48. See Overall, *Why Have Children?* For such an understanding of autonomy, see
Carolyn McLeod, *Self-Trust and Reproductive Autonomy* (Cambridge, MA: MIT
Press, 2002). In *Why Have Children?* Overall uses the phrase "bodily freedom
and autonomy." Moreover, she defines bodily freedom as "the absence of physical, legal, or social constraints on one's decisions about one's body" (Overall,
Why Have Children?, 21). Because we interpret bodily autonomy more broadly
than Overall does and in a way that captures what is problematic about external constraints on our bodies, we do not need to refer to both bodily autonomy
and freedom.
49. Overall, *Why Have Children?*, 21.
50. Judith Thomson, "A Defense of Abortion," *Philosophy and Public Affairs* 1, no. 1
(1971): 47.
51. For discussion see Crawford, "On Non-Biological Maternity, or 'My Daughter is
Going to be a Father!'."
52. Quigley, "A Right to Reproduce?," 410. Her concern is with arguing in favor of
public funding for ARTs.
53. Ibid.

REFERENCES

Baylis, Françoise, and Carolyn McLeod, eds. *Family-Making: Contemporary Ethical
Challenges*. Oxford: Oxford University Press, 2014.
Blake, Lucy, Martin Richards, and Susan Golombok. "The Families of Assisted Re-
production and Adoption." In *Family-Making: Contemporary Ethical Challenges*,
edited by Françoise Baylis and Carolyn McLeod, 64–85. Oxford: Oxford Uni-
versity Press, 2014.
Brand, Ann, and Paul Brinich. "Behavior Problems and Mental Health Contacts in
Adopted, Foster, and Nonadopted children." *Journal of Child Psychology and
Psychiatry* 40, no. 4 (1999): 1221–1229.
Brennan, Samantha. "Children's Choices or Children's Interests: Which Do their
Rights Protect?" In *The Moral and Political Status of Children*, edited by David
Archard and Colin Macleod, 53–69. Oxford: Oxford University Press, 2002.
Brennan, Samantha. "The Good of Childhood and Children's Rights." In *Family-
Making: Contemporary Ethical Challenges*, edited by Françoise Baylis and
Carolyn McLeod, 29-45. Oxford: Oxford University Press, 2014.
Brighouse, Harry, and Adam Swift. "Parents Rights and the Value of the Family."
Ethics 117, no. 1 (2006): 80–108.
Crawford, Julie. "On Non-Biological Maternity, or 'My Daughter is Going to be a
Father!'" In *Family-Making: Contemporary Ethical Challenges*, edited by Fran-
çoise Baylis and Carolyn McLeod, 168-181. Oxford: Oxford University Press,
2014.
De Wispelaere, Jurgen, and Daniel Weinstock. "State Regulation and Assisted Re-
production: Balancing the Interests of Parents and Children." In *Family-
Making: Contemporary Ethical Challenges*, edited by Françoise Baylis and
Carolyn McLeod, 131–150. Oxford: Oxford University Press, 2014.

Fontenot, Holly B. "Transition and Adaptation to Adoptive Motherhood." *Journal of Obstetric, Gynecologic, and Neonatal Nursing* 36, no. 2 (2007): 175–182.

Gheaus, Anca. "The Right to Parent One's Biological Baby." *Journal of Political Philosophy* 20, no.4 (2012): 432–455.

Hart, H. L. A. *Essays on Bentham: Studies in Jurisprudence and Political Theory*. Oxford: Clarendon Press, 1982.

Haslanger, Sally. "You Mixed? Racial Identity Without Racial Biology." In *Adoption Matters: Philosophical and Feminist Essays*, edited by Sally Haslanger and Charlotte Witt, 265–289. Ithaca, NY: Cornell University Press, 2005.

Haslanger, Sally. "Family, Ancestry and Self: What is the Moral Significance of Biological Ties?" *Adoption and Culture* 2, no. 1 (2009): 91–122.

Haslanger, Sally, and Charlotte Witt, eds. *Adoption Matters: Philosophical and Feminist Essays*. Ithaca, NY: Cornell University Press, 2005.

Koepke, J., S. Anglin, J. Austin, and J. Delesalle. "Becoming Parents: Feelings of Adoptive Mothers." *Pediatric Nursing* 17, no. 4 (1991): 333–336.

LaFollette, Hugh. "Licensing Parents Revisited." *Journal of Applied Philosophy* 27, no. 4 (2010): 327–343 LaFollette, Hugh. "Licensing Parents." *Philosophy and Public Affairs* 9, no. 2 (1980): 182–197.

LaFollette, Hugh. "Circumscribed Autonomy: Children, Care, and Custody." In *Having and Raising Children*, edited by Julia Bartkowiack and Uma Narayan, 137–151. State College, PA: Penn State University Press, 1998.

Levy, Neil, and Mianna Lotz. "Reproductive Cloning and a (Kind of) Genetic Fallacy." *Bioethics* 19, no. 3 (2005): 232–250.

McLeod, Carolyn. *Self-Trust and Reproductive Autonomy*. Cambridge, MA: MIT Press, 2002.

McLeod, Carolyn, and Andrew Botterell. "Not For the Faint of Heart: Assessing the Status Quo on Adoption and Parental Licensing." In *Family-Making: Contemporary Ethical Challenges*, edited by Françoise Baylis and Carolyn McLeod, 151-167. Oxford: Oxford University Press, 2014.

Overall, Christine. *Why Have Children?* Cambridge, MA: MIT Press, 2012.

Overall, Christine. "What is the Value of Procreation?" In *Family-Making: Contemporary Ethical Challenges*, edited by Françoise Baylis and Carolyn McLeod, 89-108. Oxford: Oxford University Press, 2014.

O'Neill, Onora. "Begetting, Bearing, and Rearing." In *Having Children: Philosophical and Legal Reflections on Parenthood*, edited by Onora O'Neill and William Ruddick, 25–38. New York: Oxford University Press, 1979.

Pearson, Yvette. "Storks, Cabbage Patches, and the Right to Procreate." *Bioethical Inquiry* 4, no. 2 (2007): 105–115.

Quigley, Muireann. "A Right to Reproduce?" *Bioethics* 24, no.8 (2010): 403–411.

Raz, Joseph. "On the Nature of Rights." *Mind* 93 (1984): 194–214.

Robertson, John. *Children of Choice*. Princeton, NJ: Princeton University Press, 1994.

Rulli, Tina. "The Unique Value of Adoption." In *Family-Making: Contemporary Ethical Challenges*, edited by Françoise Baylis and Carolyn McLeod, 109-128. Oxford: Oxford University Press, 2014.

Rulli, Tina. "Preferring a Genetically-Related Child." *Journal of Moral Philosophy*, online (2015): doi 10.1163/17455243-4681062.

Singer, L., D. M. Brodzinsky, D. Ramsay, M. Steir, and E. Waters. "Mother-infant Attachment in Adoptive Families." *Child Development* 56, no. 6 (1985): 1543–1551.

Steinbock, Bonnie. "A Philosopher Looks at Assisted Reproduction." *Journal of Assisted Reproductive Genetics* 12, no. 8 (1995): 543–551.

Thomson, Judith. "A Defense of Abortion." *Philosophy and Public Affairs* 1, no. 1 (1971): 47–66.

Tittle, Peggy, ed. *Should Parents Be Licensed?* Amherst, MA: Prometheus Books, 2004.

Vallentyne, Peter. "The Rights and Duties of Childrearing." *William and Mary Bill of Rights Journal* 11, no. 3 (2003): 991–1009.

Wenar, Leif. "Rights." In *The Stanford Encyclopedia of Philosophy* (Fall 2011 edition), edited by Edward Zalta. http://plato.stanford.edu/archives/fall2011/entries/rights/ (accessed December 31, 2013).

Witt, Charlotte. "Family Resemblances: Adoption, Personal Identity, and Genetic Essentialism." In *Adoption Matters: Philosophical and Feminist Essays*, edited by Sally Haslanger and Charlotte Witt, 135–144. Ithaca, NY: Cornell University Press, 2005.

Witt, Charlotte. "A Critique of the Bionormative Concept of the Family." In *Family-Making: Contemporary Ethical Challenges*, edited by Françoise Baylis and Carolyn McLeod, 49-63. Oxford: Oxford University Press, 2014.

CHAPTER 9

Privileging Adoption over Sexual Reproduction?

A State-Centered Perspective

JURGEN DE WISPELAERE AND DANIEL WEINSTOCK

INTRODUCTION

In a recent paper, we argued that states ought to regulate access to assisted reproduction technologies (ARTs) in order to privilege adoption among prospective parents who cannot acquire children "naturally."[1] They ought to do so, we argued, because there is a morally significant asymmetry between the interests of children who are already born and who for a variety of reasons do not have parents, and the interests of unborn children. Implicit in our discussion is the view that the very important interest that adults have in being able to parent—in the event that they decide to do so—is equally realized whatever the means through which children are "acquired"; that is, whether through natural reproduction, ART, or adoption. This interest, we argued, grounds a *pro tanto* right to become a parent, but it fails to ground an equivalent right to parent a child with whom one has genetic or gestational links. Parenting one's own biological child in our view amounts to something like an expensive taste.

In our earlier work, we argued that a pricing mechanism could be legitimately adopted to regulate access to ART, where access would be priced such that it maximizes adoption amongst children in need of a family.

However, in our scheme we also insisted pricing should remain sensitive to the real access that parents have to potential adoptees, not merely the number of children currently institutionalized or otherwise in need of a family. When regulating access to ART we must take into account the many hurdles and obstacles to prospective parents' ability to adopt children.[2] In a nutshell, the harder it is to adopt, the lower the price tag attached to artificial reproduction.

One important implication of the proposed scheme is that it appears to create an objectionable inequality between parents who can procreate naturally and those who cannot. Parents who have the ability to procreate without assistance seem to be exempted from contributing to the satisfaction of the very strong interests that potential adoptees have in finding homes within which to be raised. In our scheme, that responsibility is divested to those who are already disadvantaged by virtue of being unable to reproduce naturally.

From a moral point of view, it would seem that this unequal obligation adds insult to injury. On the one hand, fairness considerations clearly mitigate against parents contemplating ART having to take on a disproportionate responsibility in satisfying the unmet needs of prospective adoptees, for parents contemplating ART and parents considering having children through natural procreation are identically situated with respect to the interests of children in need of a family. On the other hand, purely consequentialist considerations also argue against unnecessarily restricting the pool of prospective adoptive parents by giving those able to reproduce naturally a "free pass," given that the interests of already-existing children trump those of potential children.[3]

Importantly, our focus is not on the question of how the responsibility for the satisfaction of these interests ought to be dealt with from an abstract ethical standpoint. Rather, we are concerned with the perspective of the state, and with the manner in which public policy regulates the procreative and parenting choices of its citizens. State action in this area is ethically constrained in a variety of ways that preclude our simply seeing it as an enforcer of abstractly stated moral duties. One purpose of this chapter is to outline the constraints that impede the state's ability to regulate natural procreation in particular. The latter go some way towards justifying the unequal treatment of natural parents compared to those requiring reproductive assistance. A second goal of this chapter, however, is to show several ways in which the state could nevertheless legitimately influence the reproductive choices of natural parents while avoiding the aforementioned constraints and optimizing the interests of children in need of a family.

The state-centered perspective on becoming a parent is distinguished from other ethical approaches by focusing on the ways in which state action itself both promotes and restricts opportunities in this context. In other words, we are acutely aware both of the need for state action in shaping a reproductive context within which key interests of parents and children are promoted, and of important limits on legal and policy instruments to achieve this laudable goal. The combination of several types of constraints on state action in our view amounts to a trilemma, which at first blush leaves precious little scope for the state to incentivize natural parents to contribute to the task of ensuring as many children as possible are adopted. The present section sets out the three horns of the trilemma.

Coercive Interventions

A first horn of the trilemma relates to the coercive nature of state intervention applied to procreation. The problem of coercion bears directly on the state's ability to regulate procreation and parenting because citizens are assumed to have profound liberty interests in the area of childbearing decisions. Two separate sets of reasons mitigate against coercive state intervention.

In the first place, much of the value of becoming a parent depends on this activity being pursued freely as a matter of choice, in accordance with one's conception of the good or one's self-identity as a prospective parent. To deny the requisite liberty is to erode in large part what is at value in the parenting relationship. Harry Brighouse and Adam Swift offer a sophisticated account of the importance of what they call "familial relationship goods," comprising a distinctive type of human flourishing of both children and parents that requires "permission, and social support, for activities and interactions between parents and children that facilitate the realization of the [familial relationship] goods."[4] Nevertheless, a protected perimeter of legitimate partiality is insufficient to produce the valued familial relationship goods of love, trust, and care; a necessary prior step is to refrain from coercing individuals to become parents in the first place. Coercion is infertile ground for the sort of unconditional bonding that characterizes parental relationships.

The liberty interest of prospective parents also features prominently in the converse case. The coercive means that the state would have to dispose of in order to prohibit unassisted sexual reproduction (and thereby to pro-mote adoption, at least in theory) all justly elicit horror. They would in-clude such things as mandatory abortions, mandatory sterilizations, or extensive parental licensing, which we take ethically as well as politically to be a non-starter in any society that embraces basic liberal principles.[5] The ethical case against such methods does not require much argument as it clearly violates considerations of fundamental liberty as well as the equally critical right to bodily integrity.[6] Thus, though there may be areas of public policy in which coercion is perfectly justified, in part in virtue of the very limited infringement that it imposes upon the liberty interests and the right to bodily integrity of citizens, a state that cleaves to broad liberal constraints on state action in the pursuit even of valuable goals will rule out of court coercive legislation requiring that citizens prescind from sexual reproduction and instead opt for adoption.[7]

Non-coercive Interventions

If, as the previous section argues, the liberal state is not allowed to coer-cively prohibit prospective parents from procreating naturally, what in-struments does the state have to induce natural parents in sharing in the responsibility of furthering the very great interests that potential adop-tees have in "acquiring" suitable parents? Specifically, are there any non-coercive mechanisms that might incentivize prospective parents from forgoing procreation for adoption?

It is important at this point to introduce an important factual asymme-try between the situation of potential ART users and prospective natural procreators. The assumption that we made in our earlier paper was that there was a price threshold at which many prospective parents who cannot procreate naturally are pushed out of the ART market and instead taking recourse to adoption to satisfy their desire to become a parent. The key assumption in that paper—that no moral loss occurs in the satisfaction of the prospective parent's interest in parenting by reverting to adoption rather than ART—implies that the cost barrier to ART that we envisaged does not cause harm to prospective parents.[8] In addition, no existing child suffers in this proposal, while prospective adoptees benefit from the pool of available parents being increased.

This assumption is difficult to maintain in the case of those who can procreate naturally, for the simple reason that prospective parents who are able cannot be that easily priced out of reproducing naturally. Finan-cial incentives—the leading non-coercive measure in public policy[9]—may sway some prospective parents, but our hypothesis is that when such incentives are constrained by considerations of economic feasibility, they will likely be insufficient to have effects proportionate to the case of prospective ART parents. One reason has to do with the prevailing idea that sexual reproduction is and ought to remain the "natural" default for becoming a parent, and the associated notion that parenting a child thus conceived is somehow more valuable than the alternative.[10] Another is that, even in an age of widely available methods of birth control, many children are still conceived by accident rather than planning, which bypasses incentive mechanisms. More importantly, however, offering prospective parents a financial bonus for agreeing to parent an adoptive child rapidly raises the sort of ethical concerns propounded by those suspicious of letting the market creep any further into the crevasses of our social fabric.[11] The notion that one might have been paid for raising one's adoptive son or daughter not only implies objective worries about children having a price (a form of expressive harm), but also raises the concern that it may crowd out the very conditions that develop and sustain the family relationship goods mentioned earlier.

The obvious solution to both the budget problem and the concern about expressive harm is to impose a penalty on those who insist to procreate naturally rather than reward those who opt for adoption. However, policymakers rapidly find themselves in a delicate double bind when applying financial incentives in this way. Imagine a situation in which the state proposes to impose a financial cost on those individuals who prefer to acquire children through sexual reproduction, be it in the form of a targeted "procreative tax" or a reduction in child benefits. The price thus exacted may induce some to forgo sexual reproduction and to opt for adoption. But up to a point, *ex hypothesi* the vast majority of people will simply accept the cost and engage in sexual reproduction anyway, for the reasons mentioned before. But if this is the case the scheme has the perverse side-effect of resulting in actual, rather than merely hypothetical, children to be harmed. For children whose parents chose to procreate naturally rather than adopt would grow up in households that were poorer than they would have been absent the state-imposed cost, with potentially severe effects on their opportunities for well-being.

Now, the extent of the harm would of course depend upon the antecedent material situations of parents as well as the level at which the penalty is fixed. Penalties that were merely symbolic would hardly register as harms, but then they would likely have little of the intended effect of boosting adoption. A state inclined to make use of such a mechanism to foster adoption would presumably not peg prices at a level that was so low that it would not have any impact on people's decision-making about procreative matters, nor offset costs associated with adoption.[12] The level at which it would make at least some sense to impose costs upon those who choose to reproduce sexually would on fairly realistic assumptions give rise to non-negligible effects on children—in particular at the lower end of the income distribution. The problem with financial penalties is that they constitute an unacceptable form of "child-child trade-off": either they are too low to have any real effect and harm prospective adoptees or else they are sufficiently high to have real impact, in which case they will inevitably harm some of the children conceived through sexual reproduction.[13]

A Trilemma

Let us summarize the discussion thus far. In the pursuit of the goal of increasing the proportion of parents who choose to adopt rather than to reproduce sexually, the state must balance three legitimate sets of interests. There are, to begin, the interests of children in need of adoption. The state incurs a responsibility to find these children a family grounded in the interests those children have to grow up in an environment that provides for them the familial relationship goods of love, continuing care, security, and so on.[14] The combination of the deeply ingrained view that sexual reproduction is the only "normal" way to have children, and the ease with which such children are created through sexual reproduction when no biological barrier exists, implies that the vast majority of people will likely continue to have children in this way. The state cannot merely rely on people's innate conviction that adoption is a virtuous act[15] but must develop a policy strategy to promote the desired outcome. But here we run squarely into the two other horns of our dilemma. First, to the claims of children in need of adoption we must add the interests that adults have in liberty and in bodily integrity, which we argued rules out coercive measures directly prohibiting natural reproduction (mandatory sterilization, mandatory abortion, etc.). There are, finally, the interests of those children who are born following sexual reproduction, who may be affected by the main non-coercive mechanism available to the state—to wit, financial incentives in either their positive or negative form.

The discussion thus far suggests very strongly that these sets of interests cannot all be satisfied by the kinds of policies we have been considering up to this point—hence, the state faces a trilemma. Coercive policies may be more effective at satisfying the interests of prospective adoptees, in as much as they would force those adults who wanted to parent to do so by the route of adoption. To the extent that they were effective in preventing adults from procreating sexually, they would not harm existing children. But they would be morally catastrophic adults' interests in liberty and in bodily integrity, and arguably self-defeating in terms of providing the conditions conducive to the desired familial relationship goods. Non-coercive policies, on the other hand, either have little to no effect or risk harming present or even future children in the targeted family. Escaping either of these horns suggests the state refrain from acting altogether, relying solely on prospective parents' willingness to act privately on their moral views about whether adoption is the most suitable path towards becoming a parent. But under current conditions this option would simply not be effective in promoting the interests of potential adoptees, and must be deemed suboptimal from the perspective of the child in need of an adoptive family.

LOOKING UPSTREAM: MAKING ADOPTION MORE ATTRACTIVE

Given the impossibility of satisfying all relevant interests through the kinds of policies that we have been considering thus far, should we then throw up our hands and conclude that there really is no way for the state to bring parents who are not prevented from reproducing sexually by biological factors to shoulder their fair share of our joint responsibility for meeting the needs of prospective adoptees? Does that task fall exclusively on the shoulders of those who are constrained by biology to the choice of ART and adoption?

That conclusion would be too hasty. In the previous section we suggested that a policy geared at enticing prospective parents to consider adopting a child rather than procreate naturally must directly restrict the choice set of those individuals, whether through the coercive elimination of this option or the less coercive but nevertheless harmful use of financial carrots or sticks. In this section we want to argue that the state can intervene in at least three ways in influencing the decision-making process of individuals who are considering parenting while remaining within the set of constraints that we have just enumerated. In order to avoid policies that would fall afoul of these constraints, our claim is that the state can intervene upstream in the decision-making process by removing obstacles that are present in current circumstances when parents consider different ways in which to "acquire" children. The obstacles to adoption are of (at least) three kinds: cultural/ideological, administrative, and financial. We argue that there are policies that the state can pursue on all three of these fronts, each of which makes it somewhat more likely that natural parents would consider adopting.

Countering Disturbing Biologism

Consider first the cultural and ideological obstacles to adoption. A very strong set of deeply embedded representations of family life make it the case that we tend to think of biological ties as necessary for "real" parenting. "Who are your real parents?," a question often posed to adopted children, is just taken to be synonymous with "Who are your progenitors?" Adoption, in the context of this set of representations, is seen as second-best parenting, as something that you settle for when you cannot have children naturally and when ART has proven unsuccessful.[16]

The parenting relationship is, however, not a biological but a social one. Parents are the persons who take on the role of principal promoter of the various welfare interests of children, including the interests that are inherent in an intimate family life. No biological link is required in order for this role to be taken up by adults vis à vis particular children. Nor, we would argue, is there any loss involved from the point of view of prospective parents' interests in being able to realize the goods of parenting and family intimacy in their own lives in parenting children with whom they have no genetic tie.[17] There is no loss independent of the representations that we have been referring to in this context. That is, given the presence of fairly deep-seated beliefs in the "naturalness" of parenting when it is parenting of one's "own" children as opposed to children who have been borne by others, it is possible that some people feel that they are somehow being deprived of a good in its full instantiation when circumstances dictate that they parent adopted children if they are to parent at all. But these representations must be subjected to critical scrutiny in very much the same way that we progressively question unsubstantiated beliefs about the unnaturalness of gay parents or parenting across racial lines.

We do not deny that there may be some important good in the gestational process, nor that there is a *pro tanto* moral right to being able to parent the children one has given birth to.[18] The claim here is the limited one that, first, parenting (and its attendant goods) is a relationship that does not presuppose a biological link, and that second, the belief that the relationship does presuppose such a link is a major obstacle to people being inclined to consider adoption as a way of acquiring children.[19] To this we should add a third claim: many of our social institutions are actively constructed around the default assumption that biological procreation is the norm. We know from recent research that default positions within institutional design have a powerful effect on human decision-making and that default reversals in turn may become powerful policy instruments.[20] This suggests that state ought to carefully examine the presence of the biological default across its institutions and, where possible, engage in reversing the default rule.[21]

What concrete measures might the state employ to counter the disturbing biologism enshrined in contemporary society? The state has a number of means at its disposal to affect the representations which structure agents' contexts of choice—most notably through its control of the curriculum of public schools. It would be interesting, for example, to determine to what degree sex education and home economics are underpinned by an unreflective commitment to the ideology of biologism, as we might call it, and to think about ways in which that ideology can be curbed. We might, for instance, draw inspiration from the way in which heterosexist norms about parenting are being challenged in many school systems in the world today in ways that are proving surprisingly effective.

The formal school system is not the only pedagogical tool that the state has at its disposal to counteract the heavily biologist assumptions that constitute the biological default. State-funded parenting classes, which arguably ought to be mandatory for all prospective parents, are unavoidably underpinned by views about what "normal" parenting is, and they serve to reinforce those beliefs as well. Such classes could be restructured to provide prospective adoptive parents—or perhaps even all parents— with information they need to parent an adopted child that would be on par with the information that "natural" parents receive today. In our view it is not just a matter of providing "separate but equal" information, however. The inclusion of information about adoption *alongside* information about natural parenting might go some way toward "normalizing" the situation of adopted children, and about families formed through adoption, in the public imaginary.

These are just a few examples of how to adoption-proof key social institutions that determine the choice context against which prospective parents decide how to act upon their desire to become a parent. We are aware that default reversals will require time for their effects to materialize in the social psyche of prospective parents and thus are under no illusion about the likely size of its immediate impact. But to the skeptics we say: even small changes at the margin make a huge difference in some children's lives, and one should not underestimate how small changes today may cascade into a social norm shift tomorrow.

Parents who have successfully adopted children report that cultural obstacles to adoption pale before the invasiveness and complexity of the bureaucratic obstacles. Parents who choose to adopt are subjected to a mad-
dening set of bureaucratic requirements that all purportedly aim to ensure
that the interests of prospective adoptees are met, but that are often experienced as prohibitive by parents. Many parents who have overcome the
ideological obstacles to adoption rooted in biologism are defeated by the
costliness in terms of time and the invasiveness of the requirements set
by adoption agencies. How should a state that has accepted an obligation
to secure a home for children in need of a family respond to this particular
challenge?

Let us assume that the sole purpose of these bureaucratic hurdles has
to do with the welfare of potential adoptees.[22] Agencies responsible for
matching children to families are the trustees of vulnerable children, and
it is entirely appropriate that they act zealously in their interests. Recognizing this is entirely compatible with the observation that the precise
level at which levels are presently set by virtue of the sheer level of bureaucratic interference succumbs to what we might term the *fallacy of the
status quo*. This fallacy is encountered in a great many policy domains,
and it consists of downplaying or ignoring entirely the costs associated
with the status quo relative to those that might be brought about by
policy change. Thus, for example, opponents of the decriminalization of
euthanasia and assisted suicide focus single-mindedly on the risks of
slippery slopes that might follow from a departure from the present situation, in which such practices are prohibited, and either ignore or downplay the costs in terms of needless suffering and arbitrariness in the (un-
acknowledged) dispensation of physician-assisted death.[23] A similar
situation is arguably present in the way in which adoption agencies vet
prospective adoptive parents. Costs associated with the status quo, which
in this case have to do with the needless suffering of children who find
themselves in conditions that are clearly difficult to reconcile with the
minimal conditions of well-being and human flourishing, and with the
frustration of the interests of adults who have chosen to parent but who
find themselves unable to do so because of bureaucratic hurdles and very
demanding criteria governing suitability, are not weighed on the same
scale as are the harms that might accrue to children raised by less-than-
perfect parents.

We believe this imbalance cannot be justified by the argument that the
state should primarily concern itself with its own wards—those children

that are directly in its charge by virtue of not having a set of parents discharging a duty of care. First, clearly the state in practice does not restrict itself to this subset of children and, through the department of social services or related institutions, regularly engages in the policing of parental care even where parents are present. The many children being taken from negligible or abusive parents is a case in point.[24] Second, the state's special obligation to ensure that adopted children are not placed in below-par families must be balanced by the equally weighty obligation to take into account the overall well-being and opportunities of *all* children in need of a family. Failure to do so constitutes another example of the child-child trade-off.[25]

Just as in the euthanasia and assisted suicide case, and in many others bearing the same structure, an appropriate role for the state is to enact policy that avoids the kind of fallacy just described. In the case of adoption, this might mean regulating adoption agencies so as to ensure that children are not left in worst-case scenarios, because well-meaning agencies refuse to release them into the care of parents who, though they may not be perfect in all regards, are nonetheless adequate, and certainly more compatible with the conditions for well-being and flourishing of children than the status quo would be. Though it is difficult to define with precision what the "sufficientarian threshold" involved should be, it would presumably be far more exigent than the standards that presently govern the state's role in removing children from the care of clearly inadequate parents. At the same time, the relevant threshold would likely be less stringent that current adoption procedures in an attempt to ensure that more children would be placed in decent family homes and that more individuals or couples consider adopting in the first place.

Socializing Adoption Costs

Financial costs associated with adoption are a third, highly visible obstacle to the choice of adoption among people who are able to procreate naturally. This is especially true in the case of international adoptions, which often require numerous trips and protracted stays in faraway lands, payment of agencies both domestic and foreign, and so on. Given the foreseeable costs of raising children, and the fact that these costs are at present borne almost entirely by prospective parents, it is not surprising that adoption appeals only to a very small fraction of those people who are capable of having children naturally.[26]

An obvious way in which to alter the decision space within which people decide how to acquire children is therefore to ensure that at least part of the costs linked to adoption are covered through general taxation, in much the same way that general taxation is employed to pay for the education and health needs of children in many jurisdictions. Note that what we have in mind here should not be confused with selective incentive payments discussed and dismissed in an earlier section. By contrast to those targeted incentives aimed at offering a differentiated reward for adopting a child (a potential expressive harm), the current proposal is aimed at evening out the financial inequality in the present system in which prospective parents end up paying a considerable sum for the "privilege" of taking care of one of the many children in need of a family. Our purpose, thus, is solely one of compensating for extra costs incurred (and a partial compensation, at that), not payment for "services rendered."

How might we justify drawing upon the public purse to offset the costs associated with adoption, which would only benefit a selective few? We believe that the elements required to mount a successful justification of adoption subsidization are already in view. There are several interconnected reasons to support socializing the costs of adoption. First, as we have argued elsewhere, parenting is a very important good for those persons who choose to parent, and moreover it is one that cannot be substituted for by other goods.[27] The combination of importance and unsubstitutability grounds at least a strong *pro tanto* case for state funding.

Second, that case is strengthened by the fact that the principle of equal opportunity directly applies in relation to the right to become a parent, which at a minimum suggests an equal starting base for prospective parents independent of the manner by which they "acquire" the child. But note here the important distinction between the right to become a parent and the personal preference of parenting one's own child, outlined before. Equal opportunity only applies to the former, not to the latter.[28]

Third, in the case of adoption we are, as it were, not responding to a "new need." Prospective adoptees are characterized by an already-existing unmet need, both material and emotional, to which adoption responds. ART and sexual reproduction, by contrast, are differently situated in this respect because while they clearly satisfy the interests of adults in parenting, they necessarily bring a new need into the world by *creating* a child. To the extent that the state accepts a moral and social responsibility of care for those children that do not belong to a family and equally accepts that such care is best exercised within the context of a family, there exists a clear moral imperative towards offering assistance to prospective adopters to reduce their financial burden. Furthermore, to the extent that the state here in fact divests of an obligation originally held by society as a whole, the use of public funds is appropriate.

Defraying some of the costs of adoption through taxation thus allows us to satisfy two important sets of interests—those of adults who through adoption are provided the opportunity to access the goods of parenting, and those of already-existing children who but for the taxation scheme might find themselves blocked from being adopted due to considerations of cost. The combination of these two considerations in our view generates a very strong defeasible right to having the predictable costs of adoption covered through taxation. Moreover, it bears noting that socializing the costs of adoption achieves this in a cost-effective way, as it literally shifts a large amount of the direct cost-of-care for an institutionalized child—otherwise borne by society (in other words, the taxpayer)—to the prospective parent(s) in return for a comparatively small subsidy that assists those willing to adopt to overcome this initial hurdle.

If the proposal to socialize adoption costs constitutes a strong defeasible right, as we argue here, under what conditions can it be rendered void? We can think of two types of arguments that could override our proposal: if socializing costs runs afoul of the constraint that it must not harm existing children, and if socializing costs constitutes a form of unfairness towards those who pay for the benefit of others. Let us discuss each in turn.

First, some critics might argue that taxation for the purposes of subsidizing adoption falls afoul of a principle that we relied upon ourselves in the previous section. That principle is that measures employed to encourage adoption should not end up harming already-existing children, or future children who will be created sexually or though ART in spite of the state's attempt to encourage adoption. In response to this concern, we point out again that funding adoption through taxation does not target anyone in particular. It operates quite differently from a penalty system that specifically targets parents and their children who choose to forgo adoption. Of course, we would all have more disposable income were the state not to tax us (though whether we had any more money left after having had to pay for all services out of pocket is a different matter), but to say that we are harmed by taxation in virtue of this fact is to stretch the notion of harm beyond the breaking point. Taxation affects all citizens, whatever the mode of parenting they choose. It does so on the basis of a reckoning as impartial as possible of the important interests that the members of a just society should ensure the satisfaction of. No one is unfairly singled out by virtue of his or her choice of becoming a parent. In addition, general taxation divides the burden of contributing to the adoption costs amongst a large pool of contributors, thus decreasing the extent to which a single person would be harmed by reduced income alone. And of course a progressive taxation system would drastically reduce the likelihood that those at the bottom of the income distribution would end up contributing beyond their means, thus further taking the wind out of this particular objection.

A second objection maintains that even in the absence of manifest harm, socializing the costs of adoption might be unfair to those who are net contributors. According to this view, the choice to become a parent is an expensive taste, one that should be entirely internalized by those who opt for it.[29] Now, whatever the force of this argument against those who would claim support from the state for their decision to bring new persons (and thus new baskets of need) into the world, it has no bite against those who would draw upon the public purse in order to defray the costs associated with adopting a child. First, in our view the goal of becoming a parent, for those who have decided that parenting was a non-substitutable ingredient of the good life as they construe it, cannot be readily assimilated to a frivolous taste which fellow citizens can simply disregard. Rather, it is a fundamental interest that creates at least a *pro tanto* obligation on the part of others. Casal and Williams may not accept this view, but they should not be able to dismiss a second argument as easily.

Our second argument builds on the fact, already alluded to, that adoption, as opposed to ART and sexual reproduction, does not generate new needs. Rather, it allows for already-existing but unmet needs of prospective adoptees to be met. To the extent that there is a dimension of parenting that fits the expensive taste model, it has to do not with parenting per se, but rather with a mode of acquisition of children that increases the total amount of unmet need in the world. Casal and Williams may be right that those who create a new need must bear the primary, or perhaps even the sole, responsibility for meeting it. But whatever plausibility this claim has vanishes in the case of adoption, where no new need is created. If the need is as it were "out there" by virtue of the child already existing, it would seem right that society collectively undertake the responsibility for meeting those needs.[30] *Ex hypothesi*, the progenitor of the child is already out of the picture; after all, that is what it means to give up a child for adoption. And it would seem to be unfair to saddle an individual or couple willing to undertake the care of this child with the full costs associated with adoption.

If anything, the argument can be turned on its head in this case: the willingness of some to parent already-existing children allows all others—including those who refrain from parenting altogether—to satisfy whatever obligation they might have relative to these children simply by their contribution to the public purse. It is the parents who adopt children (and who will, it should be emphasized, also be contributing to the public purse in the same way as non-parents) who will be ensuring that the myriad quotidian needs of children are met. Of course, they do this while at the same time securing for themselves a valuable private good, namely the familial relationship goods that only materialize in the parenting relation. Fairness does not demand that prospective adoptive parents receive a subsidy for the ordinary costs of parenting—the costs that each parent, independent of acquisition method, incurs by virtue of being a responsible and caring parent—merely the costs associated with the adoption process itself. In our view socializing the costs of adoption understood in this way balances fairness considerations between all types of parents (and even non-parents).

In summary, there are good reasons to financially support adoption that resemble the reasons we have to fund other programs through taxation. The interests that adoption serves are considerable, both on the part of prospective parents and on the part of prospective adoptees. Funding adoption is particularly important for the latter. Indeed, though (some) prospective parents could always employ other methods in order to satisfy their interest in parenting, the unmet needs of already-existing children require the lifting of as many of the obstacles as possible that presently incline prospective parents away from adoption. Like the cultural obstacles to do with the supposed "normality" of sexual reproduction or the bureaucratic hurdles that require prospective adoptive parents to run the gauntlet of administrative approval, the sheer financial cost of the adoption process may prove a powerful deterrent to some considering adoption a viable alternative for becoming a parent. But here the state could very easily address the problem and, if our arguments hold, has little reason to refrain from doing so.

CONCLUSION

We started this chapter by asking how we should distribute the moral obligation to ensure the many children currently awaiting adoption find a suitable family amongst the adults of a modern liberal society. Specifically we want to know whether there is something objectionable about a scheme that seems to leave the responsibility for adopting children in need of a family entirely to those unable to procreate naturally. In an earlier paper we argued that access to ART ought to be priced such that it maximizes the number of prospective adoptees finding a family. But what about those who are able to procreate naturally and thus can go ahead without any assistance from third parties? Is there anything the state can and ought to do in terms of incentivizing natural procreators to consider adoption instead?

The answer to this question, we argue, is complicated. The state is burdened by the fact that policy intervention in this area must itself operate within several constraints. On the one hand, there are limits to the use of coercive measures that directly take the option of natural reproduction off the table. On the other hand, the use of financial rewards or penalties also causes problems; this time by affecting the well-being or opportunities of the children of natural procreators affected. From the state's point of view, natural reproduction is simply not something easily regulated in the direct, downstream fashion by which we can affect access to ART.

But the argument doesn't stop here, for the state may instead opt for the regulation of natural procreation through a host of upstream mechanisms. Upstream policy instruments do not tackle the decision to procreate in a direct manner, but instead shape the choice context by redressing some of the inequalities in the present system. We discuss three proposals: countering the pervasive biologism default by ensuring education or parenting classes are adoption-proofed; reducing the bureaucratic hurdles that fail to take into account the costs to both parents and children of the present status quo; and socializing the costs of the adoption process to achieve a fair balance of burdens amongst different types of parents (and non-parents). In our view, these are practical measures that the state can enact to further promote the opportunities of children in need of a family without falling foul of any of the moral constraints that prevent the state from regulating procreation in a hands-on fashion. While there are important differences in how the state should regulate natural reproduction and ART, respectively, in the light of the need to promote adoption natural parents (and non-parents) are not exempt from social regulation.

NOTES

1. Jurgen De Wispelaere and Daniel Weinstock, "State Regulation and Assisted Reproduction: Balancing the Interests of Parents and Children," in Family-Making: Contemporary Ethical Challenges, ed. Françoise Baylis and Carolyn McLeod (Oxford: Oxford University Press, 2014).
2. See Carolyn McLeod and Andrew Botterell, "'Not for the Faint of Heart': Assessing the Status Quo on Adoption and Parental Licensing," in Baylis and Mcleod, Family-Making.
3. For a discussion of the ethical complexities entailed by this last point, see Christian Munthe, "The Argument from Transfer," Bioethics 10, no. 1 (1996): 27–42; Thomas Søbirk Petersen, "The Claim from Adoption," Bioethics 16, no. 4 (2002): 353–375.

4. Harry Brighouse and Adam Swift, "Legitimate Parental Partiality," *Philosophy & Public Affairs* 37, no 1 (2009): 56; more generally, Harry Brighouse and Adam Swift, "Parents' Rights and the Value of the Family," *Ethics* 117, no. 1 (2006): 80–108. In addition, there may be third-party interests at play, where functional families play a crucial role in securing benefits that occur beyond its members in a strict sense. See Jennifer Roback Morse, "No Families, No Freedom: Human Flourishing in a Free Society," *Social Philosophy and Policy* 16 (1999): 290–314.

5. Daniel Engster, "The Place of Parenting within a Liberal Theory of Justice: The Private Parenting Model, Parental Licenses, or Public Parenting Support?," *Social Theory and Practice* 36, no. 2 (2010): 233–262.

6. On the latter, see J. J. Thomson, "A Defense of Abortion," *Philosophy and Public Affairs* 1, no. 1 (1971): 47–66.

7. Hugh LaFollette tries to circumvent these problems by removing children and putting them up for adoption, but this of course exacerbates the very problem we are trying to resolve. Hugh Lafollette, "Licensing Parents," *Philosophy and Public Affairs* 9, no. 2 (1980): 193. We criticize LaFollette's solution in Jurgen De Wispelaere and Daniel Weinstock, "Licensing Parents to Protect Our Children?" *Ethics and Social Welfare* 6, no. 2 (2012): 195–205.

8. Somewhat more controversially, we also maintain that the resulting inequality of opportunity between those with sufficient private means to purchase ART and those who depend on state subsidy is not necessarily unfair. Jurgen De Wispelaere and Daniel Weinstock, "State Regulation and Assisted Reproduction: Balancing the Interests of Parents and Children," in Baylis and Mcleod, *Family-Making*, 145–147.

9. We do not deny that under some circumstances financial incentives can be coercive, or otherwise ethically suspect. Our point here is merely to distinguish between outright prohibition and the altering of cost/benefit ratios through financial inducement. See Ruth Grant, *Strings Attached: Untangling the Ethics of Incentives* (Princeton, NJ: Princeton University Press, 2012); Sarah Conly, *Against Autonomy: Justifying Coercive Paternalism* (Cambridge: Cambridge University Press, 2012)

10. For a non-genetic reason why parenting a child with a biological link could be valuable, see J. David Velleman, "Family History," *Philosophical Papers* 34, no. 3 (2005): 357–348.

11. Debra Satz, *Why Some Things Should Not Be For Sale: The Moral Limits of the Market* (New York: Oxford University Press, 2010).

12. Such costs include the fees charged by agencies and by donor countries in the case of international adoption, and costs associated with raising children who may in virtue of the conditions in which they found themselves prior to adoption have special needs. We discuss this aspect more later.

13. On child-child trade-offs, see De Wispelaere and Weinstock, "Licensing Parents to Protect Our Children?"

14. B. B. Woodhouse, "Waiting for Loving: The Child's Fundamental Right to Adoption," *Capital University Law Review* 34, no. 2 (2005): 297–329; Brighouse and Swift, "Legitimate Parental Partiality." We share the view with Brighouse and Swift that even the best institutional care arrangement cannot fully provide children access to these goods.

15. See Tina Rulli, "The Unique Value of Adoption," in Baylis and Mcleod, *Family-Making*.

16. Elizabeth Bartholet, "Beyond Biology: The Politics of Adoption and Reproduction," *Duke Journal of Gender Law and Policy* 2, no. 1 (1995): 5–13; S. F. Appleton, "Adoption in the Age of Reproductive Technology," *University of Chicago Legal Forum* (2004): 393–451; A. P. Fisher, "Still 'Not Quite as Good as Having Your Own'? Toward a Sociology of Adoption," *Annual Review of Sociology* 29, no. 1 (2003): 335–361.

17. For an account of the goods of parenting with which we are largely in agreement, see Brighouse and Swift, "Parents' Rights and the Value of the Family."

18. On the importance of gestation in relation to parental rights, see Anca Gheaus, "The Right to Parent One's Biological Baby," *Journal of Political Philosophy* 20, no. 4 (2012): 432–455. But note that gestation does not establish a right to become a parent of a biologically related child.

19. Daniel Friedrich has in a recent paper shown that many beliefs surrounding adoption, and underpinning the sense that many people have that the goods of parenting can only be achieved in a relationship with children to whom one is biologically related, do not survive critical scrutiny. See his "A Duty to Adopt?" in *Journal of Applied Philosophy* 30, no. 1 (2013): 25–39.

20. See notably Cass Sunstein and Richard Thaler, *Nudge. Improving Decisions about Health, Wealth, and Happiness* (New Haven, CT: Yale University Press, 2008).

21. One could argue, in line with Thomas Pogge's notion that neglecting to change an institution that maximizes just outcomes is tantamount to injustice, that the state has a negative duty to change any default rules that fails to maximally promote justice. Thomas Pogge, *World Poverty and Human Rights: Cosmopolitan Responsibilities and Reforms*, 2nd ed. (Cambridge: Polity Press, 2008).

22. Lafollette, "Licensing Parents"; Hugh LaFollette, "Licensing Parents Revisited," *Journal of Applied Philosophy* 2, no. 4 (2010): 327–343.

23. Udo Schuklenk et al., "End-of-Life Decision-Making in Canada: The Report by the Royal Society of Canada Expert Panel on End-of-Life Decision-Making," *Bioethics* 25, no. 1 (2011): 1–73, at p. 50.

24. In cases where there is a clear presumption that the welfare of the child might be negatively affected the state may decide to intervene in advance. Examples of such risk categories include expectant parents with severe (cognitive) disabilities, long-term drug addicts, violent offenders and those registered on the sex offender registry, and parents who already had previous children removed and put into social care. We are grateful to Gideon Calder for drawing our attention to this point.

25. Jurgen De Wispelaere and Daniel Weinstock, "Licensing Parents to Protect Our Children?", at p. 201.

26. For a very compelling, firsthand account of the costs associated with international adoption, see Carolyn McLeod and Andrew Botterell, "'Not for the Faint of Heart': Assessing the Status Quo on Adoption and Parental Licensing," in Baylis and Mcleod, *Family-Making*.

27. De Wispelaere and Weinstock, "Licensing Parents to Protect Our Children?"

28. This explains our treating adoption and ART differently in our previous paper. Jurgen De Wispelaere and Daniel Weinstock, "State Regulation and Assisted Reproduction: Balancing the Interests of Parents and Children," in Baylis and Mcleod, *Family-Making*.

29. Paula Casal and Andrew Williams, "Rights, Equality and Procreation," *Analyse & Kritik* 17, no. 1 (1995): 93–116, and "Equality of Resources and Procreative Justice," in *Dworkin and his Critics*, ed. Justine Burley (Oxford: Blackwell, 2004).

30. We are here abstracting from a difficult question: should the state include the claims of potential foreign adoptees—children without families born outside of the state's jurisdiction or born from non-national progenitors—amongst its responsibilities? Solving this question will have important moral and practical implications for our account, but it would take us too far to attempt a resolution in this chapter.

CHAPTER 10

Parental Competency and the Right to Parent

COLIN M. MACLEOD

INTRODUCTION

The moral right of adults to become parents[1] and to thereby stand in a special relation of authority, responsibility, intimacy, and special influence to specific children is widely and highly valued. Yet the right is unusual in some respects. First, it is a right held by specific persons to exercise authority over other persons (i.e., children) who have not and cannot consent to the authority to which they are subject. Children typically do not have the moral or legal prerogative to release themselves from the authority of their parents.[2] Second, the right to parent a specific child or group of children is routinely (though not necessarily) assigned to two (and sometimes more than two) adults who exercise the rights of parenthood jointly. In this way, the right to parent is not fully an individual right. Typically its successful exercise requires coordination and cooperation between the adults to whom the right is jointly assigned. Third, access to the right to parent is conditional on the requirement that would-be parents satisfy a standard of adequacy or competency. To some important degree, parents are guardians of the interests of their children, but in order to occupy that role parents must be willing and able to fulfill parental responsibilities to a satisfactory degree. Yet there are controversies about what constitutes parental competency of the sort requisite to establish a right to parent. These general features of the right to parent give rise to various puzzles about the justificatory basis of the right to parent as well as the nature and scope of parental rights. My aim in this chapter is to examine how considerations of competency regulate the moral right to parent. However, en route to addressing this issue I shall offer some remarks on the character of the interests of adults that partly ground and shape the right to parent. I argue that the standard of parental competency requisite to the right to parent is more robust and demanding than is often assumed. But I reject the view that competent parents must, at least in theory, be optimally good parents. Although the standard of parental competency I endorse is robust, it is, when properly interpreted, readily attainable by most would-be parents. So a robust standard of parental competency need not narrowly or unfairly circumscribe the class of adults who can enjoy the right to parent.

The chapter is organized in the following way. First, I offer a brief characterization of the right to parent that is at stake in the rest of the discussion. Second, I consider how the right to parent is related to the interests of both children and adults. I give special attention to powerful interests that adults have in becoming parents and exercising the right to parent. I explain how these interests are related to the independent interests and claims of children. I offer a critique of child-centered justifications of parental rights and propose a version of a dual interest theory of parental rights. Third, I distinguish two accounts of parental competency on which the right to parent might be thought to depend: a modest view and a robust view. I suggest that specification of a standard of parental competency should be grounded in the justice-based entitlement of children. I explain why the justice-based entitlements of children favor adoption of the robust view but that this need not narrowly limit the set of adults who may claim a right to parent. I also explain how the social division of moral labor is relevant to ensuring that parents' interests in exercising the right to parent can be secured and meaningfully exercised while at the same time helping to secure the crucial interests of children.

THE RIGHT TO PARENT

The right to parent is a moral right held by an adult or adults (e.g., a married couple) to establish and maintain a special relationship to specific children over whom the parents have authority to make a wide variety of decisions about how children are raised. Within the parameters fixed the justice-based entitlements of children and other persons,[3] adults with the right to parent have wide prerogatives to interpret, protect, promote, and develop their children's interests about a wide range of matters, such as nutrition, clothing, education, culture, leisure, social relationships, religion, where children live, and facets of children's moral development. The right to parent creates (qualified) parental authority over children in these domains and protects parents from interference by others (e.g., the state, other adults) with respect to the child-rearing decisions parents make within the relevant parameters. The potential bearers of parental rights are diverse. In addition to married heterosexual couples, adults eligible to claim a right to parent include people who are single, gay, bisexual, disabled, and so on. Merely having a biological relationship with a child is neither necessary nor sufficient to establish a right to parent.[4] The character and extent of parental authority over children changes and diminishes as children develop and become mature agents capable of successfully articulating their own interests and taking responsibility for their own lives.[5] Finally, as noted, the right to parent is conditional on some standard of parental competency. Would-be parents may be denied the right to parent because they cannot or will not adequately discharge parental responsibilities. Similarly, adults who have acquired the right to parent may lose it or have it severely circumscribed for parallel reasons.

JUSTIFYING THE RIGHT TO PARENT

The fact that the right to parent is conditional on would-be parents satisfying a standard of competency indicates that the justification of the right to parent depends crucially on the link between the right and the interests of children. One seemingly attractive way of developing this link is to adopt a child-centered view according to which the right to parent is grounded entirely in the interests of children. Since children initially lack and only gradually develop the capacities and knowledge needed to track and secure their own interests reliably, they must be assigned guardians who can identify, protect, and promote their legitimate interests until they are able to assume that role for themselves. On the child-centered view, parental rights are harnessed to the fiduciary role that parents occupy and the claim that particular adults have to exercise the prerogatives of parenthood over particular children is only as strong as the would-be parents' capacities as adequate fiduciaries of their children's interest. This view is often thought to be vulnerable to the objection that it implausibly authorizes assigning parental rights to the adults who are best able to promote the interests of specific children.[6] This raises the ugly specter, at least in principle, of redistributing children from adults who would be good parents to adults who would be better parents.

However, I believe that the concern is misplaced. The problems with the child-centered view lie elsewhere. The redistribution objection only arises in a troubling way if we assume that children have a claim to be raised in a way that *maximally* promotes their interests. Yet it is far from clear that children have an entitlement to *maximal* promotion of their interests by their guardians. Although the interests of children are extremely important and require special attention, adults have legitimate interests of their own that must be given independent recognition and weight.[7] The interests of vulnerable and dependent children have a special claim on our moral attention but we should not assume that when the interests of children and adults diverge—as sometimes happens—that priority always attaches to the promotion of children's interests. Suppose, for example, that an adult can confer a small benefit on a child by incurring a significant cost or forgoing a very valuable opportunity. In such a case, it surely does not follow that the adult morally must do what is (literally) best for the child. Whether that will be so will depend on the relative gravity of the interests at stake and what fair consideration of the competing interests requires. Perhaps the consideration of competing interests here need not be strictly impartial but at some point the interests of adults serve as constraints on the promotion of the interests of children. Once this point is appreciated, we need not suppose that a child-centered view must be committed to assigning parental rights over specific children to adults who would be the *best* available parents (i.e., those adults best placed to maximally promote the interests of children). The justification of parental rights still turns only on the way such rights secure the interests of children, but we can dispense with the idea that children, in general, have a genuine claim to be raised by the best available parents.

It seems more plausible to characterize the child-centered view as holding that parental rights are designed to help secure the interests to which children have a justice-based claim. As we have seen, it is doubtful that children have a justice-based claim to optimal parents. Of course, those justice-protected interests are likely to be quite substantial, and some would-be parents will be unwilling or unable to secure them and hence will not have a right to parent. However, in normal circumstances, most would-be parents will have the capacities to secure the legitimate interests of children. So when stripped of the implausible idea that children have some standing claim to the best possible upbringing, a child-centered view need not face the redistribution problem.

This does not mean, however, that the child-centered view offers a fully adequate account of the justificatory basis of parental rights. In my opinion, it faces two serious difficulties. First, the view suffers from a problematic indeterminacy along two dimensions: (1) it provides an insufficiently strong explanation of why particular adults have a strong claim to have parental rights over specific children, and (2) it does not explain why adults can claim a right to parent children in the face of alternative child-raising strategies in which guardianship of children is widely distributed amongst a large group of adults. To motivate the first dimension of the indeterminacy problem, consider two couples who wish to parent a particular child. Assume that both are equally well-placed to secure the relevant interests of a child and both wish to become parents. On the child-centered view, the fact that one couple has deliberately engaged in procreative activity aimed at creating a child that they can parent is, strictly speaking, irrelevant to determining whether they or the equally capable non-procreative couple can advance a successful claim to parent the offspring of their procreation. From the perspective of the child's interests, it is indeterminate which of the couples should exercise parental authority over the child. (At best, the deliberate planning of the procreative couple serves as evidence that they can be relied upon to fulfill parental responsibilities.) But this seems mistaken. The fact that one couple has, through their activity, established a strong narrative connection to a particular child is relevant to establishing their claim to parent that child. In a related vein, suppose that collective child rearing is equally good at securing the relevant interests of children as typical parenting[8] is. If this were the case then the child-centered view would be neutral on the issue of whether there is a right to parent at all. The view cannot explain why we might have decisive reasons to recognize the rights of adults to become parents and exercise parental authority over specific children. Here too the fact that so many people in so many cultures highly (and reasonably) value the project of having and raising children of their own[9] seems relevant to the grounding of the right to parent. For many people, parenting contributes enormously to the goodness of one's life. But this fact seems to have no direct justificatory force in the child-centered view.

A second problem of the child-centered view is that it provides an incomplete basis for some dimensions of the right to parent. In acquiring a right to parent, adults assume certain important responsibilities for securing the interests of their children. However, although the content of the right to parent is constrained and shaped by the interests of children, it is not completely determined by those interests. This is not because parents' interests sometimes trump the interests of their children but rather because parenting itself is a source of some of children's interests. Some of children's basic interests are, of course, "upbringing independent." For instance, the core physical and psychological health interests of children fall into this category. A child's interest in having access to nutritious food or good education is an interest she has independent of the decisions her parents make about how to raise her. However, some interests are "upbringing dependent" in the sense that they cannot be properly attributed to children in the absence of having been raised in a certain way. In this context the relation between interest attribution and identity formation assumes significance. There are, I assume, many ways in which our identities can be shaped that neither harm us by setting back an interest that we antecedently have nor promote an interest we already have. However, once our identity is shaped in a certain way we can acquire interests that are related to that identity. I think this is true of many routine facets of cultural identity. For instance, prior to being raised in a Jewish household that observes traditional Jewish holidays, a child has no interest in celebrating Hanukkah. However, the child's upbringing as a Jew (or as a child in a Jewish household) can generate such an interest. Subject to certain important constraints concerning the facilitation of autonomy in children, I think the right to parent includes the right to shape the identity of one's children by (provisionally) privileging[10] a conception of the good in family life. Moreover, this facet of the right to parent is integral to the value that parents derive from parenting. Yet this dimension of the right to parent cannot be properly grounded in how it serves the interests of children. One might, of course, argue that children have an interest in acquiring specific cultural identity on the grounds that an identity is integral to the development of autonomy in that it provides what Kymlicka calls a "context of choice."[11] Or one might argue that identity formation contributes instrumentally to the realization of antecedent interests children have, such as enjoying intimate, loving relationships with their parents.

These suggestions are plausible but they do not adequately capture the distinct interests that parents appear to have in shaping children's identity and encouraging their participation in the conception of the good adopted by parents. The point is not simply that identity shaping is compatible with or linked to the interests of children; rather, it is that the prerogatives to shape one's children's identity in line with one's own conception of the good are most credibly grounded in distinctive interests of parents. These interests are, in my view, sufficiently powerful that they play a role in justifying the right to parent and this, in turn, provides a reason to adopt a dual interest view of the right to parent.

The suggestion that a dual interest account of the right to parent provides a more adequate justification of the right to parent is not novel. For instance, Brighouse and Swift[12] have advanced an influential version of the view that grounds the right to parent in the fundamental interest that parents have in enjoying the special goods of intimacy that are uniquely available in (good) relationships between parents and children. I agree with Brighouse and Swift that the value, to parents, of intimate relationships with their children plays a role in grounding the right to parent.[13] However, I doubt that intimacy alone provides a sufficient basis to ground the crucial prerogatives to provisionally privilege one's own conception of the good with one's children. It is important to note that Brighouse and Swift concede that parents have such prerogatives to influence children and cultivate cultural or religious interests in them. "Parents have the right to determine whether the child will attend a church, a mosque, or neither; they have the right to live with the child and spend a substantial part of the day with her. They have the right to share their enthusiasms with their children, including, for example, their enthusiasms regarding their own particular cultural heritage."[14] But they insist that such identity shaping prerogatives arise only because and to the degree that they are (realistically) necessary for facilitating the special interest that parents have in intimate relationships with their children.

In my view, the attempt to ground parental prerogatives to shape the identity of children in the parental interest in intimacy is unsuccessful. To begin with, it is doubtful that intimacy strongly depends on providing parents with the prerogatives to privilege their own conceptions of the good with their children or to mediate their intimate relationships with their children through their conception of the good. It is perfectly possible for parents to enjoy deep and emotionally rich relationships with their children without requiring that their children participate in the activities or observe the rituals tied to a specific conception of the good (e.g., a specific religious or cultural tradition). It is plausible to imagine, for instance, that religious Christians can enjoy a fulfilling intimate relationship with their daughter without sharing their Christian convictions with her or requiring her to attend church. Should we therefore conclude these parents, strictly speaking, do not have the prerogative to include their daughter in various Christian activities and rituals? I do not think so. The prerogative seems to have significance to parents beyond its connection to intimacy per se.

It might be argued that the kind of compartmentalization of one's conception of the good that is envisioned here would, in fact, be difficult for many people and hence there is no practical way of facilitating intimacy without granting parents the prerogative to shape their children's identity. The practical point has, I concede, some force when it comes to crafting public policy that is hospitable to intimacy. All things considered, it may be preferable to have a state that does not attempt to determine precisely which parental practices are integral to intimacy and which are not. However, my point concerns the normative grounding of the parental prerogative to shape children's identity. The fact that we can readily imagine intimacy obtaining in the absence of the exercise of the parental prerogative to shape children's identity reveals the limitation of grounding the prerogative in intimacy.

The obvious way to remedy this limitation of the Brighouse and Swift strategy is simply to give direct recognition to the interest that parents appear to have in shaping their children's identity. The challenge, of course, is to characterize this interest in a way that renders it both weighty enough to serve as a (partial) ground of the right to parent and allows us to see how recognition of the interest is compatible with respect for the rights of children. My suggestion is that we characterize the interest as an important instantiation of the fundamental interest we have in what I call "creative self-extension." Many of the most important projects and activities we adopt and pursue have a crucial expressive component: we seek not only to pursue a conception of the good but to display its features to others[15] and to encourage their appreciation of its value. Sometimes we hope to persuade others to share our conception of the good and to collaborate with us in pursuing it but other times we seek only understanding and acknowledgement of the value of our commitments. Negotiating this expressive dimension of valued commitments involves, I suggest, extending our values and identity to others. But successfully extending our values to others may be very difficult and typically demands creativity. Hurdles arise for various reasons. Others may not be receptive to our values or our modes of expressing them or they may have existing commitments or interests that diverge or conflict with ours. There are also important moral constraints on how we may convey or encourage appreciation of our commitments. For instance, we cannot use coercion or brainwashing techniques to cultivate appreciation by others of our conception of the good. However, skillfully meeting the challenge of extending ourselves to others can be a source of enormous value in itself and is frequently integral to the implementation of our conceptions of the good.

Parenting presents an especially rewarding yet complex opportunity for this kind of creative self-extension. Children are vulnerable, dependent, and impressionable, and this means that parents typically wield power over children that they do not wield over other persons. On the one hand, this means that parents are in a very good position to exercise a great deal of influence over the values and interests that children have. So the scope for creative self-extension is wide and remains wide for many years. On the other hand, despite this power, instilling interests and values in children is a difficult and uncertain business. Children are not simply lumps of human clay without personalities of their own. They are not fully autonomous agents but they display forms of agency that cannot be ignored.[16] Children frequently resist their parents' efforts at enculturation in both small and dramatic ways, and responding to resistance or indifference can be very demanding for parents. Of course, the fact that parents care deeply for their children and assume significant responsibilities for facilitating the flourishing of their children significantly raises what is at stake when parents shape their children's identity. If we think our conception of the good is worthy of adoption by our children, we cannot be indifferent to whether our children understand and appreciate the value commitments that are constitutive our identity.[17] In this respect, creative self-extension has an important altruistic dimension: it is motivated in part by a concern to help others flourish.

Even if it is conceded, in light of the foregoing remarks, that the opportunity for creative self-extension through parenting is extremely important to parents, there remains a concern that it is inconsistent with respect for children as independent persons. It is true that some forms of creative self-extension by parents are objectionable. Children should not be treated as mere ingredients in the life plans of parents who may be manipulated to fit the conception of the good favored by parents. Legitimate creative self-extension must respect children's emerging agency and must be compatible with the facilitation of autonomy. However, while some forms of creative self-extension are disrespectful to children or amount to wrongful indoctrination, not all forms fall prey to this objection. The first point to made in this context is simply that the fact that an interest or value is cultivated or instilled in a child by parents does not itself pose a threat to autonomy. Children can also develop the moral capacities and acquire the knowledge (e.g., of other values or projects) requisite to critical reflection and assessment of elements of their identity that have been shaped by parents. For example, merely being raised in a particular religious tradition does not preclude full and meaningful critical evaluation of the tradition and its practices.

Second, providing that creative self-extension occurs with suitable sensitivity to autonomy facilitation, it need not jeopardize other vital interests that children have. As I noted earlier, once a person's identity is shaped in a given way she can acquire interests linked to the identity. We usually assume that adults have an identity of some sort along with the capacities to direct their own lives. We can manifest disrespect for adults by frustrating pursuit of their identity-related interests or by trying to undermine or subvert the identity that they endorse and have an interest in maintaining. For example, forcing a Jew to participate in Christian religious rites is an assault on an identity-related interest and is disrespectful. However, the situation is different with children precisely because they initially have no identity-related interests of this sort. So Christian parents who share their Christianity with their children by requiring them to attend church or perform other acts of religious faith do not thereby manifest disrespect for the identity-related interests of their children. Absent the identity-shaping activities of their parents, the children have no vital identity-related interests to offend.[18] In light of this, it seems difficult to hold that the cultivation of a cultural or religious identity in children by parents is disrespectful to children per se. If, as seems plausible, there are many autonomy-compatible religious and cultural identities, then parents do not wrong children by systematically favoring one of them and orienting important aspects of child rearing around it.

I hope the foregoing remarks explain why appeal to the parental interest in intimacy is not sufficient to ground all dimensions of the right to parent. Acknowledging the interest that parents have in creative self-extension supplements the appeal to intimacy interests and provides a better rationale for some distinctive features of the right to parent. The approach I have sketched explains how parents can both respect their children and shape important aspect of their religious and cultural identity. On my view, there is a plurality of acceptable cultural, religious or secular scripts that parents have the right to privilege in raising their children. The authority to choose from the large set of autonomy compatible scripts rests with parents and serves their interests but not in a way that is hostile to the interests of children. The content of an acceptable script is highly constrained but not entirely controlled by children's upbringing independent interests.

MODEST VS. ROBUST PARENTAL COMPETENCY

I now want to turn to the issue of how considerations of competency should regulate access to the right to parent. Although the dual interest view recognizes that parents have powerful interests in parenting, this need not imply that the importance of protecting children's vital interests must be balanced against conflicting interests of parents. Nonetheless, the emphasis I have placed on the value of parenting to adults might seem to weigh in favor of a modest standard of parental competency that denies the right to parent only to would-be parents who threaten to abuse children physically or mentally or who cannot attend adequately to very basic nutritional and health needs of children. After all, if the right to parent is so valuable to adults then it might seem that it may be denied only to adults who are or who are likely to be egregiously bad parents. Discussions of the proposal that prospective parents satisfy licensing requirements before securing the legal right to parent also often seem to assume that the right to parent is conditional only on a modest standard of parental competency. The issue at the center of such discussions is whether licensing can successfully, efficiently, and fairly screen out abusive or grossly negligent parents.[19] That is clearly an important issue but it begs the question whether satisfaction of a modest standard of parental competency is sufficient to acquire the right to parent. I believe the modest standard is not sufficient and that the moral right to parent is conditional on would-be parents satisfying a more robust standard of competency. I will not provide a fully developed articulation of the robust standard but I will try to explain why the modest standard is inadequate in a way that points the way towards fuller characterization of a robust standard.

The main point I want to make in this context is that articulation of the standard of parental competency fundamentally depends on: (1) identifying the justice-based entitlements of children, and (2) determining how the social division of moral labor can be orchestrated so as to effectively and reliably ensure those entitlements. I assume it is obvious that all children have a right not to be subject to physical or psychological abuse. So the modest standard of parental competency correctly insists that the right to parent is dependent on parents satisfying the minimal requirement that they refrain from abusing their children. Yet I think it is equally obvious that the justice-based entitlements of children are more extensive than the right to be free from abuse or gross neglect.

I cannot here offer a full articulation of children's justice-based entitlements. However, the following claims strike me as credible components of an account of children's entitlements. First, children are entitled to health care, good nutrition, physical exercise, and education of a sort compatible with full development of their physiological and cognitive capacities. Second, children are entitled to an autonomy-facilitating upbringing that equips them for participation in the political community but also enables critical and independent reflection and deliberation on their values and commitments.[20] Third, children have a right to be loved by those who care for them.[21] Fourth, children have a right to access intrinsic goods of childhood such as opportunities for carefree play and preservation of a degree of innocence during early phases of childhood.[22]

Securing these entitlements for children does not fall entirely to parents, but would-be parents must be willing and able to play their part in helping to meet them. But that in turn suggests that the modest standard is inadequate. On any plausible rendering of the entitlements of children, parental competency requires more than the avoidance of abuse or neglect. Yet it is important to see that a robust standard does not require parents to be optimal parents. The robust standard holds that competent parents must be willing and able assume their fair share of the moral labor in meeting children's entitlements. I have already explained why children do not have an entitlement to an upbringing that maximally promotes their interests. If this is correct and we adopt the suggestion that competency be linked to the justice-based entitlements of children, then competent parents need not be the best-available parents for a given child.

Precise specification of all the elements of a robust standard of parental competency is difficult because what can be demanded of competent parents will be influenced by the role that background institutions and social policy play in meeting the entitlements of children. For example, the degree to which competent parents must be able to ensure that their children's claims to good education and health care are met will depend on the kind of social provision of these goods that obtains. If a child has a right to education and there are no public schools then competent parents must have the wherewithal to educate their children themselves or to buy private education for their children. By contrast, in a society with excellent public schools, the demands of a robust standard of parental competency will be correspondingly lower. Here it is worth noting that the absence of excellent and accessible public education and health care can unfairly affect the class of adults who can claim a right to parent. Poor or inadequate provision of these essential public services will make it difficult for some would-be parents (e.g., poor people who lack the resources to cover the routine medical expenses of children) to meet the threshold of parental competency. If, as I have suggested, the interest in parenting is weighty, then we have a reason grounded in the right to parent to ensure that all people have adequate and reliable access to good health care and education.

Notwithstanding the caveat about how the social division of moral labor can affect the precise content of a robust standard of parental competency, the contours of the robust standard can be fleshed out in the following way. Recall that at the heart of the right to parent is the assignment to parents of special authority over children. Given the justice-based entitlements of children that I have outlined, we can say that parental authority should not be exercised in ways that: (1) result in serious (and readily) avoidable physical or psychological harm to children, (2) frustrate or impede the development of autonomy, (3) leave children hostile or insensitive to the rights and basic moral claims of others, (4) ignore or run roughshod over the distinct and sometimes idiosyncratic preferences, interests, and enthusiasms of young children and adolescents (i.e., parents should manifest suitable respect for the emerging agency/autonomy of their children), (5) deny children love, affection, or intimacy, and (6) deprive children access to the intrinsic goods of childhood. Competent parents must be willing and able to abide by these constraints. This in turn suggests that, on the robust view, competent parents should have the following general attributes.[23] First, parents should display good judgement about the content of their own children's welfare. Competent parents can, perhaps in concert with others (e.g., teachers, health care professionals, etc.) reliably identify and track the basic needs and interests of their children. Second, given both the time that children spend with parents and the wide scope of the interactions parents and children have, competent parents are attentive to their children. They regularly monitor their children's well-being and are motivated to identify and address problems.[24] Third, competent parents must be emotionally engaged with their children. They must be disposed to manifest love, affection, and concern to their children. Fourth, competent parents display respect for their children. They are disposed to acknowledge and respond appropriately to the emerging moral personality of their children.

Although the robust standard of parental competency is more demanding than the modest standard, it need not unduly circumscribe the set of adults who can claim a moral right to parent. To begin with, robust parental competency is multiply realizable: the precise constellation of personal traits parents must display to fulfill the criteria can vary quite a bit. There are many different modes of successful parenting that give adequate expression to the different facets of the robust standard. For example, love and affection for children can be communicated via a wide variety of different cultural and social conventions. Similarly, decent parents may employ different overall strategies to monitor and respond to their children's interests. Any reasonable and practically feasible interpretation of the robust standard must be sensitive to the different ways in which decent parenting can be achieved. Second, most parents are disposed to love their children and have the capacities to care for them in an effective and respectful fashion. So it is unlikely that many would-be parents will be denied the right to parent on the grounds that they do not meet the robust standard of parental competency.

Nonetheless, there may be one significant exception to the last observation, namely illiberal groups who hold conceptions of the good (e.g., various types of conservative religious views) that are expressly opposed to facilitation of autonomy in children. Such groups usually place a high value on maintenance of traditional family structures in which the prerogatives of parental authority are assumed to be much stronger than my account allows. Moreover, such groups often subscribe to doctrines that are sexist, homophobic, or intolerant along other dimensions. Arguably, many people in such groups hold views that conflict with the requirement that parents respect and support the development of the independent agency of children. Yet such parents are capable of love and can attend competently to their children's other interests. The robust standard seems to imply that such persons are not fully competent parents. Should we therefore say that they do not have a moral right to parent? Such a conclusion would be highly controversial, especially in pluralistic democracies. The solution to this conundrum lies in a division of moral labor in which responsibility for autonomy facilitation does not rest primarily with parents. Instead, schools can be relied upon to help children acquire a reflective appreciation of the plurality of different conceptions of the good held by different people. Of course, this strategy requires, among other things, severely limiting parental prerogatives to insulate their children from educational contexts in which there is exposure to different doctrines and encouragement of independent critical thinking about such matters.[25]

CONCLUSION

For many people, parenting is an unrivaled, intense, enduring, unique, and profound source of meaning. Parenting provides an opportunity to play a leading role in creating a distinctive family narrative that is reflective of our values, personalities, and preferences. The version of the dual-interest view of the right to parent I favor gives direct recognition to this facet of the value of parenting. However, when linked to a robust standard of parental competency, it does not jeopardize the legitimate interests of children. I have argued that the robust standard of parental competency that regulates who can claim a right to parent should be articulated via identification of children's justice-based entitlements. I have not offered a full account of those entitlements. But, in my view, they are sufficiently demanding so as to disqualify the modest standard of parental competency. Yet they are not so demanding as to require competent parents to be optimally good parents. Adequately securing the entitlements of children involves complex forms of cooperation between adults. A suitable division of the moral labor of caring for children is crucial to safeguarding the interests of children while simultaneously ensuring that the opportunity to parent is readily available to the adults who wish to pursue it. Finally, if the right to parent is both highly valuable to people and yet only claimable by those who satisfy the robust standard of parental competency, then we have reason to ensure both that our social institutions and practices properly prepare people to meet the robust standard and that we remove or mitigate unfair obstacles that prevent people who wish to parent fulfilling that role in a fully competent fashion. I have not explored the legal or social policy implications of the approach to the right to parent I have defended here. But I hope it provides a fruitful normative perspective from which to address such matters.

NOTES

1. For the purposes of this discussion, I assume that human procreation is morally permissible. However, the issues I discuss arise even if an anti-natalist position of the sort defended by David Benatar (*Better Never to Have Been*, Oxford: Oxford University Press, 2006) is correct. Even if it is wrong to procreate, children wrongly brought into existence need care, and so the issue of the right to parent will arise.
2. Non-immigrant citizens of states arguably do not consent to the authority of the state to which they are subject. But citizens have, at least in principle, the right to exit their state and voluntarily subject themselves to the authority of another state.
3. Although my discussion of parental competency makes various substantive claims about the rights of children (e.g., that children have a right to an autonomy facilitating upbringing), I do not provide a detailed account of how the relevant considerations of justice that ground these rights are to be developed or defended. Some of the justice-based parameters on the exercise of parental rights such as those forbidding the physical abuse of children are clear and uncontroversial. (Of course, precisely what constitutes physical abuse may generate controversy as debates about matters such as corporal punishment and circumcision indicate.) Other parameters, such as those concerning the prerogatives that parents have to confer significant educational and economic advantages on their children of the sort that disrupt equality between children are more controversial. See Adam Swift, *How Not to be a Hypocrite: School Choice for the Morally Perplexed* (London: Routledge, 2003).
4. However, as Anca Gheaus argues, the fact of an intimate gestational relationship with a child of the sort that normally obtains between pregnant women and their babies does play an important role in grounding the right to parent one's biological baby: Anca Gheaus, "The Right to Parent One's Biologial Baby," *Journal of Political Philosophy* 20, no. 4 (2011): 432–455.
5. I set aside the question of whether parents wield any residual parental rights over their adult children, such as a right to demand assistance in old age or a right to contact and visit with grandchildren.
6. Hannan and Vernon, who develop a sophisticated version of the child-centered view, amusingly dub this the "Plato worry" in light of Plato's

declared enthusiasm in the *Republic* for redistributing children: Sarah Hannan and Richard Vernon, "Parental Rights: A Role-Based Approach," *Theory and Research in Education* 6, no. 2 (2008): 173–189. Hannan and Vernon provide a useful critical assessment of ways of addressing the Plato worry found in the work of Ferdinand Shoeman ("Rights of Children, Rights of Parents, and the Value of the Family," *Ethics* 91, no. 1 [1980]: 6–19), Harry Brighouse and Adam Swift ("Parents' Rights and the Value of the Family," *Ethics* 117, no. 1 [2006]: 80–108), and Matthew Clayton (*Justice and Legitimacy in Upbringing*, Oxford: Oxford University Press, 2006). Although I am very sympathetic to many of the observations these authors make about the nature and value of parenting, my response to the Plato worry is different. In effect, I deny it is a genuine worry in the first place. It is worth noting that the Plato worry depends on the assumption that it is possible to meaningfully distinguish best parents from the merely good parents. I think this is a dubious assumption. As I explain below, the goodness of parenting has many dimensions and is multiply realizable. Above a certain (reasonably high) threshold of competence, comprehensive quality comparisons between different parents are, in the real world, epistemically indeterminate.

7. Saying this is compatible, of course, with insisting that many of the legitimate interests of children have not been adequately recognized in contemporary political philosophy or in political practice.

8. As I indicated earlier, parenting can take many forms. My point here is not to rule out parenting structures in which a number of adults exercise shared parental rights. How many parents a child can have is an interesting question about which I take no stance here save to say that parental authority cannot be successfully shared amongst a large number of adults. At some point, collective rearing of children is distinguishable from parenting children.

9. By "their own," I do not mean to signal a biologically relationship or a relationship of property ownership. Instead, the sense of "own" I intend here is one signifying a complex web of special intimate relationships between an adult and child grounded in a shared narrative history.

10. That the right to shape one's children's identity takes the form of a prerogative to *provisionally privilege* a conception of the good is important. The right is not designed to ensure that children actually adopt a specific conception of the good. Properly understood, permitting parents to shape children's identities by privileging a conception of the good does not license indoctrination or hostility to the facilitation of children's autonomy. See Colin Macleod, "Conceptions of Parental Autonomy," *Politics and Society* 25, no. 1 (1997): 117–140.

11. Will Kymlicka, *Liberalism, Community and Culture* (Oxford: Oxford University Press), 165.

12. Brighouse and Swift, "Parents' Rights."

13. Elsewhere I have offered my own characterization of the special value of intimate relationships between parents and children: Colin Macleod, "Parental Responsibilities in an Unjust World," in *Procreation and Parenthood: The Ethics of Bearing and Rearing Children*, ed. David Archard and David Benatar, Oxford: Oxford University Press, 2010. I draw a distinction between intimacy and a slightly different but related value of "cherishment." On my view, the value of intimacy arises through the meaning derived from responding to the challenges of negotiating our personal connections to those to whom we are closely

related. The value of cherishment is located in the emotional engagement we have with family members that allows us to experience especially intense forms of love and pride. However, the distinction between intimacy and cherishment is not directly relevant to the criticism of the Brighouse and Swift view that I advance.

14. Brighouse and Swift, "Parents' Rights," 102
15. The target audience may be very wide (e.g., a large community) or small (e.g., a few friends or family members).
16. For recent discussion of the nature and significance of the agency of children, see the following articles in *The Nature of Children's Well-Being: Theory and Practice*: David Archard, "Children, Adults, Autonomy and Well-Being"; Paul-Bou Habib and Serena Olsaretti, "Autonomy and Children's Well-Being"; Colin Macleod, "Agency, Authority and the Vulnerability of Children"; Monika Betzler, "Enhancing the Capacity for Autonomy: What Parents Owe Their Children to Make Their Lives Go Well"; and Anthony Skelton, "Utilitarianism, Welfare and Children."
17. This does not imply that successful creative self-extension requires that children actually adopt and pursue the projects or values that parents try to convey to them. That children come to have a reflective appreciation of the parents' conception of the good seems more important.
18. I provide a fuller discussion of the identity-related interests of children in Colin Macleod, "Interpreting the Identity Claims of Children," in *Diversity and Equality: New Approaches to Fundamental Freedom in Canada*, ed. Avigail Eisenberg (Vancouver: University of Britsh Columbia Press, 2010).
19. McFall, Michael, *Licensing Parents: Family, State and Child Maltreatment* (Lanham, MD: Lexington Books, 2009); Hugh LaFollette, "Licensing Parents Revisited," *Journal of Applied Philosophy* 27, no. 4 (2010): 327–343; Jurgen De Wispelaere and Daniel Weinstock, "Licensing Parents to Protect Our Children?" *Ethics and Social Welfare* 6, no. 2 (2012).
20. Macleod, "Conceptions"; Meira Levinson, *The Demands of Liberal Education* (Oxford: Oxford University Press, 1999); Harry Brighouse, *School Choice and Social Justice* (Oxford: Oxford University Press, 2000); Eamonn Callan, "Autonomy, Child-Rearing and Good Lives," in *The Moral and Political Status of Children*, ed. David Archard and Colin Macleod (Oxford: Oxford University Press, 2002), 118–141.
21. Mathew Liao, "The Right of Children to Be Loved," *Journal of Political Philosophy* 14, no. 4: 420–440.
22. Macleod, Colin. "Primary Goods, Capabilities and Children." In Harry Brighouse and Ingrid Robeyns (eds.), Measuring Justice: Primary Goods and Capabilities. Cambridge: Cambridge University Press, 2010; Samantha Brennan, "The Goods of Childhood, Children's Rights, and the Role of Parents as Advocates and Interpreters," in *Family-Making: Contemporary Ethical Challenges*, ed. Françoise Baylis and Carolyn McLeod (Oxford: Oxford University Press, 2014); Anca Gheaus, "The Intrinsic Goods of Childhood and the Good Society," in *The Nature of Children's Well-Being: Theory and Practice*. (Berlin: Springer, 2014).
23. I do not explore it here, but robust parental competency is *weakly indexed* to particular children: the attributes necessary to parent some children successfully can be special. For example, parenting children with significant cognitive or physical disabilities may require special parental competencies.
24. Attentiveness is different from good judgment. A person may be capable of correctly identifying a person's interests and yet may be inattentive to whether the interests are being secured.

25. This almost certainly entails significant restrictions on the extent to which parochial schools can orient a curriculum and pedagogy towards systematic promotion of specific religious doctrines or practices. Similarly, it would dramatically limit the prerogatives of parents to homeschool children and thereby deny them a suitably pluralistic education.

REFERENCES

Benatar, David. *Better Never to Have Been: The Harm of Coming Into Existence*. Oxford: Oxford University Press, 2006.

Brennan, Samantha. "The Goods of Childhood, Children's Rights, and the Role of Parents as Advocates and Interpreters," in Françoise Baylis and Carolyn McLeod (eds.,) *Family-Making: Contemporary Ethical Challenges*. Oxford: Oxford University Press, 2014.

Brighouse, Harry. *School Choice and Social Justice*. Oxford: Oxford University Press, 2000.

Brighouse, Harry, and Adam Swift. "Parent's Rights and the Value of the Family." *Ethics:* 117, no. 1 (2006) 80–108.

Callan, Eamonn. "Autonomy, Child-rearing, and Good Lives," In: David Archard and Colin Macleod (eds.) *The Moral and Political Status of Children*. Oxford: Oxford University Press, 2002: 118–141.

Clayton, Matthew. *Justice and Legitimacy in Upbringing*. Oxford: Oxford University Press, 2006.

De Wispelaere, Jurgen, and Daniel Weinstock. "Licensing Parents to Protect Our Children?," *Ethics and Social Welfare* 6, no. 2 (2012): 195–205.

Gheaus, Anca. "The Right to Parent One's Biological Baby," *Journal of Political Philosophy* 20, no. 4 (2011): 432–455.

Gheaus, Anca. "The Intrinsic Goods of Childhood and the Good Society," in A. Bagattini and C. Macleod (eds.), *The Nature of Children's Well-Being: Theory and Practice*. Berlin: Springer. 2014.

Hannan, Sarah, and Richard Vernon. "Parental Rights: A Role-based Approach," *Theory and Research in Education* 6, no. 2 (2008): 173–189.

Kymlicka, Will. *Liberalism, Community and Culture*. Oxford: Oxford University Press. 1989.

LaFollette, Hugh. "Licensing Parents Revisited." *Journal of Applied Philosophy* 27, no. 4 (2010): 327–343.

Levinson, Meira. *The Demands of Liberal Education*. Oxford: Oxford University Press, 1999.

Liao, Matthew. "The Right of Children to Be Loved." *The Journal of Political Philosophy*, 14, no. 4 (2006): 420–440.

Macleod, Colin. "Conceptions of Parental Autonomy." *Politics and Society* 25, no. 1 (1997): 117–140.

Macleod, Colin. "Interpreting the Identity Claims of Children." In: Avigail Eisenberg (ed.), *Diversity and Equality: New Approaches to Fundamental Freedom in Canada*. Vancouver: University of British Columbia Press, 2006.

Macleod, Colin. "Parental Responsibilities in an Unjust World." In David Archard and David Benatar (eds.), *Procreation and Parenthood: The Ethics of Bearing and Rearing Children*. Oxford: Oxford University Press, 2010.

Macleod, Colin. "Primary Goods, Capabilities and Children." In Harry Brighouse and Ingrid Robeyns (eds.), *Measuring Justice: Primary Goods and Capabilities*. Cambridge: Cambridge University Press, 2010.

McFall, Michael. *Licensing Parents: Family, State, and Child Maltreatment*. Lanham, MD: Lexington Books, 2009.

Shoeman, Ferdinand. "Rights of Children, Rights of Parents and the Moral Basis of the Family." *Ethics* 91, no. 1 (1980): 6–19.

Swift, Adam. *How Not to Be a Hypocrite: School Choice for the Morally Perplexed Parent*. London: Routledge, 2003.

CHAPTER 11

How Much Do We Owe to Children?*

MATTHEW CLAYTON

Parents and other adult members of the political community are required by political morality to set aside resources to discharge their
duty to raise and care for children appropriately. But how many resources
do we owe to children? For example, we might devote more or fewer monetary resources to the education of children and, thereby, recruit better
teachers or maintain class sizes that are better suited to learning. Similarly, we might or might not adopt policies that enable, encourage, or require parents to spend more time with their children, or protect parks and
other recreational facilities that are used by children more or less. We
need a conception of justice that provides sound guidance to address the
distributive issue of how much we owe to children.

Here I offer some programmatic thoughts about how to approach these
issues. My contribution is in one way disappointing, because I do not offer
concrete proposals that specify what or how much we owe to children. The
soundness of any specific proposals turns on many non-normative facts,
such as whether larger or smaller class sizes are better with respect to facilitating learning, or whether parents spending more or less time with
their child benefits their child, which I lack the expertise to address.

Rather than describe particular policy proposals, I elaborate and defend
a set of normative principles that ought to guide our policy choices. That
set of principles is a hybrid conception that draws on the work of John
Rawls and Ronald Dworkin. Briefly, Rawls articulates a set of interests
that we have in virtue of our having the status of "free and equal citizens,"
which has considerable significance for policies that ought to regulate the
upbringing of children. However, notwithstanding their significance, an

appeal to the interests Rawls identifies leaves open several questions related to how much is owed to children, and I turn to Dworkin's conception of liberal equality, particularly his account of equal hypothetical insurance, for guidance on how to offer a more complete solution to the problem. However, before elaborating and defending what I take to be the most promising conception, I describe the problem more precisely, distinguish it from other related issues, set out some background assumptions, and briefly review and reject some other possible answers to our question.

FOCUS AND ASSUMPTIONS

Many believe that how much a particular child is owed sometimes depends on how much *other* children receive. Those who endorse equality of opportunity hold this view. The fact that resource-rich parents devote considerable resources to their children gives us a reason to ensure that children of resource-poor parents receive extra resources so that they enjoy similar opportunities to others; or the fact that some children can or do enjoy only limited educational opportunities might be a reason to limit the educational opportunities enjoyed by others.[1] The issue I address does not address the question, *what is owed to particular children given what other children receive?* I bracket that question and ask what we owe to children on the assumption that every child receives or enjoys the same. If there is a case for equal opportunity, we might still ask whether opportunities for children should be set at lower or higher levels. Of course, once the fact of unequal childhoods is recognized, that might make a significant difference to the aggregate amount we ought to spend on children. If, for example, we ought to equalize opportunity, but it is impossible or undesirable to limit rich parents investing in their child's upbringing or education, then there might be a case for spending possibly huge sums to enhance the opportunities of the least advantaged. Notwithstanding its importance, however, I shall not systematically address issues concerning equality of opportunity between children here.

The problem I address is part of a more general issue concerning how to distribute resources across a life. The resources in question might be monetary resources or in-kind resources, such as time spent with parents, the size of school classes, health care provision, and so on. There appears sometimes to be a conflict between the interests of children in having a good start in life and the interests of adults in having resources and opportunities to pursue their non-parental goals.[2] The general thought is that part of the answer to our question is to extend the insights of Daniels and Dworkin, who resolve the problem of justice with respect to age-groups by asking how relatively prudent individuals would distribute resources across their own lives.[3]

The aim of this chapter is to explore an anti-perfectionist response to our question. The key feature of anti-perfectionism, as I understand it, is that political morality does not appeal to the "whole truth" about what makes one's life go well or our ethical responsibilities. Instead, it seeks principles that are acceptable to what Rawls calls "free and equal" individuals who share interests in developing and deploying the capacity for a sense of justice and the capacity to lead an autonomous ethical life. Addressing our question by reference to the choices that would be made by fairly situated and relatively prudent individuals is particularly well suited to an anti-perfectionist conception. Or so I argue.

In elaborating this framework, I make three further assumptions. First, I assume that no problematic issues of personal identity arise: I shall assume that a named individual remains the same person from conception to death. If that is not the case, then the question of how to distribute resources across a life may not map nicely onto the question of how much we owe to children, because it could be that an individual's life ends or gradually vanishes on reaching adulthood.[4] If the natural life span of a human contains several different personal identities, then our assessment of what we owe to individuals at different periods of their lives might be dramatically different. I do not offer an argument for the continuity of personal identity from conception to death in the normal case; I merely make this conventional assumption.

Second, I proceed on the assumption that procreation does not normally wrong the child who is created. If that assumption is mistaken, our answer to the question "How much do we owe to children?" might be affected, because if it wrongs children to bring them into existence, then they might be owed compensation by those who intentionally beget them. I do not believe that children who have lives worth living are, indeed, wronged.[5] But, to side-step the issue, we might assume that children fall out of the sky and are not intentionally begotten.

Finally, I address the question "What is owed to children?," but don't address the question "Who is duty-bound to incur the costs or duty-bound to ensure that children receive what they are owed?" Although the latter question raises several interesting normative issues, I do not address them for reasons of space.[6] In what follows, I assume that we might make progress with respect to identifying the entitlements of children without attending to the question of the correlative duty-bearers of these entitlements.

REJECTED VIEWS

Before I embark on the central task of trying to identify the right principles of what we owe to children, I briefly review and reject certain other answers to how we ought to resolve the apparent conflict between the interests of children and adults with respect to the enjoyment of advantage.

Minimalism

One simple, extreme view is that children are owed merely a life worth living. We can think of certain cases in which this answer, which I call *minimalism*, seems right. Suppose that my partner and I live on a deserted island. Given the paucity of provision on the island, and the lack of other people with whom to interact, if we procreate, we would be able provide the child we beget with no more than a life worth living. Now if we owed the child more than a life worth living, it would be morally impermissible for us to have a child. However, in this case, it seems morally permissible to beget the child even though we are capable of providing her with merely a life worth living: such a life would not, by hypothesis, be bad for the child—it is a life worth living—and it is the only possible life she could have. The child has no reasonable complaint.

If sound, this argument shows that sometimes—perhaps rarely, in scenarios like the island case—children are owed no more than a life worth living. But it does not show that when children can be provided with better life prospects, it is permissible to provide them with merely a life worth living. I take it as axiomatic that everyone is owed an equal share of resources: we need to know more about what an equal share is across generations and age-groups, but, on any plausible view, an equal share will, in most circumstances, afford more than a life worth living. This will often be the case because parents and other adults can normally transfer resources they enjoy to improve children's opportunities or quality of life.

Maximalism

At the opposite extreme, *maximalist* views assert that children are owed the best available upbringing. Peter Vallentyne has offered an interpretation of this view to answer the different question of how custody over children ought to be allocated (I shall call this *maximalism in custodial rights*).[7] In his view, within the set of persons who are willing to hold custody rights over her, the child is entitled to the custodian who is expected to provide her with the best life prospects.

However, Vallentyne is not committed to *maximalism in custodial conduct*: his view does not morally require custodians to provide the best life prospects for their child that they are capable of providing. For example, if other would-be custodians offer to provide only decent life prospects for the child, the child's custodians are permitted, consistent with fulfilling the requirements of continued custody, to provide her with merely better than decent life prospects even when they are capable of providing much better than decent prospects. Since it concerns only the conditions under which custody is properly allocated or transferred, Vallentyne's view is silent on the question of how custodians should *exercise* their custodial rights beyond the conduct that they contract to offer in their bid to acquire custody.[8] That a custodian can provide very good, good, or merely decent life prospects for her children without losing her custodial rights is compatible with the acceptance or rejection of the claim that she is morally required to provide the best upbringing.

I want to concentrate on maximalism in custodial conduct. It claims that if I hold custody rights over a child and there is a conflict between my interests and my child's interests in having the best available upbringing, then I am morally required to serve the child's interests. However, the view needs further specification because "the best available upbringing" is ambiguous between two interpretations, which have different implications. "Best upbringing" might mean best for the individual *as a child* or best for her *taking her life as a whole*. Consider, for example, a childhood that is replete with respect to the kinds of activity and experience that many believe are intrinsically valuable for children: imaginative, adventurous and carefree play with opportunities for valuable aesthetic experience, athletic success, fun, and amusement.[9] The consequence of having a perfect childhood understood in this way might be that this child's life as an adult might go worse in two ways. First, the intrinsic goods of childhood might involve activities that detract from acquiring the skills and capacities that equip the individual well for life as an adult: for example, fun and amusement are sometimes, for some individuals, incompatible with learning how to write well. Second, it might be that supplying opportunities for children to experience the intrinsic goods of childhood places demands on parents and other adults to supply suitable environments in which children can engage in secure, but imaginative, play. If there were a conflict between the interests of children and adults, then the implications of maximalism interpreted as the duty to supply the best childhood would be different to those of maximalism construed as providing what is best for the child taking her life as a whole. That is because when we take into account the child's life as a whole we must include in the reckoning the burdens adults have to bear to supply the goods of childhood.

These considerations suggest that maximalism in custodial conduct might take different forms depending on how we understand "best for the child." The key observation is that benefits to children as children sometimes correlate with burdens placed on parents or adults in the form of moral duties to supply certain goods.[10] If the child goes on to have children, then it will be the case that the rules in place that secure for her a good childhood will be paid for by her incurring more costs as a parent than if different rules were in operation that are less demanding with respect to the duties that parents have towards their children. What is best for us as children, then, may not be best for us taking our lives as a whole when we factor in the costs of fulfilling the duty to provide the best childhood for any offspring we might have.[11]

Perhaps we ought to be maximalists in general. After all, anything less than maximalism implies missed opportunity. However, it is, I think, clear that we should not be maximalists in custodial conduct when that is interpreted as the requirement to provide the child with the best childhood they could have. Such a view is implausible because it gives absolute priority to one's interests *as a child* even when everyone would prefer to give (or be better off by giving) less than absolute priority to her interests in that period of her life.

SUSTAINABILITY

According to the ideal of sustainability, which is popular as an account of intergenerational justice, children are owed as good an upbringing as their parents' generation received. At first sight, this view seems plausible for egalitarian reasons. Why should it be that future generations have fewer opportunities than the present generation? True, many previous generations experienced a harder life, lower life expectancy, and fewer opportunities than the present generation which, on some accounts, is a violation of equality. However, there is nothing we can do about inequality between present and past generations short of levelling down, by destroying the present generation's goods to reduce the inequality. What is within our power, however, is to ensure that our actions do not prevent our children from having the opportunities that are available to us. It seems that only an unjustified sense of superiority or self-importance on the part of the present generation could explain why we do not take steps to ensure that individuals in future generations are as advantaged as we are.

However, notwithstanding its apparent plausibility, sustainability is objectionable because it determines present parents' obligations on the basis of the activities of their parents, which seems a morally arbitrary point of reference. Consider again the observation that goods for children are correlated with burdens for parents, at least within some range. It might be that parents in the first generation (G1) willingly take on many costs to facilitate the best childhood for their children (G2). According to the ideal of sustainability, because they enjoyed an excellent childhood, G2 individuals owe their children the same quality childhood. But this makes G2's moral duties depend on the unilateral choices of individuals in G1 in a way that G2 can reasonably reject. In particular, G2 might say that it would prefer to have had a worse upbringing if the upside of that were an adulthood that is free of the burdens required to provide the best childhood for the next generation.

In addition, G3 might object to the upbringing provided by G2 parents. If so, it would not be an adequate response for G2 parents to claim that G3's upbringing was no worse than theirs, because their own childhood might have been less than they were owed. Plainly, if that were the case then questions would arise about how G2 should be compensated for the unjustly impoverished childhood they received. But the fact that they were unjustly treated does not mean that parents from G2 onwards now owe less to children.

I have argued that it is mistaken to determine the duties of G2 to their children by reference to the upbringing it received from G1. Instead, putting aside cases in which particular generations must make sacrifices for the realisation of just institutions, what we owe to children ought to be elaborated by reference to our needs and interests regardless of our place in the sequence of generations.[12] It is to the task of identifying the right way to identify those needs and interests and incorporating them with a complete lives view that I now turn.

RAWLSIAN REQUIREMENTS

John Rawls is famous for working out the political and economic implications of a liberal egalitarian conception of political morality. Because he focused on what he took to be the central questions of political philosophy—the constitution, citizen's rights and liberties, and the distribution of jobs and income—he left unaddressed many other issues, including the question of how much we owe to children. However, Rawls's fundamental ideal of "social cooperation between free and equal citizens" provides the basis of at least a partial answer to our question.[13]

There are two main components to Rawls's ideal: a conception of our interests as "free and equal citizens" and the requirement that principles of political morality be acceptable to such citizens. I review each and briefly explore how it shapes how much we owe to children.

Rawls's ideal of citizens as free and equal offers a description of our interests in developing and deploying the capacities—the "moral powers" he calls them—that are necessary to be free and equal. The first moral power is a sense of justice; the second consists in the capacity to develop, deliberate about, and pursue an ethical conception—a conception that selects between the various non-political ends one might have. Rawls asserts that we have an interest in having these capacities and the motivation to exercise these two moral powers.[14]

In interpreting what Rawls means by a sense of justice, it is important to avoid two extremes. First, an individual might have a sense of justice even if she holds certain beliefs about the distribution of wealth or the protection of liberty, for example, that are unsound. The requirement to enable individuals to develop a sense of justice, then, does not commit us to doing all we can to provide an upbringing that imparts to everyone perfect convictions about how our important political institutions ought to be governed. However, second, it is not the case that our interest in having a sense of justice is secured merely by knowing that there is a moral dimension to various public issues. That content-independent interpretation of a sense of justice is inadequate because we have an interest in having a sense of justice because each of us has a right to be treated justly, and each of us is, in turn, under a duty to treat others justly. Since that is the case, it is important for us to have an adequate understanding of our moral rights and duties.

Rawls distinguishes between *justice* and *legitimacy* to negotiate between these two extremes. Justice obtains when our major political and socioeconomic institutions are appropriately arranged so that each citizen receives her due. But these institutions might be legitimate—in other words, have justified authority over us—even when they are not fully just. They are legitimate, according to Rawls only if they are (1) suitably democratic—taking into account in a fair, deliberative decision procedure the views of different individuals who disagree about ethics and justice—and (2) not too unjust.[15] Indeed, he itemises the parameters of political legitimacy and, by extension if I interpret him correctly, a sense of justice. Legitimacy obtains, first, only if citizens enjoy democratic rights and the familiar liberal freedoms of conscience, speech, association, and occupation and protection of these rights and freedoms are given priority over other public aims; and, second, only when there is a distribution of social and economic resources such that citizens have the wherewithal to make effective use of their rights.[16]

Accordingly, the Rawlsian answer to the question of how much we owe to children is: at least an upbringing that allows them to develop the capacity for, and the motivation to exercise, a sense of justice so understood. That seems to be a demanding requirement. It requires a rich educational experience in which children learn, among other things, to cooperate with each other, respect each other as equals, deliberate about public matters on terms that other free and equal citizens can affirm, comply with collective decisions, but also to have the gumption to challenge the majority's view where they believe it to be unjust.[17] The institutional preconditions of the development of such a sense of justice turn on various empirical questions, such as the importance of integration between students with different identities as a means of ensuring that citizens and leaders have appropriate knowledge of people who are unlike themselves and the desire to act politically for the sake of everyone.[18] Although I cannot explore these matters further, it is clear, I think, that this interest alone generates a reasonably costly duty on the part of adults to provide children with an education that enables them to become well-functioning citizens.

If the development of Rawls's second moral power—the capacity to develop, deliberate about, and pursue an ethical conception—is taken to be an aim of upbringing, as I believe it should be, it generates a similar set of implications and some additional ones.[19] An education that imparts to an individual the capacity to develop a sense of justice will also be one that develops her capacity to imagine, reflect on and pursue nonpolitical goals, because there are certain intellectual, physical, emotional, and motivational skills that are common to any goal-directed activity, whether the goals in question are political or non-political. Nevertheless, an understanding of the details of different ethical traditions that have attracted, or continue to attract, people's allegiance also seems necessary for an individual to be able to imagine how her life might go if she changed her non-political goals. That places further demands on adults beyond those required to cultivate a sense of justice.

Although it is clear that adopting a Rawlsian account of political morality has significant implications for what is owed to children, it remains incomplete in several of respects. First, it is unclear from the above account how weighty these reasons are. The interests cited are satiable: that is, they specify a threshold of capability and do not necessarily require us to improve people's proficiency with respect to the two moral powers above that threshold. Still, certain individuals beset by cognitive, psychological, or emotional impairments may be brought up to the threshold only at very great expense or with considerable support. It seems too demanding to claim that everyone who is capable of developing the two moral powers is entitled to an upbringing that secures that development irrespective of the cost involved. The costs might not be purely financial. As teachers who work in schools in which mainstreaming pupils with special needs is practised well know, the costs of enhancing the development of those with certain behavioral problems are often borne by other children whose educational needs are satisfied less than they might be. Thus, we need to delineate the requirement to satisfy the two moral powers further and ask whether there are cases in which it is justifiable not to bear certain costs that are necessary to enable particular individuals to be free and equal.

Second, there may be other low-functioning individuals for whom freedom and equality specified by reference to the two moral powers is unobtainable. Some severely cognitively impaired people fall into that category. Plainly, the Rawlsian considerations above do not speak to them. Perhaps there are different kinds of provision that would enable some to become more just or ethically reflective, albeit not enough to describe them as fully free and equal. There is a small, very severely impaired minority, however, who cannot get close to freedom and equality, and our account of what we owe to children ought to include their claims. A complete view must deal with the issues they raise in an plausible manner.

Finally, the Rawlsian account is incomplete because the interests on the basis of which it justifies its principles are artificially restricted to exclude certain questions that need answering. A clear case is health care. In most of his writing Rawls brackets issues of justice that arise in the distribution of health care. When he does address the issue he offers little guidance that would enable us to identify the fine-grained proposals we require from a conception of justice in health care.[20] Similarly, Rawls doesn't address the case of children except in relation to their potential for development into well-functioning citizens. For these reasons we need to look beyond Rawls for views that might supplement his conception.

Before I proceed with that task, however, it is worth emphasizing the second main component of Rawls's account, the requirement that principles of political morality be acceptable to free and equal persons, for that feature places constraints on how we may proceed. As Rawls argues, given the persistent ethical disagreement exhibited by any society that satisfies our interests in developing and deploying the two moral powers, if the conceptions of justice we advance in politics are to be accepted by free and equal citizens those conceptions must be anti-perfectionist: they must not rest on controversial ethical foundations, such as the affirmation or rejection of particular religions. Instead, our arguments must be premised on ideals that can be justified to all free and equal citizens. Rawls's own conception of primary goods is one way of trying to identify a set of claims that can gain political acceptance across the plurality of ethical views. However, I have suggested that that account is incomplete in various respects and it is not clear how it could be rendered more complete. A different, but complementary, way of proceeding would be to deal with the distributive issues we face by asking how equally situated individuals would choose when faced with the possible consequences of different proposed principles. Since I believe that this approach is underexplored, I finish by considering how it might be used at least to orientate our thinking about how much we owe to children.

HYPOTHETICAL INSURANCE UNDER CONDITIONS OF EQUALITY

We are after a more fine-grained conception of our duties to children than the Rawlsian conception provides, but one that remains consistent with the moral constraint that the conception must be acceptable to free and equal individuals.

Our account cannot be one that simply rests on a conception of what is best for each person. Such a perfectionist conception might have the following two features. First, we identify how much is owed to each individual taking her life as a whole. Second, taking due consideration of her goals, talents, and situation, we then allocate that sum appropriately across the different temporal periods of her life so that it goes better than it would under any alternative distribution between its temporal stages. Such a view might not disregard the aims and ambitions of the person in question, because on many conceptions of well-being, living well depends in part on pursuing one's valuable goals. Nevertheless, this view remains perfectionist and, to that extent, unsuitable as a basis for determining how much we owe to children, because it subjects individuals to an allocation of resources across their lives that is justified by a controversial account of what a good life involves.

Instead, we ought to answer our question by asking how much suitably situated individuals would allocate to their own childhood. This solution bears similarities between the account of distributive justice with respect to health care advanced by Normal Daniels and Ronald Dworkin. Daniels insists that distributive issues that arise between age groups should not be theorized as conflicting *interpersonal* claims, but as an allocation problem within a single life. Accordingly, first we try to identify what is a fair share of resources for an individual taking her life as a whole. Thereafter, we ask how, if she were prudent, she would distribute those resources across the different stages of her life.[21]

A similar approach is taken by Dworkin in his account of justice in the distribution of health care, which uses the device of hypothetical insurance.[22] Dworkin notes that we are affected by unequal brute luck with respect to our morbidity and mortality and we need a way of compensating those who suffer brute bad luck. Suppose that individuals enjoyed a fair (equal) share of external resources—wealth and income and occupational opportunity. We ought, he argues, to determine health care policy—both the size and distribution of the health care budget—by asking what well-informed individuals would choose by way of medical insurance if they did not know whether as individuals they were lucky or unlucky with respect to the distribution of luck. As a part of this exercise, they assess whether they want to take out more or less expensive insurance packages for different periods of their lives. Dworkin accepts that, because of its hypothetical nature, we can proceed only on the basis of certain speculations about what would be bought in such an insurance market. Nevertheless, he argues that as a matter of justice everyone is entitled to the provision characterized in the insurance package that would be purchased by the average individual, with these arrangements financed out of general taxation.

We need not go into the details of Dworkin's account. For our purposes, it is notable that one of its attractive feature is its anti-perfectionism because, rather than justifying a particular health policy on the basis of a controversial conception of well-being, it defers to people's own judgments with respect to how much they value being the recipient of different kinds of health care at different stages of their lives. Specifically, in the hypothetical insurance schemes each asks herself how much *she values* good or excellent health in the knowledge that more health care sometimes comes at the cost of the enjoyment of other goods, such as wealth and income to spend on personal projects, education, good pensions, and so on. Because health policy is the product of that kind of fair consultation exercise it seems to satisfy the acceptability criterion mentioned earlier, at least when constrained or informed by the interests elaborated in the previous section.

Can we adopt a hypothetical insurance scheme to determine our distributive obligations to children? I think we can, but to do so we have to revise the scheme a little to iron out a problem that arises if we run the scheme by asking adults how much they would set aside for their childhood. The problem is simply that if it is adults who buy insurance, they know that their childhood is in the past and, therefore, they may well find the question difficult to answer in a way that is not self-serving. To avoid this problem, we might revise the hypothetical choice by asking the following question: how many resources would you devote to your childhood if you (1) had a fair share of resources and opportunities taking your life as a whole; (2) were well informed about the costs and effects of the different choices available with regard to the nature of your childhood and adulthood; and (3) knew that you would live another life from birth to death, but did not know the particular circumstances of that life: for example, whether your social circumstances or biological endowment will be advantageous or disadvantageous, or your particular talents, character, and goals. Assuming that one will live again means that adult choosers need to reflect on the value of childhood in their lives as a whole. It forces them to focus on the problem of what it is reasonable to provide to children by addressing the question—how much of my fair life share would I devote to my own childhood if I were to live again through all the different life stages and I knew the costs and effects of different choices? This is the kind of thought experiment we need to run to get reasonably fine-grained policies with respect to children that are responsive to the values of fairly situated individuals and, for that reason, acceptable to free and equal persons.

I said at the outset that I would disappoint the reader by not producing concrete policy-specific answers to our question. But I want to finish by making a few observations about certain relevant considerations that individuals within our thought experiment would take into account when making their choices and about the general political implications of the hypothetical choice approach. In the first place, we would take into account the opportunity costs of different choices. As Daniels explains, we have good reason to invest heavily in children, at least when it comes to issues of health, because such investment reaps better health outcomes over the life span: improved educational outcomes in general and improved understanding about health, in particular, have health benefits throughout one's life.[23] For this reason, investing in children has fewer opportunity costs compared to giving resources to adults, at least within a certain range and for certain goods. Health care and educational provision for children are rational investments because of the sizeable returns they reap throughout one's life. One does not give up much, if anything, by this investment: one might have more money by being healthy and well educated than if one lacked these attributes—refusing to fund these childhood investments out of a concern to increase opportunities for consumption as an adult would be self-defeating.

For this familiar reason, then, investing a considerable amount in childhood is rational. Whether that amount is more or less than the average spending on children's health and education in our society is open to dispute. It is difficult not to conclude, however, that the resources currently devoted to those significantly below the average is lower than justice would permit. Knowing the long-term beneficial consequences of being well educated and healthy with respect to their opportunity to lead the life they value, individuals in the hypothetical insurance scheme planning for their life would set aside considerable monetary resources to insure against the possibility that their familial or social circumstances prevents them from acquiring the desired level of understanding, skills, and knowledge. If so, then everyone is entitled to such investment as a requirement of egalitarian justice. Indeed, this argument goes beyond the one made in the previous section, which claimed that citizens' interests in having a sense of justice and the capacity for independent ethical thought and pursuit justify education investment. The argument here is that even more investment than that required to satisfy those interests is justified if the health and occupational benefits adults gain from educational investment are relatively high.

As well as considering the opportunity costs of different policies, individuals in our hypothetical insurance scheme have to take a view about the importance of childhood activities and experiences in their lives. People's views about this question are more difficult to identify. I mentioned earlier Colin Macleod's view that there are intrinsic goods that are particularly relevant in childhood—spontaneous, carefree, and adventurous play, for example. Such goods are, he argues, valuable for us as children independently of whether they also contribute to our development into well-functioning adults. Individuals in our thought experiment might agree with Macleod. If they do, they need to ask several questions to figure out the extent to which such goods ought to be provided. What kinds of arrangement need to be put in place to deliver such goods? For example, does the provision of the goods of childhood require more contact time between parents and their children than is typical in societies with high rates of participation in the labor market; does it require the maintenance of particular kinds of public spaces and recreational facilities and transport to access them? What are the costs of these arrangements? In addition, if the provision of Macleod's childhood goods is reasonably costly, they will need to take a view of how important these goods are to their well-being, taking their lives as a whole.

If we were to live our lives again and the price of having greater access to these childhood goods is having fewer disposable resources in adulthood or additional duties to be with one's children, for example, then we need to think about how much we value these goods in comparison with the goods we would have to sacrifice as adults to supply them. Reasonable people will answer this question in different ways. Some who reflect on the quality of their own childhood might regret the absence of various opportunities to engage in music, art, sport, and play. Others might think of childhood as a period in which one cannot lead a flourishing life, because it lacks certain essential qualities, such as the capacity to deliberate rationally about various options or the exercise of certain faculties. Reasonable people will disagree about whether childhood or adulthood contributes most to well-being, which will influence their judgements about how many resources to devote to that period of their lives beyond those resources that are necessary to finance the acquisition of Rawlsian interests.

I mentioned above, as one reason to turn to Dworkin's model, the indeterminacy of appealing to Rawls's interest with respect to a range of questions, such as how much we owe to individuals for whom possession of Rawls's two moral powers is very costly, or to severely impaired individuals who are not capable of leading a free and equal life so understood. One view that has some initial intuitive attraction—the priority view—asserts that, morally, it is more important to attend to the needs of the worse off even when the available resources allow us to improve their quality of life much less than we can improve the lives of individuals who are better off.[24] However, the priority view seems to be mistaken, at least when adopted as the only principle in play. There is surely a limit to the burdens we as adults are required by justice to take on in such cases. It seems too burdensome, for example, to expect reasonably well-off parents to sacrifice their non-parental interests beyond a certain level for minor gains for their severely impaired children. Of course, some who align themselves to the priority view say that we also have a reason to promote people's quality of life and to prioritize those individuals whose lives can be improved to a greater extent. Those who adopt such a pluralist view accept that there is a conflict between our reason to prioritize the worse off and our reason to act beneficently, but they rarely attempt to explain how we are to resolve this moral conflict.

The revised hypothetical insurance scheme I propose allows us to supply more determinate answers to these questions. It invites us to consider how much ought to be set aside to deal with the possibility that one's life is severely impaired in these ways. In doing so, I stipulate that individuals making insurance decisions are motivated by the desire to become free and equal persons, but they are also sensitive to considerations of cost and, accordingly, do not give absolute priority to improving their sense of justice and capacity for reflection about the good life. When only insignificant improvements to one's two moral powers are available, for example, it would not be rational to choose such an improvement when that requires significant reductions in the opportunities one might enjoy if one were not severely impaired. In this way, the insurance model allows us to identify more precisely the duties of justice we have to those who fall below the capability threshold for freedom and equality; it does so by making reference to the decisions that free and equal persons would take when they contemplate the different kinds of life they might have in a fair context of choice.

The general position I am propounding asserts that we are entitled to the childhood provision that would be chosen by equally placed well-informed individuals tasked with the responsibility of allocating resources across their own lives. That may seem objectionable within a liberal conception because, in effect, we are deciding how to allocate resources between different age groups by reference to the views of the *average person*, which is insensitive to the range of views available. What promised to be resolution of the problem that is sensitive to individuals' ambitions turns out, on reflection, to be one that fails to accommodate individuals with idiosyncratic or minority views about the intrinsic importance of childhood. Or so the objection goes.

The objection lacks force, I believe, because it is unclear how we could get more sensitivity to people's ambitions than that exhibited in the hypothetical insurance scheme. Within the scheme it is possible to select policies that offer a range of different kinds of provision and well-informed individuals will, no doubt, exercise that opportunity: they assume that they will live another life but, not knowing what character or particular needs they will have in that life, it is rational to cater to individuals with diverse childhood interests, talents, and circumstances. This feature of the scheme gives it considerable sensitivity to relevant differences between people. And, more generally, when we assess the scheme's liberal credentials, we need to compare it with alternative models for determining what and how much we owe to children: models that appeal to the correct view of well-being. True, some will claim that the childhood provision selected by the average person is better or worse than she would have chosen. But we need a way of deciding what adults owe to children and, given the impossibility of tailoring our conception of children's rights and adults' duties to individuals' particular values, the scheme is more accommodating of people's values than one that decides these matters according to a particular disputed conception of well-being. When judged in comparison with alternative methods for identifying our duties, then, it seems that the objection fails.[25]

This reply reveals the essential feature of equal hypothetical insurance as a model. It is a way of identifying answers to distributive questions that are fair and responsive to people's ambitions (and fair, in part, because they are ambition-sensitive). Because of its responsiveness to our ambitions, the scheme is appealing to those committed to principles of political morality that are acceptable to free and equal persons.

As I said at the outset, I have not supplied concrete policy prescriptions that follow from this account of the duties of adults to children. Instead, I have set out the normative foundations of an answer to our question that draws on Rawls's account of freedom and equality and Dworkin's account of hypothetical insurance. The latter gives us hope that we might be able to identify reasonably fine-grained answers. To do so, there is a need for social scientific study to try to identify how fairly situated well-informed individuals would choose to allocate resources across a life on the assumption that they would live again through all the different stages of life. In the meantime, it is, I think, clear that the opportunities provided to those born into disadvantaged circumstances in our society are significantly less than they are entitled to from the point of view of justice.

NOTES

* Earlier versions of this chapter were presented at conferences at Pompeu Fabra University and the University of Western Ontario. I am grateful to the participants at these events and to Tom Parr and Andrew Williams for their helpful comments and objections.

1. For a view of equality of opportunity that gives us a *pro tanto* reason to act in these ways, see Harry Brighouse, "Educational Equality and School Reform," in *Educational Equality*, ed. Graham Haydon (London: Continuum, 2010), 26–44.

2. If parents have a child then we might distinguish at least three interests they have. They may have an interest in retaining custody over their child and an interest in fulfilling their parental responsibilities, but also an interest in pursuing the goals they have that are independent of their role as parents. It is possible that the first and third interests conflict with children's interests.

3. See Norman Daniels, *Just Health Care* (Cambridge: Cambridge University Press, 1985), and *Am I My Parents' Keeper? An Essay on Justice between the Young and Old* (New York: Oxford University Press, 1988); Ronald Dworkin, *Sovereign Virtue: The Theory and Practice of Equality* (Cambridge, MA: Harvard University Press, 2000), Chapter 8, and "Justice in the Distribution of Health Care," in *The Ideal of Equality*, ed. Matthew Clayton and Andrew Williams (London: Palgrave, 2002).

4. For elaboration and discussion of this idea, see Derek Parfit, *Reasons and Persons* (Oxford: Oxford University Press, 1984), Part Three.
5. For a different view, see Seana Shiffrin, "Wrongful Life, Procreative Responsibility and the Significance of Harm," *Legal Theory* 5, no. 2 (1999): 117–148.
6. For discussion of the question of whether the costs of child rearing should be shared between all adults or between only parents, see Paula Casal and Andrew Williams, "Equality of Resources and Procreative Justice," in *Dworkin and His Critics*, ed. Justine Burley (Oxford: Blackwell, 2004); Serena Olsaretti, "Children as Public Goods?" *Philosophy and Public Affairs* 41, no. 3 (2013): 226–258.
7. Peter Vallentyne, "The Rights and Duties of Childrearing," *William and Mary Bill of Rights Journal* 11, no. 3 (2003): 991–1010.
8. I articulate Vallentyne's idea with the device of an auction, because it presents his idea vividly. It might be, however, that the device of an auction is less good than some other mechanism for identifying the best custodian.
9. Colin Macleod has suggested that childhood should not be theorized simply as preparation for adulthood. There are what he calls "intrinsic goods of childhood," the enjoyment of which makes an individual's life go well *as a child* irrespective of whether those goods also prepare her well for life as an adult. See Colin Macleod, "Primary Goods, Capabilities, and Children," in *Measuring Justice: Primary Goods and Capabilities*, ed. Harry Brighouse and Ingrid Robeyns (Cambridge: Cambridge University Press, 2010).
10. For simplicity I do not distinguish between the duties of adults and the duties of parents. There are surely significant differences between these duties, which need to be incorporated into an account of how much is owed to children. I do not consider them here for reasons of space.
11. In a more complete account, we might add and discuss the complicating feature that the burden of raising and caring for children might be placed equally on every adult or more heavily placed on parents. And we would need consider how the fact that begetting children is usually avoidable makes a difference. But for simplicity, I set these issues aside.
12. Rawls's principle of just savings countenances the possibility that some generations are required by justice to save to realize just institutions. See *Justice as Fairness: A Restatement* (Cambridge, MA: Harvard University Press, 2001), 159–161.
13. The two key texts to which I refer are *Political Liberalism*, paperback edition (New York: Columbia University Press, 1996) and *Justice as Fairness: A Restatement*.
14. Rawls, *Political Liberalism*, 29–35.
15. Ibid., 427–429.
16. Ibid., xlvii–lx.
17. For a fuller elaboration of the educational implications of the development of a sense of justice, see my *Justice and Legitimacy in Upbringing* (Oxford: Oxford University Press, 2006), ch. 4.
18. For this argument, see Elizabeth Anderson, "Fair Equality in Education: A Democratic Equality Perspective," *Ethics* 117, no. 4 (2007): 595–622, and *The Imperative of Integration* (Princeton, NJ: Princeton University Press, 2010).
19. Rawls himself claims that this moral power might not be one that we have an interest in cultivating in our daily lives.
20. See Rawls, *Justice as Fairness: A Restatement*, §. 51.
21. Daniels, *Am I My Parents' Keeper?*, especially Chapter 3.
22. Dworkin, "Justice in the Distribution of Health Care"; *Sovereign Virtue*, Chapter 8.

23. Daniels, *Just Health: Meeting Health Needs Fairly* (New York: Cambridge University Press, 2008), 176.
24. For discussion of the Priority View, see Derek Parfit, "Equality or Priority?" in Matthew Clayton and Andrew Williams (eds.), *The Ideal of Equality* (Basingstoke: Palgrave, 2000).
25. Here I follow Dworkin's reply to a similar objection made in a different context. See Dworkin, *Sovereign Virtue*, 340–345.

REFERENCES

Anderson, Elizabeth. "Fair Equality in Education: A Democratic Equality Perspective." *Ethics* 117 (2007): 595–622.

Anderson, Elizabeth. *The Imperative of Integration.* Princeton, NJ: Princeton University Press, 2010.

Brighouse, Harry. "Educational Equality and School Reform." In *Educational Equality,* edited by Graham Haydon, 15–70. London: Continuum, 2010.

Casal, Paula, and Andrew Williams. "Equality of Resources and Procreative Justice." In *Dworkin and His Critics,* edited by Justine Burley, 150–169. Oxford: Blackwell, 2004.

Clayton, Matthew. *Justice and Legitimacy in Upbringing.* Oxford: Oxford University Press, 2006.

Daniels, Norman. *Just Health Care.* Cambridge: Cambridge University Press, 1985.

Daniels, Norman. *Am I My Parents' Keeper? An Essay on Justice between the Young and Old.* New York: Oxford University Press, 1988.

Daniels, Norman. *Just Health: Meeting Health Needs Fairly.* New York: Cambridge University Press, 2008.

Dworkin, Ronald. *Sovereign Virtue: The Theory and Practice of Equality.* Cambridge, MA: Harvard University Press, 2000.

Dworkin, Ronald. "Justice in the Distribution of Health Care." In *The Ideal of Equality,* edited by Matthew Clayton and Andrew Williams, 203–222. London: Palgrave, 2002.

Macleod, Colin. "Primary Goods, Capabilities, and Children." In *Measuring Justice: Primary Goods and Capabilities,* edited by Harry Brighouse and Ingrid Robeyns, 174–192. Cambridge: Cambridge University Press, 2010.

Olsaretti, Serena. "Children as Public Goods?" *Philosophy and Public Affairs* 41 (2013): 226–258.

Parfit, Derek. *Reasons and Persons.* Oxford: Oxford University Press, 1984.

Parfit, Derek. "Equality or Priority?" In *The Ideal of Equality,* edited by Matthew Clayton and Andrew Williams. Basingstoke: Palgrave, 2002.

Rawls, John. *Political Liberalism,* paperback edition. New York: Columbia University Press, 1996.

Rawls, John. *Justice as Fairness: A Restatement.* Cambridge, MA: Harvard University Press, 2001.

Shiffrin, Seana. "Wrongful Life, Procreative Responsibility and the Significance of Harm." *Legal Theory* 5 (1999): 117–148.

Vallentyne, Peter. "The Rights and Duties of Childrearing," *William and Mary Bill of Rights Journal* 44 (2003): 991–1010.

INDEX